JOHN STONEHOUSE,
MY FATHER

JOHN STONEHOUSE, MY FATHER

THE TRUE STORY OF THE RUNAWAY MP

Julia Stonehouse

ICON

Published in the UK and the USA in 2021 by Icon Books Ltd
Omnibus Business Centre, 39–41 North Road, London N7 9DP
email: info@iconbooks.com • www.iconbooks.com

Sold in the UK, Europe and Asia
by Faber & Faber Ltd, Bloomsbury House, 74–77 Great Russell Street,
London WC1B 3DA or their agents

Distributed in the UK, Europe and Asia
by Grantham Book Services, Trent Road, Grantham NG31 7XQ

Distributed in the USA
by Publishers Group West, 1700 Fourth Street, Berkeley, CA 94710

Distributed in Canada
by Publishers Group Canada, 76 Stafford Street, Unit 300, Toronto,
Ontario M6J 2S1

Distributed in Australia and New Zealand
by Allen & Unwin Pty Ltd, PO Box 8500, 83 Alexander Street,
Crows Nest, NSW 2065

Distributed in South Africa
by Jonathan Ball, Office B4, The District, 41 Sir Lowry Road,
Woodstock 7925

Distributed in India
by Penguin Books India, 7th Floor, Infinity Tower – C, DLF Cyber City,
Gurgaon 122002, Haryana

ISBN: 978-178578-741-6

Typeset in Adobe Garamond by Marie Doherty

Printed and bound in Great Britain
by Clays Ltd, Elcograf S.p.A.

Julia Stonehouse with her father, John, 1985.
Photograph Terence Donovan © Terence Donovan Archive

This book is dedicated to Michael P. O'Dell and Harry Richards — two gems among men.

On 20th November 1974, British member of parliament, John Stonehouse, faked his death in Miami and, using a forged identity, entered Australia hoping to escape his old life and start anew. This is his true story. It involves spies, secret services, politics, high finance, and the love of two women.

Contents

1

Going Crazy

B etween the 6th and 11th of November 1974 my father flew from London to Miami, to Houston, to Mexico City, to Los Angeles, to Atlanta, to Miami, to Chicago, to San Francisco, to Tampa, to Miami and back to London. He'd planned to fake his own death and go to Australia, so when he arrived at Miami on the 6th he'd passed through immigration as Stonehouse and then doubled back to join another immigration line and entered again on a false passport in the name of Joseph Markham. He was psychologically shattered and trying to break free of the personality of John Stonehouse, but was unable to do so.

When he arrived in Miami, he booked into the beach-side Fontainebleau Hotel and phoned the National Bank of Miami to confirm his lunch meeting there the next day, to discuss the possibility of them buying a large block of shares in his banking company – originally called the British Bangladesh Trust, but now renamed the London Capital Group. He was hoping that a last-minute change of fortune could save him from the dire financial predicament he was in. He later wrote a book to explain his faked death and disappearance, *Death of an Idealist*, in which he said this meeting was 'a straw to clutch', asking, 'Would it give me hope and pull me back from the brink of the extinction I was planning for myself?'[1]

He woke early the next day to a beautiful tranquil morning and started making contingency arrangements. He needed somewhere to hide a set of dry clothes, so he walked along the beach and was surprised to find that, next to the Fontainebleau, the Eden Roc Hotel was shuttered closed, and its exterior area dilapidated and deserted. He'd stayed there as a minister on a tour of the States, and as he now stood by its dirty swimming pool he remembered his once confident and cheerful self. He wrote that he felt 'as though I was looking back on myself through a long series of distorting mirrors. At the other end I could see the old me looking backwards through the same distorting mirrors with an expression of horror and incredulity.' As he stood there, a broken man, he looked back on the successful man and the once successful man also looked at him. 'I looked over the passage of time – in both directions – and shuddered.'[2]

He drove to the airport and bought a ticket to Houston in the random name of George Lewis, no ID required. He also bought a suitcase and clothes, and put them in a big luggage locker, along with the false Markham passport and other documents in that name. He drove to the Fontainebleau, then walked back to the Eden Roc Hotel with a spare set of clothes and hid them in a telephone kiosk near the swimming pool he'd been at earlier. At the lunch meeting with the bank executives there was no positive news, and no pulling back from the brink. He was going. Back at the Fontainebleau, he put his Stonehouse passport and money into his document case, leaving them in his room and leaving his ticket for Los Angeles on the bedside table. He had planned to go there the next day to meet Harry Wetzel, the president of an aerospace company, the Garrett Corporation. Then he changed into swimming shorts and a shirt and headed for the beach. Leaving his shoes and shirt on the verandah, he got in the sea. He felt the water washing away the tensions of his past, like a baptism. He swam towards the Eden Roc; the sea and beach were deserted. After changing into the spare clothes he'd left in the phone kiosk, he strolled to the road, hailed a taxi to the airport, collected his suitcase with all the Joseph Markham paperwork, and flew to Houston.

From there he flew to Mexico City, exiting the USA as Markham. The plan was to catch the once-weekly Qantas flight from Mexico

City to Sydney, but there had been an agonising delay causing him to miss the flight by ten minutes. The quickest way to get to Australia now was to catch a flight from Los Angeles, so the next day, the 8th, he caught a plane to LA, entering the USA and booking into the airport Marriott Hotel as Markham. He wanted to rest until the flight later that night, but he'd stayed at that hotel before as Stonehouse, and the memories came flooding back. The planned meeting with Harry Wetzel had not been cancelled and his offices were only yards away. They'd been due to discuss a report he was writing for the Garrett Corporation on the future of the British aircraft industry which, as a former minister of aviation, he knew a great deal about. He decided to attend the meeting anyway, although he would now be late, and walked there. With each step he felt Markham ebbing away and Stonehouse returning. On his last visit to Wetzel, he'd noticed a book of M.C. Escher prints on the bookshelf, and it now seemed as he sat in that office that his state of mind was reflected by Escher's labyrinthine puzzles and faultless blending of day into night, night into day, up to down, and down to up. By the time he returned to the Marriott Hotel, Markham had gone and it was Stonehouse who opened the room door. He felt disembodied: one half in California; the other missing in Florida.

In mental turmoil, he phoned my mother. She remembers it as a short, garbled call, in which he said 'he couldn't take it anymore'. She thought he meant that he couldn't take any more stress of trying to make business deals, not that 'it' meant his whole life. He told her he might not be back in time for the Remembrance Day service at his constituency, due to take place in two days on Sunday 10th, and asked that if he wasn't back, could she go in his place. She wasn't surprised to find him calling from LA, as he had planned to be there, but what she didn't know was that his passport and clothes were in Miami, and he'd stayed the previous night in Mexico City.

Reluctantly, he decided to return to London. He later wrote, 'The pain and anguish of returning to Stonehouse was intense. Markham, for his part, resented the intrusion on his plans; he could see no point in returning to the empty charade in Britain, but Markham would not fight the blood ties which were dragging Stonehouse back like a powerful magnet.' There were no available direct flights, so he flew to Atlanta, arriving at 4am on Saturday 9th, and caught a connecting flight to Miami. When he arrived back at the Fontainebleau Hotel it was clear that nobody had noticed he'd been gone almost two days. He felt as though he didn't really exist. After a short nap, he woke to the full horror that he was once again in his Stonehouse personality: 'The horror of it hit me like a sledgehammer.'[3]

Once more, he felt he had to escape. Again, he left all the Stonehouse belongings in his room, took some clothes for Markham to the Eden Roc Hotel, and went for another baptismal swim in the vast blue ocean. He wrote later that this time it was different: 'Markham was stronger and determined to succeed. The philosophical haze of the previous swim was replaced by a harsh strong light. I could see it all clearly now. Stonehouse must definitely die.' He caught a taxi to the airport but there were no available direct flights to LA or San Francisco, where he could get a connecting flight to Australia, so he flew to Chicago where he easily picked up a plane to San Francisco. As he sat there, heading West once again, more internal turmoil struck. 'I felt suddenly oppressed, like a reluctant lemming. Why should I throw my being over the precipice even if I was doing it only metaphorically, and only in space and time, and with the technology of jet travel to help me? From the depths of my being an emotion of tremendous intensity rose within me. I went to the rear of the plane into the tiny toilet compartment and screamed at the reflection in the mirror. "Why do you do this to me?" But who was screaming – was it Stonehouse or was it Markham? The struggle between the two was tearing me to pieces.'[4] In emotional agony, he wept.

Stonehouse won that battle: 'The umbilical cord was not severed after all. I must return to Miami and recreate my own identity.' In

San Francisco he bought a ticket back to Miami and, for the second consecutive night, flew from West coast to East coast arriving, after a detour to Tampa because of engine trouble, back in Miami. It was now Sunday the 10th of November and, once again, nobody at the hotel had noticed he'd gone missing. He felt it was fate – he could not escape. Meanwhile, my mother was walking in his place behind the band through the streets of Walsall and towards the church to remember the armistice and the fallen soldiers, silently anguishing about whatever mental trauma her husband was going through on the other side of the Atlantic. He flew overnight to London, feeling 'like a condemned man, with the noose already around my neck, being dragged along to a hideous circus'.[5] He arrived on the morning of Monday the 11th, went to his office in Dover Street, then to the House of Commons, and carried on apparently as normal. Nobody noticed he was silently exploding inside his head.

Two days later my parents celebrated their 26th wedding anniversary by having dinner at their favourite restaurant, La Busola. My mother felt relieved that my father seemed to have recovered from his 'I can't take it anymore' moment a few days earlier in America and didn't realise that he was already operating in two distinct mental dimensions, and that this would be their last anniversary dinner. As she sat across the table from him, my mother had no idea my father had constructed an elaborate persona in the name of Joseph Markham, complete with bank accounts and plans to emigrate to Australia, plus bank accounts in yet another name – Clive Mildoon.

My father had kept from my mother the extent of his financial difficulties, and the fact that for five years he'd been having an affair with his secretary, Sheila Buckley, who was 21 years younger than him. My mother knew my father had been under intense emotional pressure since 1969, when Josef Frolik, a defector from the StB, the communist Czech secret services, accused him of being one of their agents. That allegation, although unsubstantiated, had lost him his job in government and led to a group of right-wing establishment figures generating further rumour and unfounded allegations, which compounded his anxiety and stress. My mother also knew that my father took prescription drugs to counter the insomnia caused by all his problems. What nobody knew, however, was that those drugs were driving him crazy.

My father's bathroom cabinet was full of bottles of Mandrax and Mogadon. After he died in 1988, Sheila told the *Daily Mail*: 'What I should have done which I now blame myself for was to insist he had medical help. He had been to see the House of Commons doctor and had been on Mandrax pills to sleep for the last two years. It should have been a warning to me but I did nothing about it.'⁶ My father was getting Mandrax (methaqualone) and Mogadon (nitrazepam) from a variety of sources, none of whom knew the extent of his drug taking. In those days, doctors carried around little green prescription pads and when my father saw an MP who was also a GP walking down the corridor of the House of Commons, he'd get a prescription from him. And from another, and another, and also from his own doctor. For two years he was self-medicating on a cocktail of the two drugs, essentially without medical supervision. An increased risk of suicide is a side effect of both drugs, and a tolerance of Mandrax develops rapidly so larger and larger doses become required for the same effect.

Mandrax, known in the street drug trade as mandies or in the USA as Quaaludes, was widely prescribed in the 1970s for insomnia and anxiety, but has been banned in the UK and USA for over 30 years because of its now-recognised negative impact on mental health, including depression, anxiety, paranoia, mental confusion, poor decision-making and the increased risk of suicide. Taken with alcohol, Mandrax can be fatal. Mogadon is still available, but its recognised side effects include depression, with or without suicidal tendencies, impairment of judgement, and delusions. Today, people taking Mogadon are advised to consult their doctor if their behaviour becomes bizarre, and in 1974 my father's behaviour was certainly that. Schizophrenia can develop as a result of psychological assault, which he was definitely suffering, but it's also a reported side effect of benzodiazepines such as Mogadon. I believe the cocktail of Mandrax and Mogadon caused my father to spiral out of control and made him do some absolutely mad, out of character things, and contributed to what he called his 'psychological suicide'.

At my father's trial, his barrister, Geoffrey Robertson, questioned Dr Maurice Miller MP, who my father sometimes 'consulted' at the House of Commons, and Miller told the court that over the course of 1974 my father's character had changed and he 'frequently sank into deep anxiety states'. Geoffrey Robertson later wrote 'none of the independent experts in psychology or psychiatry we consulted had any doubt but that he had been clinically depressed. The private self lost faith in the public man: he seriously contemplated suicide, but designed instead a psychiatric equivalent: he would kill off John Stonehouse, MP, and return as Mr Markham or Mr Muldoon [*sic*] – anonymous and unambitious men whose ordinary joys he would savour.'[7] But in the mid-70s nobody knew about the catastrophic effects Mandrax and Mogadon can have on a person's mental state: not Dr Miller, not the General Medical Council, not the NHS, not Geoffrey Robertson, not the family, not Sheila, not the Judge and jury and not, even, my father.

Depression is a strange thing in that a person can exist in a dual mental state, walking a parallel course: continuing to behave normally, and yet sometimes sinking into a dark, hopeless, suicidal space. Often the person's family have no idea they're experiencing the dark space and only see the person behaving normally. This is how we were before my father's disappearance. Afterwards, we were aware of the dark times, and experienced them with him. Yet he could still appear to other people as normal, and that was a big part of his problem after he was discovered in Australia, and throughout the following legal proceedings.

In the 1970s, mental health problems in men weren't much talked about; men were expected to 'deal with it' and carry on. My father had a show to keep on the road, including employees he was responsible for, and a family. He didn't have a group of male friends who could've supported him. He didn't play cricket, rugby, football, golf, or any other ball game, so there was no tight team of sporty men who might understand him in his hour of need. The only game he played was the solitary game of chess, at which he usually beat his opponents. And by 1974, he'd come to detest the tribalism and hypocrisy of British politics, and pride would never have allowed him to reveal to old comrades what he was going through. Indeed, they were part of the problem.

Meanwhile, he could feel the dark cloak of suspicion that he was a communist spy enveloping him. The rumour wasn't going away, it was circulating. On 20th September, two months before he disappeared, the satirical magazine *Private Eye* published a story saying two Labour MPs were under investigation by Special Branch, linking payments and spying to the Czech embassy. No names were given, but because the newspaper community, parliamentarians, and much of the establishment could guess this piece referred to John Stonehouse, it was a hard psychological blow. On the 15th November, *Private Eye* published 'Bungler Dashed' – a play on the word 'Bangladesh', a country my father was closely associated with. The article outlined my father's career in the most disparaging terms and was a strange piece for the *Eye* because it was completely humourless and just a gratuitous character assassination full of false facts and inaccuracies.* When he was made aware of it a few days later, my father was furious and issued a writ and notice of seeking an

---

* My father thought this article had the fingerprints of George Wigg all over it. The Machiavellian Wigg had been Harold Wilson's former security liaison with MI5 and MI6. My father was so upset about the article, and my mother so worried about his reaction, she wrote to former home secretary Roy Jenkins, who was in Brussels at the time, saying the Labour Party was out of control and he needed

injunction through solicitors Allen & Overy, who listed ten separate points of complaint. He was too late to stop publication, but hoped to get unsold copies withdrawn from the shops. Unfortunately he was unsuccessful.*

On the 19th, my father flew back to Miami. This time he was travelling with Jim Charlton, the deputy chairman of his trade and export company Global Imex, and my mother hoped Jim's presence would help him maintain emotional equilibrium. She was wrong. The next time my father went swimming in Miami's inviting sea, he wouldn't be coming back.

to get back and sort them out. He sent a nice reply, saying that she was not the only one to suggest this.

* I assume that the reason my father's writ was unsuccessful was because *Private Eye* argued that nine of the ten points had been published previously and had not been legally challenged then, and the unpublished tenth point had not been contested as yet.

2

Who Was John Stonehouse?

My father grew up totally immersed in socialist politics. He was born in 1925 and as a baby spent most of his time in a pram parked at the back of draughty halls where his mother would be attending meetings, either of the Labour Party or the Women's Co-operative Guild – of which she became president. The same routine carried on when he was a toddler and child. My grandfather was a trade union man, so my father's entire childhood was, in one way or another, spent absorbing socialist ideology. The Women's Co-operative Guild was part of the larger co-operative movement, which included the Co-operative Wholesale Society, an organisation that bought food staples in bulk and distributed them to members at cost. Each purchase gave the member a 'divvy' – a dividend, which would later be in the form of stamps that could be collected in little books and exchanged for goods. Co-ops were democratic organisations where members voted to appoint officials and, still today, anyone who has a store card from a Co-op shop can vote for the management.

My father's parents were William and Rosina, and John was the youngest of their four children. Both their fathers worked in Royal Navy dockyards: William's as a shipwright; and Rosina's as a boiler-maker. At the age of fifteen, William began his six-year apprenticeship as an engine fitter at HM Dockyard Sheerness, later becoming a post office engineer and very active in the trade union. He died a few weeks after retiring and the esteem in which he was held was reflected by the fact that hundreds of people attended his funeral in the pouring rain. 'Rose', as we called her, was a councillor and alderman for 34 years, and sheriff and mayor of Southampton in 1959–60. She worked tirelessly her whole life not only for the two major political forces in her life – the Labour Party and the co-operative movement – but for all kinds of charitable causes including the Royal National Institute for the Blind, the Sunshine Homes for Blind Babies, and the National Association for Mental Health. During the Spanish Civil War my grandparents, and many other socialists, took in child refugees, and Rose went out scrubbing doorsteps to get the money to buy extra food to feed them. On a personal level, however, she was difficult. Initially, Rose wasn't keen on my mother, thinking her too young at seventeen to marry her son. She wanted John to marry a woman who ran a wool shop in Southampton and offered my mother £1,000 to call off the marriage. Obviously, she declined. Rose wasn't a nice grandmother; I don't remember her saying a kind word to me, yet alone sending a birthday card. Her visits were not keenly anticipated, because she'd say things like, 'Finish the food on your plate, don't you know there are children dying of starvation in Africa?' On one visit to her, I found a particularly manic passage of Shostakovich playing at full volume on her radio and when I asked if the neighbours minded, she dismissed me with a curt 'No'. My father was always kind and attentive to her. When she was close to death, I watched him spoon-feed her with infinite love and patience.

When the Second World War broke out in 1939 my father was fourteen and staying in Tours, France, on a school exchange trip. The father of Guy – the French exchange student – was a stamp dealer and my father learned about stamps from him, to the extent that he started trading stamps himself while still a teenager, an activity he maintained his whole life. Children under fifteen weren't allowed to travel alone in France, but my grandparents sent money to the shipping office at Le Havre and my father nevertheless travelled via Paris to Le Havre, arriving at 1.30am, and sleeping on a stone bench on the dockside. The next morning, he collected the money and spent a couple of days in a hotel until he managed to get a place on the second-to-last boat to leave Le Havre for Southampton. He was a scholarship student at Richard Taunton's grammar school, and as they'd already evacuated to Bournemouth, he joined them there. At sixteen, he got a job as an assistant probation officer, which introduced him to a whole new world of people's troubles. On one occasion he accompanied a parolee to prison in Wales and there was an argument at the gate because they thought he was the prisoner – he looked too young to be the probation officer. My father was an air cadet as a teenager and, as soon as he could, joined the Royal Air Force and trained as a pilot on Tiger Moths and Dakotas, in Phoenix, Arizona. Although he got his 'wings', the war was over before he got the chance to fly in combat and he spent the remainder of his service educating flight staff about to be demobbed. On a RAF scholarship, he then studied Government at the London School of Economics (LSE), graduating with a BSc in Economics with second class honours.

When my father was 22, he met my mother, Barbara, then sixteen, at the Hammersmith Palais dance hall. He was tall, handsome and loved to dance. My mother was already a card-carrying member of the Labour Party, which she joined after learning about the benefits of European co-operatives from her teacher, Miss Auber, at St Marylebone Central School. When my parents were courting, my father took my mother home late one night and they discovered she'd left her keys at home. She was living with her mother and stepfather on the top floor of a house in Highbury New Park, in Islington. A bathroom window had been left open so, in his brogue shoes with shiny leather soles, my father climbed four storeys up the drainpipe, crawled into the small window, came downstairs and opened the front door. He had a heroic streak like that. Later, as a journalist, he went deep into the war-torn Congo to find out what was going on while the other reporters sat around in a safe bar, drinking and copying each other's inaccurate stories. And at the tail end of the Bangladesh War of Independence, he crossed the border from India to see for himself what was happening there. Danger didn't hold him back.

My parents were married at Hackney Town Hall, eighteen months after they met, with the wedding party jumping on two buses to get to an Italian Restaurant on the Kingsland Road to celebrate. My mother was very beautiful, with deep blue eyes and flawless skin. Her mother, too, was a great beauty and was 'spotted' by film producer Harry Lachman when she was eighteen and working as an usherette at the Fortune Theatre in London. She signed a film contract with British International Pictures and found herself in Nice, France, playing opposite Monty Banks in the 1930 comedy film *The Compulsory Husband*. Although her meteoric rise from Islington working-class girl to movie star generated much press interest, Lilian didn't enjoy the new glamorous lifestyle, preferring the company of her large family who joked that she and her sisters Maude and Elsie had carried out every possible job in London's theatres, except stagehand. After abandoning the film world, Lilian developed a career as a singer and dancer on the London stage.

By sixteen, my mother was working for the Society of British Aircraft Constructors in Savile Row, with whom she attended her first air show, but one day, while waiting for my father at LSE, she saw an advert on the noticeboard for a junior secretary at the Fabian Society, an organisation that promotes democratic socialism. Despite the pay cut, she took the job and loved it. At the time, the chairman of the Local Societies Committee was Arthur Skeffington MP, and the secretary of the committee was the beautiful and intelligent Dorothy Fox. Under these two leading lights of the socialist movement my mother was encouraged to read up on the literature. Because the Fabian bookshop and offices were at 11 Dartmouth Street, a convenient ten-minute walk from the Houses of Parliament, she was also encouraged to go there and listen to debates, as well as attend Fabian weekend and summer schools held at Dartington Hall in Devon and Frensham Heights in Surrey. The atmosphere was electric, positive and optimistic, just what the world needed after the carnage of a war instigated by fascism. Together, and then later with my sister and I, my parents attended socialist youth camps all over Europe. In this way, they met many of the people who would later become active in politics in Europe, as my father had met students of politics from all over the world at LSE. These were the idealistic and networking years, and a lot would happen before my father came to write his book, *Death of an Idealist*.

As a teenager and young man, my father was a youth club leader, and later was MD of the International Union of Socialist Youth's travel service, which specialised in organising youth exchanges, study tours and summer schools – while trying to keep the communists from taking over youth and student groups. He served on various sub-committees of the London County Council and was vice chairman of a children's home in South London. He was a lecturer in adult education for Surrey County Council and for various co-operative societies. Most of his extra-curricular activities were voluntary. I've seen it said many times that my father was just greedy for money, but he was a volunteer at a farmer's co-op in Uganda for two years – supported financially by my mother working at British Insulated Callender's Cables (BICC), and for eight years he was an unpaid board member and then president of the London Co-operative Society (LCS). He also insisted on being unpaid as chairman of the British Bangladesh Trust. He did all these things because he believed in the causes, and, ironically, they all led to immense disappoint-ment: in Africa in the way politics developed, including Idi Amin's brutal control of Uganda; the take over and near destruction of the LCS by the communists; and the dangerous factionalism within the Bangladeshi community leading to the destruction of his reputation.

My father was very active in the co-op movement from an early age, being an active member of the Woodcraft Folk – the co-operative movement equivalent of the boy scouts – and thus had an early intro-duction to a social organisation wherein he took various leadership roles. Later, he became involved in co-operative society committee work, becoming a board member of the LCS in 1956 until 1962, then president between 1962–4. All this work was on a voluntary basis; as president he received £20 a year for expenses. It soon became clear to him that communists were trying to prevent the LCS developing into a modern trading organisation. He told a co-op sub-committee in January 1961: 'If we are content to merely allow our organisation to tick over as it has been doing, we shall find ourselves well and truly outstripped within the next decade'.[1] He told *The Grocer* magazine in April 1963 that 'due to historic circumstances, the LCS control structure has grown into a rather complex bureaucracy which tends to centralise detailed trading decisions, blunt initiative in the execu-tive ranks and delay action'. He continued, 'In practice many officials prefer to shelter behind committees rather than taking personal responsibility. The system encourages timidity and inaction.'[2] What he was really fighting against was the communist-infiltrated '1960 Committee' of LCS board members. Their candidates for re-election to the board in May 1963 were David Ainley, Harry Clayden, Sybil White, David McCallum and Ernest Randle – all, except the last, members of the Communist Party since the 1930s or 1940s.

In a Co-operative Reform Group election leaflet urging the 1.3 million co-op members to vote for non-communist candidates, he laid out the political reality: 'Those who have studied the devel-opment of the international Communist movement tell us that the Communists hate and fear no one so much as the Social Democrats. Wherever the Communists have succeeded in overthrowing the gov-ernment, they have turned like sharks on those Socialists who had been their collaborators. This is because the Communists cannot permit the existence of a reasonable alternative to their method of achieving "Socialism". For this reason they cannot afford to see the Co-operative movement succeed on any terms other than their own.' He begged the members to vote: 'Last year, only 12,000 people out of a membership of approximately 1,300,000 actually used their votes.'[3] That's less than 1 per cent of the electorate, but a similarly apathetic turnout in 1963 would cause the communists to get a tighter hold on the LCS, and bring about the demise of what was, at the time, the largest retail organisation in the UK. My father fought the communists tooth and nail within the organisation he'd grown up with and loved. I know this because I spent a fair amount of time as a child licking stamps and stuffing envelopes with anti-communist material. When commentators suggest my father spied for the communist StB because he was a secret sympathiser, they must be unaware that he spent almost ten years of his life, unpaid, battling communism. And if they say he did it for the money, there was no amount of money in this world that would convince my father to risk incurring the wrath of his anti-communist mother, who knew well the invidious nature of communism, which was rife in her day.

A constant feature of my father's political life was anti-colonialism. The Movement for Colonial Freedom used to hold meetings at the Quaker Friends House opposite Euston Station and afterwards participants would often continue discussions at our house in Islington. Day and night the house rang with anti-colonial discourse, with my mother providing impromptu meals for the guests. Anti-colonial sentiment extended across the world at the time and my father was friends with many of the movement leaders, some from Africa but also, for example, Lee Kuan Yew of Singapore. He also travelled to speak in support of their cause at independence rallies, such as with Dom Mintoff in Malta. My parents attended so many independence celebrations that Prince Philip once said to my mother jokingly, 'We must stop meeting like this.'

❖

My father was easy-going and generous. When we lived in the big house in Islington, my parents once lent it to Hephzibah Menuhin, sister of the violinist Yehudi, and her husband, Richard Hauser, while we went on holiday to Elba for three weeks. Hephzibah was preparing for a performance of Bela Bartok's *Piano Concerto No. 1,* so my parents hired a grand piano from the Wigmore Hall for her to practise, and had it installed in the first-floor study. Luckily, we had double-size front doors, so it could get in the house. Hephzibah didn't need it, in the event, because she used a table-top dummy keyboard to practise. Instead, her daughter Clara used the grand piano to play chopsticks. When we returned from holiday, we found a large group of young men talking on the steps outside and as we walked around the house, found more groups of men in every room. Hephzibah was in the kitchen, sitting around the table with Clara and her nanny, and various other people, singing 'Que Sera Sera'. She'd forgotten we were coming back that day. All the men were sleeping at our house, having recently been released from prison and having nowhere else to go. Prisoner rehabilitation was one of Richard's social projects – as with Hephzibah, one among many. Apparently, she'd borrowed sheets from our neighbour, Jane Carton who, with her husband Ronnie, compiled *The Times* crossword. Some people might have kicked up a fuss on finding nearly twenty ex-prisoners sleeping in their house, but my parents weren't like that. They just turned around and booked us into a hotel in Bloomsbury for a week while Hephzibah and Richard found alternative accommodation for their jolly band of misfits.

Both my parents were very kind. One day it was pouring with rain and as I stepped in the back door of a taxi, a young girl stepped in the door on other side. Neither of us wanted to get back into the rain so we shared the taxi and, on the journey, I heard her story. Beatrice Kasozi was sixteen years old and on the run from the brother of the Ugandan President, Idi Amin, who wanted to marry her. Her parents were opponents of Amin and her father had been shot while

driving his car, but luckily dodged the bullet. Kampala was dangerous, all kinds of gruesome murders were taking place, and it was
thought best for Beatrice to get out of town. Her father had sent
some money to a contact in London who was supposed to look after
Beatrice, but he'd never shown up. She was almost penniless, and
alone. When I told my parents this, they immediately took Beatrice
into their home and she became a member of our family.

Everywhere I've gone in my life, I've met people who were helped
by my father. Travelling around East Africa in the late 60s, I met
many people who remembered so well his efforts on their behalf in
their struggle for justice and independence. For years I couldn't pay
in an Indian restaurant using a cheque or card because many 'Indian'
restaurants are run by Bangladeshis, and when they saw the name
they'd say 'No, no, you must accept our gratitude, come again, any
time, no charge.' To avoid them being out of pocket I had to ensure
I carried cash to pay. I came across many people in random circumstances who would tell me their experience of him, like the time I
went into a dry-cleaning shop and the woman behind the counter,
seeing my name, asked the usual 'are you related?' When I said 'yes',
she implored me to thank my father because he'd been a tremendous
help to her son when they were both in the same prison. 'Tell your
father my son is doing really well,' she said, beaming.

As a father, John Stonehouse was tolerant, supportive and amusing. As well as reading books to us, he made up great stories of his
own, usually bizarre and hilarious. When I was a teenager attending the large Mount Grace Comprehensive School in Potters Bar, a
couple of friends and I asked the dinner lady why in the first sitting
kids got three sausages, and in the second sitting they got two, and in
the third sitting just one. It was more than sausages of course; third
sitting got dregs on a regular basis. Soon we were all called to the
headmaster's office where we were made to line our toes up against
the carpet before being given a lecture about interfering. He said to
me, 'This is not LSE, Miss Stonehouse.' This was shortly before the

Christmas holidays, when a huge volume of snow fell. We lived right across the road from the school and the night before it was due to open again, I told my father I was going to leave the headmaster a message, and told him my plan. He decided to come with me, and we climbed over the gate in our wellington boots and went to the small field under the headmaster's first floor window and wrote with our feet, in huge letters, 'FUCK YOU.' We didn't tell my mother, because she wouldn't have been impressed, or my sister Jane, because she'd tell the whole school it was us. The next morning the kids were in hysterics when they saw this message from their classroom windows, until the caretaker broke the wording with a big broom. Nevertheless, the message had got out there and my father and I had a good laugh about it.

He only once told me not to do something and that was when I was about ten. 'Where have you been?' he asked casually. When I said 'Sunday school,' he made me sit down and listen to a history of religious wars, and an explanation of how so much war has been approved and encouraged by religious establishments of all faiths. At the end of it he said 'when you're older you can decide for yourself whether you want to go to church but, for now, I won't allow it.' Clearly, his own Roman Catholic upbringing – and my grandmother was very active in the church – had not convinced him of the church's moral superiority.

Many people of my generation were burdened by their parents' racist, homophobic, or class-ridden prejudices – legacies they had to struggle to overcome. My siblings and I never had that, which meant we could start life unencumbered by those negative attitudes. My father couldn't care less what colour someone's skin was, what race or creed they were, what their sexual orientation was, where they came from, or how much money they had. Essentially, he believed in human equality and judged people on whether they were kind to their fellow human beings. I don't remember him once criticising my friends; it simply wasn't his natural style to find negative things to say about people. That trait changed with time and experience, especially with regard to the press and parliamentarians in the House of Commons.

My father became a Labour and Co-operative Party member of parliament in a by-election on the 28th February 1957, representing the West Midlands constituency of Wednesbury until February 1974 when the seat was abolished by boundary changes. He then stood for and became the MP for the adjacent constituency of Walsall North, whose boundaries were changed to incorporate some of the old constituency of Wednesbury. Nobody ever accused him of not being a highly conscientious and hard-working constituency MP and in this he was much supported by my mother's extremely efficient services as an unpaid parliamentary secretary.*

When Harold Wilson won the general election in 1964, he appointed my father parliamentary secretary at the Ministry of Aviation and over the next six years he would become parliamentary under-secretary of state for the colonies, minister of aviation, minister of state for technology, postmaster general and minister of posts and telecommunications. In 1968 he was appointed a privy counsellor, one of a select group that offer ministerial advice to the Queen. However, when Wilson lost the election in June 1970, shortly after the StB defector accused my father of being a spy, he was not offered a position in the opposition shadow government. His political career was over.

---

* Historic parliamentary proceedings as recorded by Hansard are available online, and so my father's entire parliamentary record is available to view at https://api. parliament.uk/historic-hansard/people/mr-john-stonehouse/index.html.

3

'Hold Your Heads High and Behave as Though the Country Belonged to You'

When I was nine, I came out of the front door of our house in Islington and stepped into a big puddle of industrial superglue. It was disconcerting not to be able to move my feet. For a minute there I thought I was paralysed. We never found out who'd done it, probably the same people who painted 'BLACKS GO HOME' in big letters over the pavement outside our house. Or maybe it was the people who painted the large swastika on our front door.

When I was ten, the phone rang and a man told my father, 'we know your daughter Jane gets on the overground train at Canonbury Station and gets off at Gospel Oak Station and walks across the park on her way to school. One day we're going to take her.' My sister did indeed go that way to her school, Parliament Hill. We never found out who'd phoned. It had hallmarks of the South African secret police, BOSS, but it could equally have been the racist British fascists. We were always under some threat or another. One day I remember the police crawling all over the house looking for a bomb because there was a ticking noise. It turned out to be the constant drip of rainwater from the wrought iron plant guard around the first-floor window ledge. We laughed in relief when we realised that, but this is indicative of how our lives were.

By this time, we'd lived in Uganda for two years and my father had been to Africa several times since. On one trip he'd been investigating the political and economic conditions for Africans in the British colonial territories of Kenya and what was then called Northern Rhodesia, Southern Rhodesia, Nyasaland and Tanganyika (now Zambia, Zimbabwe, Malawi and Tanzania). Officials in the Federation of Rhodesia and Nyasaland, based in Salisbury (now Harare), took objection to his activities and threw him out, declaring him a Prohibited Immigrant.

In 1952, we'd set sail for Africa on the maiden voyage of the SS *Uganda*. A fire erupted in the luggage hold half-way down the Red Sea and the male passengers were warned they might have to help put it out. It was a chaotic scene as the captain and everyone else, excluding my father and sister, were being seasick. A friendly cleric was praying for everyone while also vomiting over the side of the ship. My parents were taking a harp and washing machine to Kampala for Shirley, wife of George Shepherd, who my father would be joining as a volunteer for the Federation of Partnerships of Uganda African Farmers. We arrived in Mombasa on the 19th August; I was eighteen months old and my sister, Jane, was three. Somehow we got to Kampala with the harp and washing machine intact, and approached the house where we'd be living. My mother remarked how beautiful the tree outside was. It seemed to be covered in bright yellow flowers, but as the vehicle drew closer, the 'flowers' flew like an explosion in all directions, revealing themselves to be birds. This was Africa – colourful, exciting, surprising – and we loved it.

The house belonged to a Ugandan family, the Kitemerikes, and we shared the top floor with the Shepherds. There was no water or sanitation, but there was music and dancing and people were coming and going all the time and, aside from the bats and cockroaches, it was great fun. My mother wondered what Shirley thought she was going to do with the washing machine and supposed, being Americans, they were living in hope. George was a Doctor of Philosophy and had met my father when they were both at the London School of Economics. He'd been in Kampala almost a year before we arrived.

Both he and my father were unpaid volunteers, although they were given free accommodation and had a few expenses paid. My mother would support us by working as the secretary to the East African managing director of BICC, a large company that installed electrical cables between the pylons that opened up the supply of electricity in East Africa.

When my sister contracted cerebral TB, BICC provided us with a company bungalow where Jane could be better taken care of with the luxuries of running water and electricity. After moving in, my sister and I spent two days splashing around in the bath water, turning the taps on and off, enjoying the novelty of running water. Although I was only three-and-a-half when we returned to the UK, Africa left deep impressions. My earliest memory is stopping in our open-top Land Rover to watch the animals, with my sister and I on the back seat, and a giraffe coming over, leaning down and licking my sister's cheek. It was like sandpaper, she said. My mother remembers as hair-raising an occasion when we were driving along a dirt track and a herd of wildebeest came charging towards us. Luckily they separated when they reached the Land Rover and continued running on either side of the vehicle.

We lived in Uganda for two years, with my father and George working under the leadership of Ignatius Musaazi, director of the Federation of Partnerships of Uganda African Farmers (FPUAF). This made them essentially employees of the FPUAF, when it was almost unheard of for white men to work for black men. In Africa at the time, the usual position was that black people worked for white people, and that's how the whites, and the colonial governments, liked things. The FPUAF was an African-run organisation, distinct from the co-operatives that had been set up by the colonial government which Ugandans felt made them no better than serfs working for the white man. George and my father were tasked with assisting in the formation and organisation of co-operative societies and setting up the Uganda Consumers Wholesale Supply Co. Ltd.

The idea was to develop African trade and commerce from the start of the process to the end. It involved the collection of crops such as cotton, maize and coffee from many smallholdings, and selling them in bulk, thus achieving a better price for the farmers. Also, along the lines of long-established co-operative societies in the UK, retail co-ops would buy in bulk and sell at wholesale prices, cutting the cost to the consumer.

Encouraging the participation of Africans in trade and commerce proved difficult for a number of reasons. Most had only known self-sufficiency or exploitation by whites or Indian middlemen; the co-operative business model was something that had to be shown and proved. The FPUAF itself was disorganised, and some people within it saw it as an opportunity to exploit. Mr Sallie wrote to my father, complaining that Mr Joseph had not issued a sale receipt for some cloth in a shop and when the customer came back to collect it demanded the twenty shillings payment again. Mr Kafero also made a complaint about Mr Joseph, saying he was rude in speaking English to customers when knowing they couldn't speak it. My father and George travelled all over Uganda, buying and selling, and while they were doing the co-op's business from the front of the truck, one of the members was selling shares for a fake company at the back. When they complained about this, the share-seller was voted in as a director of the FPUAF by the other members. Disenchanted, George packed up and left for the USA. Despite the difficulties, there were some wonderful people in the FPUAF who really understood the advantages of a co-operative society, and were committed to achieving them.

My father travelled around East Africa, making contact with old friends from LSE and meeting new friends, all involved in the anti-colonial struggle. Kenya was different to Uganda in that it had a large number of white settlers, and land was being withheld from Africans. This led to understandable resentment. Africans wanted independence, and to be free of the paternalistic attitude of the whites who, at the same time, did nothing to create the institutional structures that could lead eventually to one man one vote. How would democracy follow independence if the colonial government did nothing to promote it? Kenya was repressive, and the result was the Kenya Land and Freedom Army (KLFA), also known as the Mau Mau – ostensibly an independence army but actually a brutal organisation. The colonial government gathered up tens of thousands of innocent people while trying to identify Mau Mau members. Most were never given a trial but were detained for years. Even when acquitted, men would remain imprisoned for more years, leading to deeper resentment. This only helped the Mau Mau to find converts. With the vicious circle of violence on both sides, no forward movement in terms of African development was being made. The black Kenyans felt a sense of hopeless frustration. My father collected information on the torture and killings being carried out by the British colonial authorities in Kenya, and sent that information – including names, dates and events – back to the UK. His activities brought him to the attention not only of the colonial authorities, but also of BOSS – the South African secret services. The CIA were creeping around, and when my parents saw some of their reports they realised the CIA were being informed by people who had no idea what was going on in Africa.

By the time we left Uganda at the end of my father's contract, the colonial authorities had us under surveillance. They didn't like the fact that my father worked for Africans, lived with Africans, socialised with Africans, ate with Africans, tried to help Africans become financially independent, and was supporting African independence. When my mother, sister and I arrived at Kampala airport to catch the plane to London, an undercover agent took our photograph. He didn't say anything. Another photographer took our photo as we approached the steps of the plane to London, and said: 'Your girls look lovely in those suits, I wish my daughters had such beautiful clothes.' We were wearing skirts and jackets made of soft, lightweight, grey wool, and patterned shirts, and they were exceptional because they'd been made by my mother's paternal grandmother who, before the war, had been a court dressmaker and made clothes for the royal family. She'd mailed the outfits to Uganda so we'd have something warm to wear when we arrived back in the UK, after running around in light cotton dresses for two years. The photographers had been sent to get evidence that we'd actually got on the plane and left the country. Presumably, they also took photos of my father, who'd left a couple of weeks before. The photographers worked for Special Branch, part of the colonial government.

We returned to a deeply racist Britain. This wasn't simply a reaction to the British Nationality Act of 1948, which allowed people from the colonies and newly independent Commonwealth states to take British citizenship and live here; the British had been educated to a sense of superiority, and that was hard to shift. Even though the war-torn country and new National Health Service needed more workers, when they arrived, they got the cold shoulder, complete with signs saying things like: 'No blacks, Irish, or dogs'. In 1958 there were riots in Notting Hill, and in Nottingham there were clashes involving racialist groups and their opponents, following a resurgence of Oswald Mosley's British Union of Fascists' ideology, popular in the 1930s.

Parliamentary reports from this period show just how entrenched this racism and, concomitantly, white entitlement was. On 31st May 1957, the House of Commons debated the East African Commission report and Mr Sorensen MP said, 'Let us by all means realise that we have as much right – we, the white people – to be in Africa, or in certain parts of Africa, as the Africans themselves,' and 'we should respect also, however foolish it may seem to us, the reluctance of the African to change his way of life ... It may be a stupid, it may be a primitive way of life; it may seem to us a foolish, unenlightened way of life; but it is their way of life.' In a debate four days later, on the Central African Federation, Kenya and Tanganyika (Racial

Policy), the conservative MP Archer Baldwin said, 'To say that the Highlands ever belonged to the Africans is not correct. There was no land which belonged to them. With shifting cultivation they eroded a piece of the Highlands and then moved on somewhere else, and then did the same thing again. It was only after the Europeans got there and stopped them fighting that the position which exists today was brought about.' The position he is talking about, of course, is that white farmers had appropriated the fertile land. Archer Baldwin was knighted the following year.

These attitudes were what my father was fighting against. On 28th November 1957, he asked the secretary of state for the colonies what funds had been allocated to the building of both African and European residential estates in six specific towns. The answer was that absolutely nothing had been spent on any African housing, and that £291,500 had been spent on housing for white people in Ndola, £188,000 in Kitwe, £55,000 in Luanshya, and £85,000 in Chingola. Nothing had been spent in the other two towns, Lusaka and Mufulira, apparently.

A leading light in the UK anti-colonial movement was Labour MP Fenner Brockway, who was a driving force behind the Movement for Colonial Freedom, of which my father became vice chairman. In their 1961 brochure, when Brockway was chairman, they explain their aims: 'The M.C.F. stands not only for the political freedom and the independence of all peoples, but for their freedom from military and economic domination. It is thus opposed to neo-colonialism, and now that independence has been gained by so many countries devotes much of its activity to exposing the persistence of imperialism.' In a debate on 3rd May 1957, Commonwealth and Empire Resources, Brockway referred to a United Nations report, saying 'These figures show the amazing fact that 30.6 per cent of the value of the total products of Northern Rhodesia goes in interest, dividend and profit each year to financiers in Europe and in America. My hon. Friend the Member for Wednesbury (Mr Stonehouse) described the wage levels of African workers in the copper fields. When, on top of those disgraceful facts, is added this proportion of one-third of the total value of production of the Colony which passes to external financiers, one begins to understand the degree of exploitation which is taking place in the Colonial Territories.' When anti-colonial MPs such as Brockway and my father challenged this financial status quo, the British establishment could feel their bulging wallets being stolen, and they didn't like it.

When we'd returned from Uganda in 1954, my parents found that the American tenants they'd rented our house to in Hounslow had painted it baby blue from top to bottom: ceilings, walls, floors, stairs, bannisters and furniture. My mother was aghast, and immediately took steps to find an alternative property. Her family lived in Islington, where she'd gone to primary school, and they told her that the local landowners, the Northampton Estate, were selling off their housing stock. My mother went directly to their offices and told them she and her husband would have a deposit from selling their house in Hounslow and were able to get a mortgage, and acquired a house for £5,000. So it was that we came to live in a huge four-storey Victorian villa with a garden overlooking the delightful River Walk, near my mother's grandmother and a street away from her great aunt Caroline. The house was too large for us, so my parents rented out the top floor to lodgers, but that still left plenty of space to accommodate the many African revolutionaries and British anti-colonialists who regularly held meetings there. My mother was a great hostess and my parents held terrific parties with interesting guests. They were young and idealistic: in 1956, my father was 31 and my mother, 25. The brightest socialist minds and many future African leaders were their friends. My sister and I often played with the children of barrister Seretse Khama and his British wife, Ruth, whose interracial love story is the subject of the film *A United Kingdom*.

Seretse became the first prime minister, then president, of Botswana, and his son, Ian, became the fourth president of Botswana, until April 2018, helping the country achieve remarkable economic growth.

When they'd lived in Hounslow, social breakfast get-togethers had become a feature of the household. My father was a student at LSE at the time and fellow students would come and stay and there'd be animated political discussions in the evenings, which would continue over breakfast. It was a good opportunity to introduce people to each other and make time to talk. The same routine of breakfast get-togethers continued in Islington, with a stream of guests including Pierre Trudeau, who became prime minister of Canada, and Joshua Nkomo, who led the Kalanga people of Matabeleland in white-ruled Southern Rhodesia and the political organisation ZAPU – Zimbabwe African People's Union. (He would be arrested in 1964 and spend ten years in prison but ultimately became a vice president of Zimbabwe.)

In the 1950s, Southern Rhodesia was a tinder box waiting to explode. It was self-governing, although a British Crown colony, and came under the Federation of Rhodesia and Nyasaland, also known as the Central African Federation (CAF), an overarching political grouping that would include the three areas: Southern Rhodesia (later Zimbabwe); Northern Rhodesia (Zambia); and Nyasaland (Malawi). The problem in Southern Rhodesia was land. The Land Apportionment and Tenure Act of 1931 had made it impossible for native Africans to own land, Africans only being allowed to work 25 per cent of land on a collective basis, while the minority white population could own 45 per cent of the most fertile land. Over the years the law changed somewhat but, essentially, Africans were legally barred from owning their own country. All kinds of hurdles were put in their way. Hence, the tinder box.

In February 1959, my father went on a fact-finding mission officially arranged by the Northern Rhodesian Government. They had no problem with the tour; the objections came from the federal government who felt themselves to be independent of the British

Government, even though they were actually part of colonial Britain. There was a sense of separation developing between the white settlers in Southern Rhodesia and their government in the UK, which would come to a head when, aiming to create an independent state of white minority rule like in South Africa across the border, the leader of Southern Rhodesia, Ian Smith, pronounced a Unilateral Declaration of Independence (UDI) on 11th November 1965. He chose Armistice Day to remind the British in the UK that the Rhodesians had fought alongside the mother country in the Second World War, hoping perhaps this would invoke a show of solidarity to their cause.*

* When the white Rhodesians declared UDI in 1965, the Labour government of Harold Wilson vacillated. In the Cabinet Room at 10 Downing Street on the 13th October 1966, the secretary of state for defence, Denis Healey, laid out the military challenge: the Rhodesian army was 10,000 strong; they had an armed police force of 12,000; three squadrons of modern ground attack aircraft, and one squadron of Canberra light bombers; there was no base closer than Aden; and the nearest port was Dar es Salaam, 1,000 miles away. There are those who think he exaggerated these figures and logistical problems to cover up the fact that Britain's soldiers were still busy fighting the 'secret' undeclared war in Malaysia, against Indonesia. The Minutes read 'The campaign itself might well be short: but thereafter we should be committed to occupying the country, with a bitterly hostile European population and with no Africans capable of running the country.' (Ref: The National Archives: CAB 128/46/21, Document 25.) Another factor was that the Cabinet didn't know how deeply the apartheid government of South Africa would get involved, and the UK relied on them for uranium and gold, plus they needed access to the military facilities of the Simonstown base. Although mandatory sanctions were imposed, British Petroleum (BP) offloaded their oil onto French ships which sailed to South Africa, from where it was taken overland and across the border into Rhodesia. America continued to buy chrome. It had not gone unnoticed by all black Africans that while the British were quick enough to put down a black rebellion by whatever military means necessary, when the rebels were white they did nothing. Harold Wilson added to this insult when emerging from negotiations with the Rhodesians by saying we couldn't fight 'our kith and kin' – meaning the whites. A guerrilla war ensued involving Joshua Nkomo's ZAPU and the larger group, ZANU, led by Robert Mugabe. Tens of thousands died. Largely on the kudos of having been involved in the fifteen-year war against the minority white rule that followed UDI, Mugabe became prime minister in 1980, and president in 1987, clinging to power for another 30 years.

In 1959, my father was concerned that Southern Rhodesia would turn into a blood bath like that occurring in Kenya, where white land settlement was also the major issue. He gave two speeches on 'The Labour Party's Colonial Policy' at the invitation of the Southern Rhodesian African National Congress, in Salisbury and Bulawayo, which would get him thrown out of the country by the federal government as a Prohibited Immigrant. He'd been talking about the struggle of the working class in Britain, then got to the part the white authorities found objectionable: 'So you must work for your rights in peace and then you will be much more likely to have the rest of the world behind you. Your slogan should be: "Work hard, educate yourselves, and organise." Use the right way, and you will win. If you use the wrong way you will be giving the most powerful weapons to those people who do not want to achieve the same things as you do. I ask you to have pride in your country. Hold your heads high and behave as though the country belonged to you. If you behave in a way that you are ashamed of, you cannot be surprised if people who are now your friends do become ashamed of you.' A reporter who was present at one of the speeches, Clyde Sanger of the *Central African Examiner*, put the speech in context, in response to a report in the *Rhodesia Herald* in which my father had been called a 'pedlar of mischief'. Sanger made the point that 'over and over again and with considerable courage he condemned the use of violence'.[1] Even though he was advocating peaceful means of struggle, the whites took objection to the words 'Hold your heads high and behave as though the country belonged to you' because, as far as they were concerned, it did belong to them. When my father arrived at Ndola Airport in Northern Rhodesia (now Zambia) a crowd of white people were waiting to throw tomatoes at him.[2] A week after returning to London on 12th March 1959, he attended a meeting at Central Hall where a fight broke out during which a young man shouted at him, 'Traitor to the white race.'[3] To put these events into historical context, this was three years before Nelson

Mandela would be arrested across the border in South Africa and go on to endure 27 years in prison.

My father's anti-colonial attitude dovetailed into events much later on. When the ex-MI6 conservative MP Stephen Hastings called for an inquiry into the Frolik allegations against my father in December 1977, he had personal reasons to do so. His father was a Rhodesian farmer, while Stephen himself had been in talks with Ian Smith, the leader of the white supremacists. He had links with South Africa, and the guerilla war was still going on. Hastings opposed the sanctions being imposed on Rhodesia, and wanted to find reasons to bring anyone who supported the black Africans into disrepute.

Few British politicians in the 1950s and 1960s would put into words the nub of the matter – colonialism was about slavery, racism and financial exploitation. They preferred the narrative that white people 'civilised the natives'. But my father was never shy in bringing the true nature of colonialism into sharp focus. In support of the Tanganyika Independence Bill, on 8th November 1961, he said in the House of Commons, 'Less than a hundred years ago British public opinion was electrified by the terrible reports of the slave trade in Tanganyika. At that time that country was being depopulated at the rate of tens of thousands a year by the slave traders who had gone into the interior from Dar es Salaam and who were using Zanzibar as their headquarters. It was partly as a result of this House setting up a select committee in 1871 to investigate the slave trade that the British public began to take an interest in doing something constructive for that part of the world. Now, less than a hundred years afterwards, we in this House welcome … the independence of this vast territory which had its very heart, its very soul and its very body torn out for something like four hundred years from the 15th century to the middle of the 19th century. We and the rest of the world have a debt to repay to Tanganyika for the damage done.'

When my father returned from Australia he made a statement in the House of Commons about his bizarre behaviour in 1974. It included these words: 'as a back-bench Member of Parliament, I campaigned vigorously for African independence … Much of my back-bench activities at that time … were concerned with advancing this cause. I believed in it sincerely and passionately. But those ideals were shattered in the late 1960s and the 1970s as Uganda and some other countries I had helped towards independence moved from democracy to military dictatorship and despair.' At the time my father said this, Idi Amin was in the process of killing somewhere between 300,000 and 500,000 Ugandan people, and Nelson Mandela was incarcerated by the racist South African apartheid regime, where he would remain long after my father had died. Events in Africa eroded my father's political and emotional foundations and, of course, they contributed to his depression. Hopelessness had replaced optimism.

4

The Bangladesh Fund

I have my father's collection of photos of bloodied, dead people lying on the streets of East Pakistan, which would become the independent country of Bangladesh, and it was the slaughter of 250,000 people there in 1971 that drew my father into the situation. When the British hurriedly partitioned India in 1947 at the end of colonisation, the two land areas deemed majority Muslim became 'West' and 'East' Pakistan, with 1,000 miles of India sandwiched between them. But the majority, who lived in the East, felt oppressed politically, financially and militarily by those in the West, and wanted independence. Demonstrations were peaceful, an election was won, yet the West Pakistanis were not prepared to allow separation. The easterners, Bengalis, reacted by killing those from the West, which brought about a military crackdown in March, with many Bengalis killed in turn. Ten million refugees fled to India. My father was asked by the charities War on Want and Oxfam to go on a fact-finding mission, and so his involvement with the independence movement began.

In Calcutta he met the 'Bangla Desh' Government in Exile including Tajuddin Ahmad, who was acting prime minister while PM Sheikh Mujibur Rahman was imprisoned in Pakistan. My father spoke advocating independence for Bangladesh in the House of Commons and elsewhere, and arranged for 'Bangla Desh' stamps to be made in the UK and shipped to Bangladesh, as a way of stating it was actually a country, despite what the West Pakistanis were doing.

He also became a Trustee of the Bangladesh Fund, which had been set up to collect money from UK Bengalis who wanted to support the Government in Exile, whether by arms or relief. Another Trustee was Mr Justice Abu Sayeed Chowdhury, who became president of Bangladesh. The money was collected by Bengalis in the UK, and deposited directly by them into a designated bank account. None of the Trustees had physical access to the financial collections.

The Indian government didn't want any more weapons going into the war zone, but international pressure persuaded them to send in the Indian army, and they defeated the 'West' Pakistani army. In December 1971 the fighting ended, and on the 8th January 1972 Sheikh Mujibur Rahman was released from imprisonment in Pakistan. My father was in Dhaka when he returned in triumph to Bangladesh and, in front of a million jubilant people at the racecourse, a cheque for £412,083 from the Bangladesh Fund was presented to Rahman by Abu Sayeed Chowdhury. The cheque was drawn on the account at the National Westminster Bank in Tothill Street, London, and became the first foreign reserve of the new nation. My father was made an honorary citizen of Bangladesh in recognition of what he had done for them.

Almost three years later, on 20th November 1974, my father disappeared in Miami. A week or so later rumours began to circulate that a large sum of money had gone missing from the Fund in 1972, before it reached Bangladesh. On the 29th, my mother told *The Sun* newspaper that such gossip was 'despicable'. On the 1st December 1974 the *News of the World* reported that unspecified 'documents about the relief fund' had been given to the law offices of former solicitor general Sir Dingle Foot by a retired vicar and minorities activist, Michael Scott, after he was told by 'some Bangladeshis' that the 'fund had topped £1½ million'. The first detailed newspaper report came out a day later, in the *Daily Mail*, whose headline read 'Yard mystery of Stonehouse fund'. Rev. Michael Scott was quoted as saying 'I started receiving complaints about the fund in 1972 and the police were informed.' Nothing had been done about the complaint and a Bengali barrister, Fazlul Huq, said he believed a diplomatic cover-up was very likely. The article said 'Official accounts of the fund which closed in September 1972 show receipts of £412,083. Bengalis have claimed that more than £1 million was donated.' So, according to the article, £587,917 was missing, the 'Yard' – by which they meant Scotland Yard, the HQ of the Metropolitan Police – had done nothing, and there was a diplomatic cover-up. The source of the accusation was unnamed 'Bengalis' and they had apparently told Scott that 'The complaints concerned collectors who were uncon-nected with the trustees.'[1] It seems they were saying that, as well as official collectors of donations for the Bangladesh Fund, there were people collecting money to put in their own pockets. There has never been proof of any such fraud and it seems the 'Yard' thought there was nothing to investigate. Even though the article made it plain that the unsubstantiated and uncredited accusation was 'unconnected with the trustees', my father would come to be accused in the British press of having stolen (approx.) £600,000.

The donation collectors had put the money into their local branches of the National Westminster Bank and none of the trus-tees had access to it, either before deposit or after. The Fund was officially audited, and another audit was carried out by the new Government of Bangladesh when they received it. There never was £1 million collected. That was a figure completely made up by the unnamed 'Bengalis' who suspected that unofficial collectors had taken money. When the *Daily Mail* article came out, Mr Justice Abu Sayeed Chowdhury, a trustee of the Bangladesh Fund and future president of Bangladesh, issued a denial that any money was missing and that appeared as three lines hidden deep within the newspaper, where nobody saw it. What they had seen was 'Stonehouse stole £600,000 from charity', and that would cast aspersions on his integrity, right up to the present day. On 6th December, four days after their 'missing' Fund money article, the *Daily Mail* published another Bangladesh-related story, headlined '£1 million riddle of Mr Fixit, MP'. In this, they said my father had made at least £1 million from business deals in Bangladesh. This was completely unfounded and my mother was furious. The following day they had to run 'What £1m, says Mrs Stonehouse'.

The December 1974 *Daily Mail* article about 'missing' money generated other press reports, full of innuendo. In December 1977, Department of Trade (DTI) investigators Michael Sherrard and Ian Hay Davison, appointed to carry out an exhaustive examination of my father's business and personal finances, published their report. It said: 'Mr Stonehouse was one of three trustees of the Bangla Desh Fund – sometimes known as the Bangladesh Relief Fund. We were aware of rumours in the press that he might have misappropriated or made use of the funds of that charity. Although not strictly within our terms of reference, we kept a weather eye open for any evidence of improper dealings with the funds of that charity or the possible mixing of such funds by Mr Stonehouse but our work did not reveal any hint of wrongdoing in this connection. We have seen many witnesses hostile to Mr Stonehouse: not one of them has suggested that he interfered in any way with charity monies. It is only fair to Mr Stonehouse to say that, so far as our investigations can show, such rumours are without foundation.'[2]

But stolen charity money was a story too juicy to let go and the press just couldn't help themselves, so a year after the DTI report was published, on the 17th November 1978, *The Times* ran an extremely damaging editorial, saying, 'It is impossible to gauge to what extent the disappearance of £600,000 from the Bangladesh Fund (of which he was a trustee) may have sown unjustified public suspicions about international charitable enterprises in general.'[3] We couldn't believe what we were reading. A letter from my father's solicitor, Michael O'Dell, was printed in *The Times* the following day: 'At no time have the police or any other responsible body ever suggested that Mr Stonehouse was involved in any way, shape or form, in the disappearance of one penny from the Bangladesh Fund.'[4] Bruce Douglas-Mann MP also wrote to *The Times*, on 21st November: 'Inquiries which I have made reveal no grounds whatever for suggesting that any of the money gathered by hundreds of self-appointed collectors for this fund in 1971 (in the immediate aftermath of the invasion of what was then East Pakistan by West Pakistan) disappeared after it reached the trustees.'[5]

This was happening two months after my father's heart had stopped, when radioactive dye was released into his heart to facilitate X-rays at Hammersmith Hospital, which he recovered from after electric shocks were administered, and ten days after he'd had bypass heart surgery, while still serving a seven-year sentence in jail. The last thing he needed was this. He was furious, and from his hospital bed wrote to the editor of *The Times* about 'that shocking canard concerning the Bangladesh Fund. You refer to a missing £600,000 without any evidence or basis whatsoever. In fact there is nothing missing from the Fund. Once the figure of a missing £1 million was being bandied about. Why don't you use that amount? Or even £6m? Why should the journalistic licence you take to yourself be limited to a mere £600,000?' This letter, like so many other letters of denial over the years, would never be published.

And because of such irresponsible reporting, the myth carries on. Today I read on the *Mail Online* website a report from 8th January 2011 by Geoffrey Levy: 'There was also £600,000 missing from a charitable fund he had set up at the Bangladeshi bank to help victims of devastating floods there.'[6] First, nothing was missing; second, he didn't set it up 'at the Bangladeshi bank'; and third, it wasn't to help victims of floods, devastating or otherwise.

❖

My father's support of Chowdhury, Rahman and the new country of Bangladesh would bring him enemies from opposing factions within the Bangladesh political community and even, perhaps, in the form of the Pakistani secret services. Today Rahman is known as the 'Father of the Nation,' but in the early 1970s Bangladesh, and the Bangladeshi community in the UK, was awash with conflicting political interests. On the 15th August 1975, three-and-a-half years after becoming the prime minister of Bangladesh in January 1972, Rahman was killed along with most of his family and personal staff, by army officers who drove tanks into the presidential residence. They were backed by Rahman's former colleagues in the Awami League, and the Bangladeshi factionalism that would cause my father so much trouble brought to an end the dream that had begun with a speech my father heard, with a million others, in Dhaka, when Rahman had just returned from imprisonment in Pakistan following the end of that terrible war: 'Bengal is rich, there will be no exploitation as we will be a democratic and socialist state and a secular one too.' With Rahman's assassination, Bangladesh would be subject to more coups and counter-coups, and years of conflict and death. For my father, it was another idealistic hope dashed.

5

Lost in Translation: Could Be, Would Be, Might Be, May Be, or Will Be?

My father's life would have taken a completely different route if Kazi B. Ahmed had not walked into the House of Commons, uninvited, and asked to see him. Ahmed was a 27-year-old Bengali who thought it would be a good idea to set up a banking vehicle for the 85,000 wage-earning Bengalis living in the UK who wanted to remit monies to Bangladesh but, following the carnage of the 1971 war, were no longer prepared to use Pakistani banks. This proposed banking facility had nothing whatever to do with the Bangladesh Fund, which had been closed by this time. Banking was not something my father thought about, or knew about, but he agreed to meet with Ahmed again, this time with his solicitor, Julian Lipton, on the 25th January 1972. The following day they met at my father's offices at 26 Dover Street, Mayfair, with some prominent Bengali businessmen and my father's accountant friend, John McGrath.

My mother was against the whole idea. She thought my father should just stick to his trade and export businesses: Export Promotion and Consultancy Services (EPACS) and Global Imex. These had been set up entirely on my father's own financial assets and he took no salary from EPACS in 1971, only £1,000 in 1972, and £2,000 in 1973, essentially foregoing a salary to build up the companies. The businesses were gaining expertise and clientele and my father didn't need any diversions, especially as he was also a serving member of parliament. Exports were something he knew a lot about, and he was good at his job. Indeed, he'd been appointed a privy counsellor in June 1968 on the citation 'services to export'. I remember attending the annual dinner of the Wednesbury Divisional Labour Party in March 1967 and hearing Roy Jenkins, then home secretary, telling the audience: 'Your member has put in a good deal of hard salesmanship for this country in all parts of the world. Hardly any other person in this country can claim to have sold getting on for £100 million worth of exports purely on his own efforts. No one has made a greater contribution than John Stonehouse.'[1]

But, unfortunately, my father was persuaded to pursue the banking project. He wasn't at all sure that the idea would come to anything; clearly it was unfeasible if reliant on individual Bengalis alone, and would need the support of British institutions. The first step was to consult with the Bank of England. He told everyone concerned that he didn't want to be seen as gaining any pecuniary advantage and that if the bank went ahead he would only be chairman if the role was unpaid. On this basis, my father visited Leslie O'Brien, the governor of the Bank of England, along with Ahmed, a businessman called Nazir Uddin, and the accountant John McGrath. They were met with a surprisingly positive response, and some helpful introductions, and the unlikely project proceeded forward. Although the original idea was that it would be called 'The British Bangladesh Bank,' the Bank of England officials made it clear that the word 'bank' could not be used until the Department of Trade issued a certificate, which could not be granted until at least one year's sound trading had occurred under the supervision of management experienced in banking. It was decided that for the time being it would be called the 'British Bangladesh Trust Limited' (BBT).

As unpaid chairman of BBT, my father spent the next nine months raising pledges for share capital. Various banks, institutions and private individuals pledged financial support – with the banks recognising there could be commercial value for their clients wanting to do business with the recently independent country of Bangladesh.

In June 1972, my father's export company, EPACS, acquired the lease for the property adjoining its office, 27 Dover Street, and paid for the ground floor conversion to a banking hall, and the refurbishment of offices above. They also paid for the staff who were employed, and all the necessary printing. These expenses were later repaid with no interest being charged.

The BBT was approached by a man called Suhail Aziz who said he was a regional secretary of the Awami League – the political party in Bangladesh that had led the independence movement. It was initially agreed to give him a job, but he kept increasing the amount of pay he required, plus he wanted a directorship, his own office and a full-time assistant. Eventually he was told he wouldn't be required. The disaffected Aziz didn't leave it there and was about to cause all kinds of trouble.

News about BBT was spreading and it was time for the Bangladeshi community to be informed about the venture being proposed. Meetings were set up around the country to explain the purpose of the BBT, but when my father and his PA, Philip Bingham, arrived at the meeting places they were told that Aziz had been there before them, telling Bengalis not to put their money in the BBT or purchase shares. For the purpose of these meetings, my father had asked the editor of a Bengali newspaper, *Janomot*, to write a leaflet in Bengali. It was not a banking 'prospectus' – a legal document on which shareholding is offered – which was only ever printed in English; it did not invite anyone to make a payment, or a financial pledge; it was simply designed to make it clear that, although linked to my father's name, BBT had nothing to do with the Bangladesh Fund to which people had made donations, and was instead a banking facility. The leaflet stated that although the name of the facility included the word 'Trust' at present, that could be changed to 'Bank' in the due course of time, once all the official Bank of England requirements had been met. That last sentence seems straightforward enough, but all my father's difficulties would come to stem from the use of the words 'could be'.

The problem with the translation of the Bangladeshi leaflet, is that in the poetic and fluid Bengali language, the words 'could be' can also be translated as 'would be', 'might be', 'may be', or 'will be'. That distinction was used by my father's Pakistani or Bangladeshi enemies to cast aspersions on his integrity. The *Sunday Times* received a letter from a man called Samad Khan, who wrote that the promotional material said 'the Bank of England will give its permission' to convert the Trust into a Bank in twelve to eighteen months. On 19th November 1972, the *Sunday Times* published an article critical of the proposed flotation, saying 'the most crucial feature of this BBT flotation is the claim in the Bengali leaflet handed out with the English prospectus that the Bank of England *will* [their italics] give permission' for BBT to become a bank in twelve to eighteen months. This was shortly before the subscriptions were due to open – the legal process by which monies for the BBT are received – and the attack on my father's credibility would lead to a reduction in the expected funds from banks and investment companies. This compounded the negative impact of Suhail Aziz's activities within the Bengali community, which had been expected to invest £500,000 but, in the end, only provided £15,000 of capital to the project.

The *Sunday Times* article had been written by Richard Milner and Anthony Mascarenhas, a man my father knew. Mascarenhas was an Indian Goan Christian who was working as a journalist in Karachi, Pakistan, when invited with other journalists to what was then East Pakistan to see what the Pakistani army had been doing there. They wanted the journalists to report on the killing of West Pakistanis in March 1971, but Mascarenhas instead wrote a long article entitled 'Genocide', which exposed what the Pakistani army had been doing in retaliation, which was killing perhaps over 100,000 Bengalis. The article was published in the *Sunday Times* on 13th June 1971, and influenced the Indian prime minister Indira Gandhi to send the Indian army into East Pakistan to bring the genocide to an end. Before publication, Mascarenhas had to get his family out of

Pakistan, and they moved to London, where he became a hero of the Bengali community. At around the same time, my father had arranged for stamps to be designed and printed in the UK, marking 'Bangla Desh' as an independent state and these were 'issued' on the 27th July; on the 1st August a big rally was held in Trafalgar Square, where my father spoke for Bangladesh's independence from Pakistan; on the 27th August both my father and Mascarenhas attended the opening of the 'Bangladesh Mission' at 24 Pembridge Gardens, Notting Hill, which was to become the international HQ of the not-yet-established new country. The mission was short of money to furnish the premises, so my mother arranged for this to be done by a short-term rental of smart furniture from a cheap theatrical hire business in Isleworth, and bought them crockery from Woolworths. At the inauguration, my father gave a speech and Mascarenhas led the prayers. When the *Sunday Times* article of 19th November 1972 was published, my father was upset that Mascarenhas could be so accusatory, given they were supposed to be on the same side. My father was told by the Head of Security at the Indian embassy that Mascarenhas was a Pakistani spy, which seemed unlikely as he'd exposed their army's genocidal activities. Yet, this was what he was told, and given that the Milner/Mascarenhas article challenged my father's integrity, he came to believe that Mascarenhas was a spy or a double agent, and that coloured how he reacted to the article, which was badly, because it negatively influenced the Bengali community and dashed the hopes and expectations of the BBT project. My father also wondered whether it was a simple case of jealousy, with Mascarenhas thinking he'd been replaced as hero of the day.

Another complaint in the *Sunday Times* article was that the BBT prospectus had not explained that my father was a beneficiary of BBT, in that the landlord of the premises they occupied was EPACS, of which my father was a director. When DTI inspectors Sherrard and Hay later asked the various professional advisors about this non-declaration of the lease details in the prospectus, they had different takes on it. The auditors said the solicitors had advised them that it did not need to be disclosed because there was no concluded contract between BBT and EPACS and it was, in any event 'de minimis' – too trivial to merit consideration. The solicitors said that at the time of the prospectus there was nothing to disclose because no financial arrangements with regard to the premises had yet been made. The stockbrokers, Williams de Broe, were represented by Peter Pettman, about whom the DTI inspectors wrote: '[He] appears to have been under the erroneous impression that disclosure was not required because there was to be no application for a Stock Exchange quotation.'[2] Peter Pettman was wrong, and perhaps partly responsible for the omission in the prospectus. He told the *Sunday Times* reporters, 'We have had it scrutinised by the Stock Exchange, just so they could have a sight of it – that's all.' In 1977, the DTI inspectors concluded that, on the matter of the lease declaration, 'we do not think that anyone intended to mislead the public',[3] but in 1972, Mr Pettman had been put on the spot by the *Sunday Times* and perhaps he was feeling defensive because, if he was quoted accurately, he proceeded to destroy the project's credibility. The article said: 'Viewing the BBT flotation largely as an exercise in raising money from UK companies wanting to establish useful connections with Bangladesh, stockbroker Pettman is astonishingly frank about its merits as an ordinary investment. "It would not be advisable to put money into it at this stage," he says.'[4] About this quote the DTI inspectors wrote 'Mr Peter Pettman made comments interpreted as adverse and this added to the general suspicion directed at the Offer. This heightened the effect of the criticisms implicit in the article of 19th November 1972.'[5] It was eight days before the short three-day window of opportunity to buy shares in BBT, which opened on 27th November, and the publicity couldn't have been much worse.

The *Sunday Times* article now became a weapon in the hands of someone who was determined to cause my father further trouble. He sent some papers, including the *Sunday Times* article – anonymously

– to the Department of Trade (DTI), accusing my father of fraud under the Companies Act. The allegation was that he'd used the word '*will*' in the Bengali leaflet – which the anonymous writer was calling a 'prospectus' – which the leaflet most definitely was not. The handwriting on the package was already known to the DTI, who'd had dealings with the man before, regarding an unrelated matter, and my father recognised it too. Nevertheless, the DTI were obliged to investigate the 'anonymous' allegation, and so it was that Mr Newman arrived at Dover Street, holding the *Sunday Times* article in his hand. After their investigation, the DTI concluded that nothing illegal had occurred and no action should be taken.

Meanwhile, junior officers at the DTI had taken it upon themselves to send the papers to Scotland Yard's Fraud Squad. This wasn't their decision to make, and they seemed unaware that their superior officers were carrying out an investigation. Nevertheless, in February 1973, Detective Inspector Grant of Scotland Yard arrived at my father's offices, and explained that he was investigating the Bengali leaflet and the accusations in the *Sunday Times* article. My father phoned the editor of *Janomot*, the Bengali newspaper, and he translated the offending sentence: it '*could be*' renamed as a 'Bank' if the Bank of England approved. Both Grant and Newman obtained their own translations, each different from the next: in some it was '*could be*', in others '*would be*', '*might be*', '*may be*', or '*will be*'. Grant spent months going through all the paperwork and interviewing Bengalis who had invested small amounts in the Trust – who assumed something must be very seriously wrong if Scotland Yard had taken the trouble to come all the way to their 'Indian' restaurants in the north of England to interview them. People believe 'there's no smoke without fire', and reputational damage inevitably ensued. Confidence in my father had completely drained away by the time both Scotland Yard and the DTI decided there was no case, civil or criminal, to answer. By then, the damage had been done and my father was a nervous wreck. He wrote, 'The pressure of what I felt was unjust persecution was warping my mind and was making me incapable of normal rational relationships.'[6] That might have been because since the *Sunday Times* article came out in November 1972 he'd been popping Mandrax into his mouth to deal with the anxiety and insomnia it had caused.

After my father disappeared in November 1974, the Department of Trade and Industry investigated the activities of the BBT and their report said: 'He was determined to defeat the attack by surviving it at any price. In this he identified himself with BBT. He regarded the article as a challenge from an unjustly powerful enemy and he resolved to join battle and fight to the apparent death. His sense of proportion lost, his judgement distorted and his bitterness increasing with each sign of adversity, he abandoned the rules, repeatedly and with ingenuity broke the law, and destroyed his own idealism.'[7]

When the subscription lists closed at 10am on Thursday 30th November 1972, BBT had raised £651,140 in applications for shares, but 52 per cent of it had come directly, or mostly indirectly, from my father, his companies, the family, his nominees, staff and directors. The prospectus had said that no more than 10 per cent would come from directors, as that is the law. Finding this money involved taking out huge personal and company loans and they all had to be paid back. This was the beginning of a money-go-round that got faster and faster, breaking many regulatory rules along the way. He thought they could trade out of the situation and sell on the shares they'd purchased, but the timing couldn't have been worse. A financial crash was just around the corner.

I've often read that my father faked his own death because 'he was under investigation' by the DTI and Scotland Yard. This is a misrepresentation of what happened. The words 'he was' can be taken to mean 'he was at the time he disappeared' or, the reality – he was, but he was cleared and no charges brought, almost two years before he disappeared. Newspapers, knowing the facts are that he was cleared, twice, will still write 'he was under investigation' because it's open to interpretation, and implied drama sells newspapers. The lawyers will allow this deliberate obfuscation because the reader is being left to draw their own conclusion: that he was being investigated *at the time*, and that's what he was running away from. It might seem a small point, but there are hundreds of similar examples of subtle misrepresentation of the facts, and they all add up.

The *Sunday Times* were well aware that their article about the BBT on 19th November 1972 had led to two investigations – by the DTI, and Scotland Yard's Fraud Squad, both of which proved there were no civil or criminal charges to answer. Still, why let a good story die when there are column inches to fill and money to be made? So, two years later, a few days after my father was arrested in Melbourne, on the 29th December 1974, they resurrected the story once again, saying the leaflet 'could be taken as a Bengali prospectus'. They didn't mention that two lengthy investigations had been made into that 'prospectus', as they disingenuously called it, and nothing untoward had been found, that no charges were brought. But they had an agenda, and a narrative: '… one of the few things that can be said with absolute certainty is that, far from its being the product of a brainstorm, his flight was a carefully planned, cunningly executed operation which could not have been carried out without the active help of at least one co-conspirator in this country.'[8] By introducing the concept of 'conspiracy', which can carry a sentence of life imprisonment in the UK, they added more pressure to the situation. It was a malicious piece of journalism, and we were all shaken to the core, with my father devastated once again.

How ironic it seemed in Australia to be accused of undertaking 'a carefully planned, cunningly executed operation' when making basic, simple mistakes had ensured my father was under Australian police investigation less than two days after arriving in Melbourne. This was not 'a cunningly executed operation' but the actions of a disturbed man trying to escape a series of repercussions that ensued following the attack in the *Sunday Times*.

6

Secrets and Lies

My father's problems began in 1969 when Josef Frolik, a defector from the communist Czech secret service, the StB, accused him of being one of their agents. Frolik had no proof, had never seen my father's file, or given him any money. The head of MI5 didn't believe Frolik because he was a known liar: his unfounded fabrications included stories about Prime Minister Edward Heath, left-wing MP Michael Foot, and trade-union leader Ernie Roberts. But right-wing elements within MI5 wanted to use the Frolik misinformation for their own purposes and they made sure the rumour about my father being a spy spread to the press and to parliamentarians. As the information came from MI5, people believed it. A miasma of suspicion and contempt fell over my father and he was doomed. Nobody likes a traitor, and that was particularly the case during the 1970s, when the threat of nuclear attack by communists was so real the UK government were distributing booklets about it, and broadcasting a series of public information films on TV called 'Protect and Survive', which described how everyone should make 'fallout rooms' in their homes, complete with stockpiles of emergency supplies.

The Czech spy allegation had a life of its own and, although it was never proved, and my father was never charged or convicted, it threw a dark and dangerous cloak of suspicion around him which he could never shake off. On the 14th December 1977, while my father was incarcerated in jail, Josef Frolik's name was mentioned 53 times in the House of Commons by a triumvirate of right-wing Conservative

MPs, who were calling for a full inquiry into the allegations made by Frolik. That cause was subsequently taken up by another Conservative MP, Patrick Mayhew, who spent six hours recording conversations with Frolik in America, precisely to elicit information about my father from him. When the prime minister asked Mayhew, on 12th July 1978, 'does Frolik say he <u>knew</u> Stonehouse was a spy?' (his emphasis), Mayhew replied: 'no: he said that Husak told him that he was going to approach Stonehouse – and said that he did so – and Frolik says that he does not know whether Stonehouse gave Husak any information.'[1] Frolik knew nothing. Husak was also an StB agent in London and features in my father's file, which I have acquired from the Czech secret service archives in Prague.

The Mayhew tapes were referred to in a private meeting between the Labour prime minister, James (Jim) Callaghan, and Labour ex-prime minister, Sir Harold Wilson, in the Cabinet Room at 10 Downing Street on the 14th July 1978. Callaghan made notes of the meeting, saying he told Wilson 'the Tories were making trouble on this, they were not trying to hook Stonehouse, they were trying to hook *him*' (emphasis my own).[2] The right-wingers hoped to bring Harold Wilson into disrepute for having given a government job to a communist spy. This had been the focus of the MI5/MI6 Stonehouse leaks from 1969 onwards because the CIA, in particular, had the notion that Harold Wilson himself was a KGB spy. The Labour governments of 1974–9 had razor-thin parliamentary majorities and were in a precarious position politically. The right-wingers were keen to bring them down with a scandal, just as the conservative government of Harold Macmillan had crumpled after the revelation that their war minister, John Profumo, had been having an affair with Christine Keeler, who'd also slept with a man from the Russian embassy. The right-wingers were desperate because the country was in a mess, and they had plenty of wealthy supporters, especially after March 1974 when the Labour government raised the rate of investment income tax to 98 per cent for highest earners.

All that communist defectors had, between them and a life of terror and poverty at home, was the hope that the CIA or MI5 or MI6 would buy their gossip and give them a new, cosy, all-expenses-paid life in the West. Their only capital was information, and if they didn't have it, they'd make it up. Their lives may have depended on it. In all I've read on the subject of defectors, not one person has a good word to say about them. Yet, curiously, at the same time as being suspicious of their motives and veracity, the security services and various commentators often quote defectors' 'evidence' as if it came from the mouth of the Virgin Mary. In my father's case, the relevant defectors were Josef Frolik and Frantisek August – who are discussed in detail in later chapters of this book – and 'Affirm'.

In the spy allegation story there are two distinct time frames: before the famous StB file was made available to view by researchers in 2008, and after. In 2009, *The Defence of the Realm – The Authorized History of MI5* was published, and that has now become the go-to reference source on the subject of my father being a spy. Although Crown Copyright, it was written by Christopher Andrew, who is Emeritus Professor of Modern and Contemporary History at Corpus Christi College, Cambridge. As a work of reference, the book has excellent credentials. Nevertheless, I am going to contest just about every word Andrew has to say concerning John Stonehouse, which led to his damning conclusion that he was 'the only British politician (so far as is known) to have acted as a foreign agent while holding ministerial office'.[3]

Excluding notes, index, appendices etc., *The Defence of the Realm* is 851 pages long, with about one-and-a-half pages on my father – in other words, not much. Ten of those lines are taken up describing (and misquoting) a sex scene from a novel my father wrote, *Ralph*. In this, there's a honeytrap scene which Andrew says 'may have drawn on his own experience', and 'if it is at all autobiographical, tends to support the claims in Frolik's memoirs that Stonehouse had been recruited by the StB after falling victim to a honey trap during a visit to Czechoslovakia in the late 1950s'.[4] Clearly it's absurd to refer to a work of *fiction* as any kind of 'support' for an allegation of spying. Andrew refers to Frolik's memoirs, but doesn't repeat what Frolik actually wrote: 'The man in question was an MP who had been involved in some sort of homosexual trap,'[5] because Andrew doesn't believe my father was homosexual. The subject of homosexuality came up in a note to the prime minister, Harold Wilson, from his principal private secretary (PPS), Ken Stowe, dated 4th July 1977. Referring to information from Cabinet Secretary John Hunt, Stowe refers to Frolik's allegation 'about an unnamed Labour Minister who became involved in Czechoslovakia and this was believed to be a reference to Stonehouse, although in some respects Frolik's description of the man was quite inapplicable to Stonehouse'.[6] This is the diplomatic way of saying they didn't think he was gay. The more important point, however, is that there's absolutely no mention whatsoever in the StB file about a honeytrap – homosexual or heterosexual, and, indeed, there are many references to the fact that my father had not been compromised in any way at all.

In Frolik's 1975 memoirs, *The Frolik Defection,* he doesn't mention my father by name and the relevant text is only 200 words long, including hyperbole and general comments about democracy. It's hardly a rich mine of information. Moreover, Frolik himself said that his memoirs were unreliable. On the 15th December 1977, Cabinet Secretary John Hunt told Prime Minister Callaghan what Frolik had said about this book: 'that passages which were inconsistent with what he had originally reported (to the Security Service and to the CIA) could be ignored.'[7] Frolik also told MP Patrick Mayhew that 'much of his book that had been published had been written for him by a crooked publisher'.[8] Meanwhile that publisher, Leo Cooper, when interviewed by the BBC's security correspondent, Gordon

Corera, said 'he was sure the security and intelligence services had a hand in the book'.[9]

Christopher Andrew writes, 'In 1980 evidence from an StB defector codenamed AFFIRM persuaded both the Security Service and the Thatcher government that Stonehouse had been a Czech agent. Since, however, it was decided that the defector's evidence could not be used in court, Mrs Thatcher agreed that Stonehouse should not be prosecuted.'[10] Cabinet papers tell the story. Sir Robert Armstrong, who was cabinet secretary at the time, wrote to Mrs Thatcher on the 7th July 1980, reminding her about Mayhew's six-hour recording of Frolik in the summer of 1978, about which she had been informed at the time, then says, 'New information has now become available from a new CIS defector. According to first reports, he claims to have been Mr Stonehouse's controller from March 1968 to some time in 1969, while he was stationed at the Czech embassy in London; he claims to have taken over as Mr Stonehouse's controller from Robert Husak (who was named by Frolik as a member of the CIS who had been ordered to contact Mr Stonehouse) in Czechoslovakia in March 1968; and he says it was clear from a file which he had read that Mr Stonehouse was a conscious paid agent from 1962, had after taking office in 1964 provided information about Government plans and policies and about technological subjects including aircraft, and had been paid over the years about £5,000 in all (although none of it by this defector).'[11]

By the 11th September, the attorney general had been informed and Armstrong tells Thatcher, 'It seems that he takes the view that the new evidence would not be sufficient to sustain a successful prosecution.'[12] On the morning of the 6th, Mrs Thatcher had a meeting with the home secretary, the attorney general, and Sir Robert Armstrong at which the attorney general said he was 'sure that Mr Stonehouse had been a spy for the Czechoslovaks but he had no evidence which he could put before a jury. The new information … was not of the kind which would secure a conviction, and in any case the defector was not prepared to come to this country and take part in a trial.'[13] The attorney general was Michael Havers, who was not a man who shied away from prosecuting innocent people on little or no evidence. In 1980, it was still not known publicly that Havers, representing the Crown and the director of public prosecutions (DPP), played a crucial role in the imprisonment of eleven innocent people who collectively served 113 years in prison, and suffered one death in custody, in two notorious miscarriages of justice in 1975 and 1976: the cases of the 'Guildford Four' and the 'Maguire Seven'. In the case of the Guildford Four, the DPP suppressed alibi evidence and even suppressed confessions by the actual guilty parties, and in the Maguire case, there was discredited forensic evidence. Havers must have had some idea of the injustices being played out. So this is the man who feels confident in saying he is 'sure that Mr Stonehouse had been a spy' even though 'he had no evidence which he could put before a jury'. If even Michael Havers can't find a case in the 'evidence' of the defector, then I think it's fair to assume there wasn't much there, if any. At Downing Street on the 6th October, the discussion centred on whether Stonehouse should be interviewed by the police or secret service regarding the 'further evidence'. But Michael Havers thought that, having served his prison sentence and having had heart surgery, 'it was quite likely that he would make a public fuss and claim that he was being persecuted by the Government', adding, 'The Security Service thought that they would not gain anything by interviewing Mr Stonehouse.'[14]

Andrew doesn't mention 'Affirm's identity by name, but the most likely contender is Lt. Colonel Josef Kalina (StB alias 'Karhan', spy number 195046, d.o.b. 07.03.1925). He was one of three First Secretaries at the Czech embassy – from December 1966 to September 1969. As Kalina was the head of the StB group within the embassy, with eighteen personnel under him, it seems likely in the time frame – when my father was a minister – that someone of Kalina's seniority would be the more appropriate match for

'Affirm'.* Looking at the StB file and its records of meetings, the only other candidate is Karel Pravec, alias 'Pelnar', who defected in 1980, which is about the same time as 'Affirm' was said to have defected, but who strikes a pathetic figure in the reports, constantly whining that he can't get hold of my father by phone or any other means. On the 20th January 1970, 'Pelnar' files a report saying, 'We paid him a lot of money and didn't get anything from him,' and 'Have not had contact for one-and-a-half years.' Working backward in time, that takes the last contact to July 1968, which conflicts with 'Affirm' saying he was the controller 'from March 1968 to some time in 1969'. However hapless 'Pelnar' appeared in my father's 1960s file, today he is living in a massive five-bedroom house in New Jersey. No wonder so many Czech StB defectors headed for the USA, where the gullible CIA were prepared to fund their new life of luxury.

In his capacity as minister of aviation and minister of technology, my father had arranged for a VC10 aircraft exhibition flight to take place in Prague in 1966, with a view to the Czech National Airlines buying some. (He was also trying to sell the VC10 to Middle East Airlines, Kuwait Airways, Ghana Airways and others.) On the 13th March 1967, Kalina (agent 'Karhan') reported that he met my father, who told him the Czechs had another week to decide on the purchase of the VC10s otherwise they'd be selling them to Austrian Airlines instead. This meeting could well have occurred. Kalina says his next meeting was on the 3rd April, when the VC10 was again discussed. Kalina is the only person in the StB file to mention my father's actual name, 'Stonehouse', rather than the aliases, during the period they claimed he was an agent, and he did this on 2nd February and 8th March 1968 – and on both occasions the

* Josef Frolik told a US Senate Committee that Josef Kalina was 'a below average intelligence officer and is a product of patronage'. (Ref: 'Communist Bloc Intelligence Activities in the United States,' 94th Congress, Committee on the Judiciary, United States Senate, 18th November 1975.)

VC10 was supposedly discussed. 'Affirm' said that my father 'provided information about Government plans and policies and about
technological subjects including aircraft'. Well, given that he was
trying to sell the Czechs aircraft, which my father could speak about
in broad technical terms because he was a trained RAF pilot, that
could be true, but as for 'Government plans and policies', Kalina could
have picked up information from Hansard and the newspapers and
packaged them as 'information' from his supposed agents. Kalina
had a habit of writing reports and then hand-writing 'Katalina' (the
code name the StB used for my father at this time) at the bottom,
as if allocating 'information' retrospectively to a likely candidate.
There's no proof that my father attended most of the meetings Kalina
reports. The strongest evidence that Kalina was 'Affirm' is that 'Affirm'
says he didn't pay my father any money, and this is true of Kalina,
whose reports don't show payments of 'odmena' – rewards – and he
only claims expenses. They always claimed expenses, and the more
meetings they claimed to have, the more expenses they could claim.

Christopher Andrew writes, 'AFFIRM's evidence was largely
corroborated a quarter of a century later when some of the contents of Stonehouse's lengthy StB file were revealed in the Czech
Republic. As AFFIRM had claimed, his original codename had
been KOLON ("Colonist", a reference to two years he had spent in
Uganda). Stonehouse had been recruited while an Opposition backbencher to provide "information from Parliament and Parliamentary
committees", using the money he received to fund his social life.
The StB, however, were disappointed by the amount of intelligence
Stonehouse provided once he became a minister.'[15] This is the sum
total of Andrew's evidence that Stonehouse was 'the only British
politician (so far as is known) to have acted as a foreign agent while
holding ministerial office'. This is what 'Affirm' said was in the
file: 1) he had the code name, 'Kolon' – true, but he actually had
four code names and in 'Affirm's time the StB were using 'Twister',
and before then 'Katalina', so why not refer to them?; 2) he'd been

recruited while an opposition backbencher – there's no evidence for that; only that he'd been to Czechoslovakia for the Co-operative movement and they'd opened a file on him, as they did for every foreigner who set foot on the eastern side of the Iron Curtain; 3) he was to provide 'information from Parliament and Parliamentary committees' – anyone could pay a few shillings to purchase a daily record of every word spoken in the House of Commons by taking a stroll to the HMSO office in Holborn, and there's only one document in the file that could be minutes from a committee, and I discuss this innocuous item in full in a later Chapter; 4) he used the money to fund his social life – they had to say that because he'd not been compromised and they needed an excuse; and 5) they were 'disappointed by the amount of intelligence Stonehouse provided once he became a minister' – we can agree on that because there is practically nothing in the English language in the StB file from the entire period he was a minister.

The spy allegation was very hurtful to my father and caused him deep stress from 1969 to 1988, when he died of a heart attack aged 62. Before the file was made public in 2008, my father and the whole family had to endure speculation, based on complete ignorance, fuelled by the machinations of right-wing political activists. But after 2008 there was really no excuse for the continuance of this myth and Andrew should have taken more trouble over examining the contents of the StB file. He could have contacted us and asked the simple question: did you live at the only address the StB ever had for you – '22 Aldwyne Road'? The answer, 'No', would have shot a hole in the story he's been going around telling the world: that the StB contacted my father at that address to arrange future meetings, using dated cuttings from *The Times*. In fact, that large Victorian villa on (correctly spelled) Alwyne Road was occupied by four families paying rent to the Northampton Estate, and we were not one of them. Andrew could have asked the family for an example of my father's handwriting so he could identify the forgeries in the file: two maps, two envelopes, two notes of about six words each, and two words added to a Christmas card. With forgeries go lies, and the StB file has many of them. But instead of doing any basic research, Andrew has assumed my father was guilty, and naively or conveniently lapped up the StB's lies. And here's the reason why: Andrew thinks my father is guilty of being a spy because he was guilty of so much else – according to the ubiquitous but incorrect narrative that washed over the entire nation, courtesy of the press.

7

The Madness of 1974

On 1st January 1974, under the Conservative government of Edward Heath, Britain was put on a 'three-day week' because there was a shortage of electricity to fuel homes and businesses. The miners had gone on strike and there wasn't enough coal to supply the power stations. Until it ended on the 7th March, the nation was shivering at home and went shopping holding candles in their hands. Industrial action was just one of our problems. During 1973 and 1974 Britain suffered the worst financial crisis to hit the country since 1931. The price of oil had doubled after the Organization of the Petroleum Exporting Countries (OPEC) refused to sell oil to Britain because of its support of Israel during the Yom Kippur War; interest rates of 18 per cent were crippling businesses and private individuals alike; there was a stock market crash; and falling property prices had reduced the value of collateral against business loans. The secondary banks were in dire financial trouble and by the end of 1974 the Labour government became so worried about the domino effect of collapsing banks, they instigated a 'lifeboat' bail-out scheme to pump £1,300 million into 30 institutions. Most of the money came from the big four clearing banks, but it included £120 million from taxpayers through the Bank of England.

On the 25th January 1974, *The Times* carried an article by Christopher Sweeney: 'Defector reveals MPs' part in spy ring'. It read: 'the three then MPs who were named by him had not been arrested at the time because sufficient evidence could not be found to stand up in court ... the three were confronted with the available evidence and "their usefulness was finished ... the London people have other means up their sleeves to damage these men and they have already done so".[1] My father had all the newspapers delivered to the house so he would've read the interview in *The Times* and I expect he choked on his cornflakes when he saw that Frolik was going public with the 'fact' that three MPs had been recruited by the Czech StB. Although no names were given, he knew that his name would be among them and that, despite there being no evidence, it would only be a matter of time before those names would be floating around the bars in parliament and into the press gossip machine. It was sinister and ominous to read 'the London people have other means up their sleeves to damage these men and they have already done so'. This raised questions: had MI5 interfered with his business relations, and had they put an end to his political career?

The answer came after the 28th February election, when he wasn't offered a ministerial position in Harold Wilson's hung parliament, 33 seats short of a majority. Wilson is on record as saying he wasn't happy that when my father was postmaster general (PMG) he'd under-mined the chancellor by offering the Post Office Engineering Union a pay rise higher than the 5 per cent the government wanted to give them, but less than the 10 per cent the union's conference demanded. Their strike action on 14th July 1969 had closed down most telegraph and international phone services, and 25 per cent of inland calls, and they were resolved to carry on striking. But the fact is that when the position of PMG was dissolved in October 1969 and replaced by minister of posts and communications – to reflect the fact that the two branches of post, and telecommunications, were made into separate organisational entities, my father was appointed as the new minister – so Wilson can't have been that unhappy with his work. What had happened between the last Labour government of June 1970, and this one in February 1974, was that the spy rumour had gained traction, and Wilson had to be careful it didn't reflect badly on himself. And, as we were to learn, the very accusation of being a spy allows people to dump other unfounded allegations at your feet. No doubt too, the very fact that the DTI and Scotland Yard had carried out investigations into BBT during the previous year had damaged my father's reputation. It didn't matter that no civil or criminal charges had been brought because that had not been reported in the press, to counter the bad publicity of the original accusations. In any event, my father was now acutely aware that he was out in the political cold.

My father was becoming increasingly paranoid and with each setback, each anxiety attack, each episode of depression, or bout of insomnia, he popped another Mandrax or Mogadon into his mouth and became even more paranoid. He was spiralling out of control. Things were not improving at BBT; they were getting worse. It was a miracle the accounts of 30th June 1973 passed the audit, and to some degree this was the fault of the auditors themselves, Dixon Wilson. The DTI inspectors said it was 'astounding' that the auditors failed to 'identify that the true purpose of the bulk of the loans was to fund the purchase of shares in BBT itself' and 'We are driven to the conclusion that the auditors were thoroughly slipshod in dealing with material matters. They told us they thought that the responsibility lay with the lawyers.' Meanwhile, the solicitor, Mr Levine, said 'the primary responsibility towards the public must be the auditors'. The auditors review the totality of the files.' The senior partner at the auditors was Sir Charles Hardie, who did not escape the criticism of the DTI inspectors: 'Sir Charles, in our view, took a deliberate risk, believing that no great harm would ensue. Mr Levine, on the other hand, seems to us to have lacked the objectivity appropriate to his actual position as the company's advisor.' While the professional advisors blamed each other, the inspectors blamed them both: 'The circumstances of this case do not entitle the solicitors to hide behind the skirts of the auditors nor the auditors behind those of the solicitors.'[2]

The essential problem was that the original share issue had not got enough support from outside and my father and his companies had thrown into the big black hole every asset at their disposal and, more dangerously, every loan they could obtain. As well as his trading companies of EPACS, Global Imex and Connoisseurs of Claret, dormant companies were drawn into the crisis as nominees and a complex inter-company system of loans began. When it came to a company's year-end, another of his companies would lend it money for a short period so its accounts looked OK. This is called 'window dressing', and it was known to happen on a larger scale too. In return for the favour of one bank covering the year-end shortfall of another, a reciprocal favour would be offered. The DTI report said: 'It is clear from other Department of Trade Inspectors' Reports that this practice was common among secondary banking companies about the time with which we are concerned and in this respect, at least, BBT was typical. It took and placed deposits over its own year-end so as to increase the total of its advances and deposits and helped other concerns in a similar way. The largest such transaction in which BBT engaged was over the night of 31st May–1st June 1973 when no less than £1 million was deposited with Cornhill Consolidated Company Limited (Cornhill) against a deposit from its affiliate, Highcastle Securities Limited. Cornhill's financial year ended on 31st May.'[3]*

My father was sailing very close to the wind, and he knew it. The audit of 30th June 1974 was approaching and he feared the irregularities he'd been engaged in would be revealed. The DTI inspectors said in their report, 'This is not a case in which the promoters were bent on wrongdoing or seeking to feather their own nests at the expense

---

* The DTI report contained seven recommendations for changes in financial regulations. Following the publication of the report, a Mr G Clark of the DTI made this suggestion for a change in the law to the minister concerned: 'Companies should not be permitted to lend money on the security of their own shares. This would involve clarification of Article 10 of Table A [of Section 54 of the Companies Act 1948] which can be construed to authorise companies which make loans in the ordinary course of business to accept their own shares as security for such loans.' (Ref: 'Loose Minute' from Mr G Clark to Mr HC Gill, 11th November 1977, The National Archives File BT 299/346, page 1.)

of the company or its shareholders or creditors. Mr Stonehouse embarked on the course of serious wrongdoing when stung by bad publicity which attended an offer of shares to the public. He was propelled into crime by his pride.' They also said, 'We do not suggest that Mr Stonehouse's object was to gain and retain control of BBT; but by his own conduct he found himself forced into the position of being its actual and effective controller. As time went on, his attempts to free himself failed. He was enmeshed in his own web, which grew more tenacious as he struggled to escape from it.'[4] There were only two ways out: persuade another bank to invest in BBT, possibly an American one that needed international connections; or make a lot of money on exports to plug the financial cracks.

To this end, my father was flying all over the world trying to finalise trade deals. One day he'd be in New York, another in Sudan, another in Beirut, another in Romania, and another in Yemen. He was involved in negotiations all over the world concerning selling communications equipment to the government of Kenya, police transmitters to Bangladesh, an ICI refinery and a fertiliser plant in Bangladesh, another fertiliser plant and rail equipment to Sudan, a cotton mill in Tanzania, a hotel complex on the Gulf, cement deals involving Iran, the Gulf, Libya and Cyprus, and so it went on. He also tried to arrange bilateral trade deals such as, for example, arranging for Sudan and Bangladesh to exchange jute and cotton. He had a contract with the Government of Mauritius to promote export zones, and took a group of British industrialists there to explore the opportunities. He never stopped trying to link people and make deals and because he was the only person in his companies who could bring in this business, the successes and income were all down to him as, too, was the pressure of failure. A £6.5 million deal to supply Romanian cement to Nigeria couldn't be finalised because the shipping costs became too expensive, while a contract to supply cement to Iran was broken at the last minute when a cheaper French alternative came along. Given the importance of bringing serious money into his companies, the disappointments were crushing. In April and May, he'd been working hard on a deal to supply electronics from a British company, Racal, to North Yemen, involving negotiations with President Abdul Rahman al-Iryani. But by the first week of June the political situation was looking distinctly shaky and, indeed, on the 13th there'd be a military coup d'état led by Ibrahim al-Hamdi which would overthrow al-Iryani, and put an end to the Racal deal. The stress of Global Imex losing a potential £40,000 in commission was, I believe, the straw that broke the camel's back.

His life was becoming unbearable. Try as he might, nothing was going his way. Perhaps he'd just been fighting too long, and the pressures of a lifetime were no strong ground to stand on while weathering this financial storm. He'd erected a great big house of financial cards and the slightest breeze could bring the whole edifice crashing down around him. He wanted to walk away from it all. Instead, he remembered that in Frederick Forsyth's book, *The Day of the Jackal*, another identity could be obtained by presenting a birth certificate to the Passport Office. He imagined himself escaping the world of John Stonehouse and becoming someone else, someone without all these difficulties. It was an enticing fantasy and, drugged into craziness by eighteen months of taking Mandrax and Mogadon, he set about making it a reality.

When interviewed by police six months after the events, Mrs Markham couldn't remember the name my father gave, or the exact date he visited her in Brownhills, Walsall – it was likely to have been the second week of June. Without saying what his occupation was, he told her he was carrying out a survey of widows' pensions and their taxes. Mrs Markham couldn't remember whether the man asked her if Joseph had had a passport, but as that had been his object-ive, it seems very likely that he did. In early July, my father phoned Manor Hospital in Walsall, giving them his name and telling them he had monies to distribute to young widows and asking if they could give him names of men who'd recently died. The Deputy Patient Services Officer, Mr Perks, after verifying that he was, in fact, John Stonehouse MP, gave him about five names. When interviewed by the police six months later, Mr Perks said he couldn't remember if Mr Markham was on the list, but remembered supplying the name of Donald Clive Mildoon – because he knew a doctor with a similar name. A week or so later, on a Saturday morning, my father visited Mrs Mildoon at her newsagent shop in Walsall Road, Wednesbury, introducing himself as John Stonehouse MP and saying he'd read of her husband's death in the newspapers. Mrs Mildoon had indeed placed a notice in the local paper, the *Express and Star*. He said he was contacting her because he had a Motion going through the Commons about children of one-parent families. Then he asked if they'd been abroad and Mrs Mildoon told him they'd gone to Austria in 1971 so although he didn't specifically ask if Clive Mildoon had ever had a passport, he had his answer. He would later acquire copies of birth certificates for Clive Mildoon and Joseph Markham, and falsely obtain one passport in the name of Markham. On Christmas Eve 1974, Mrs Mildoon read on the front page of the *Express and Star* that John Stonehouse had been found in Australia using the name (Donald) Clive Mildoon. It must have been a terrible shock to Mrs Mildoon, and to Mrs Markham, to find their husbands' names being used in this way.

Throughout everything that's happened with my family, over all the years, this is the one thing we find so terrible. On behalf of my father, I apologise to the Markham and Mildoon families and hope they can accept that this bizarre behaviour was only brought about by terrible stress and the effects of mind-twisting prescribed drugs. It's unbelievable to us, the family, that my father should do something as cold-hearted as having a conversation with two widows with a view to adopting their husbands' names. It's so out of character for the John Stonehouse we knew, we can only attribute it to madness, one symptom of which is that the person does mad things. As a family, we often felt that the press would have been happier if my father had just killed himself and become a statistic, seen perhaps as a victim of the financial crisis which, by the summer of 1974, was in full swing. Instead, he found new lives to inhabit, ones that were totally separate from the man he had come to hate.

The DTI inspectors wrote that, 'By mid-July, it was clear to Mr Stonehouse that "the game was up" and his counter-measures bore the mark of desperation. To the auditors' questions dishonest replies were given. The auditors insisted on disclosure of advances to directors and their companies of £262,961 (used to purchase BBT shares).'[5] On the 15th July my father went to the General Register Office in Kingsway, WC2, and applied for a birth certificate in the name of Clive Mildoon, using the name 'H. Humphries'. He'd collect it a couple of days later. On the 17th or 18th, again at the General Register Office, this time as 'S.J. Lewis', he applied for a birth certificate for Joseph Markham, collecting that on the 19th or 22nd July.

Around this time, he first went to the Astoria Hotel at 39 St George's Drive, London SW1, telling them he'd be wanting a single room for one night a week in the middle of the week. He'd stay there for the first time a month later. On the 22nd, he opened a deposit account at the Midland Bank on Vauxhall Bridge Road in the name of Markham, giving his address as 39 St George's Drive, London SW1. Between this day, and the 16th September, he'd deposit £17,520 into this account. On the 27th, he got a Post Office Giro account for Markham. On the 1st August, he went to the Passport Office in Petty France, SW1, with a passport application in his hand in the name of Joseph Arthur Markham, age 42, of 30 Eccleston Square, SW1. He had two photographs of himself countersigned with signatures he had forged of Neil McBride, an MP who was very ill and would pass away on the 9th September. The application form said that he needed the passport by the 7th as he was travelling to France and Spain. One official checked the form, and another issued a receipt for payment. Passport number 785965A was issued the next day, and collected on Monday 5th August by a man who signed the receipt as 'J.A. Markham'. Now it was real. He was officially another man.

On the 20th August, Mr Markham registered with Management Business Services, of 243 Regent Street, London W1, a company that received and forwarded mail, took telephone calls, and provided telex and secretarial services. He was given the registration number 726, paid cash in advance for the service commencing 1st September, and said he'd be collecting his mail in person. He'd go here at least once a week and collect two or three letters each time. On the 21st August, Mr Markham stayed at the Astoria Hotel for the first time, and as he left the next morning he said that he'd be getting some mail there and asked if they'd hold it for him, and he'd collect it. He'd stay at the Astoria a further four Wednesdays: 28th August, 18th September, 2nd and 16th October. He'd arrive about 6 or 7pm, and come downstairs for a cup of tea around 9am, having already been out to buy newspapers. In addition to staying on these nights, he'd frequently phone to see if there was mail and on at least two occasions collected it while a taxi waited outside. In October, the receptionist signed for an item of registered mail and gave it to him later.

Whereas a year earlier, BBT had managed to pull the wool over the auditor's eyes, in 1974 they were dealing with Albert Stokes, a partner in Dixon Wilson, and he was altogether more eagle-eyed. The DTI wrote of him, 'By 28th August he had compiled a formidable catalogue of the wrongdoings of Mr Stonehouse and others associated with the company. Mr Stokes, we think, is the person entitled to the principal credit for his tenacity in penetrating what was, by then, a jungle dense with improprieties.'[6]

On the 3rd September, Markham opened an account at the Bank of New South Wales on Threadneedle Street, saying he was considering emigrating to Australia and, on the same day, opened an account at the Strand branch of the Australia and New Zealand Banking

Group. On the 4th, he made the first of two phone calls from Management Business Services, to number 834-0588, the Midland Bank where he had the deposit account. In the meantime, the bank had been asked by American Express for a reference for Mr Markham. As there was a substantial deposit, they wrote back 'we have no reason to suppose that he is not suitable for your purposes', and by the 23rd September, Markham had an American Express credit card in his hand. The call to the bank on the 4th had been to ask them to buy £5,000 worth of shares in the British Leyland Motor Corporation, and the call on the 13th is likely to be when he asked the bank to purchase on his behalf £5,000 of General Electric Company shares.

On the 18th September Stonehouse caught the 19:55 flight to Zurich, stayed over, and the next morning, as Markham, opened an account at the Swiss Bank Corporation with a deposit of $7,500, then opened an account at the Swiss Credit Bank, before popping to Brussels for the afternoon. The next morning, he deposited $7,500 into the Swiss Bank Corporation before catching the 12:35 flight from Zurich to London. Both these cheques came from personal Stonehouse funds, from the sale of stamps. Two days later, *Private Eye* published a piece at the top of page three saying, 'Delicacy and good taste prevent me from mentioning the names of the two Labour MPs who are at present under investigation by the Special Branch for their connections with an East European embassy. However, I should point out that the Czech embassy, which covers espionage and dirty tricks for the whole Soviet bloc, allocates £20,000 a month for "gifts", "retainers" and "consultancies" to politicians, journalists, civil servants and others who might prove useful.'[7] This was Frolik and rogue elements in MI5 spreading poison again, and my father probably thought this just confirmed that 'Plan B' was the only way to get away from this hurtful and dangerous slur. Escape beckoned, like a balmy breeze enticing him towards a new life, free of the financial, political and emotional stress and, perhaps above all, the stress of being called a traitor to the country he'd worked hard for all his life.

On the 24th September, he asked the Midland to send £7,000 to his Markham account at the Bank of New South Wales in Threadneedle Street, and on the 30th, he asked them to sell the shares and transfer the balance of his account there too. By this time, the Midland had been approached by several other banks and credit card companies to provide a financial reference for Markham, which they didn't normally give for deposit accounts, only current accounts, and they'd had to reply, 'we are unable to speak for your purposes'. This meant a refusal for Barclaycard and the National Westminster Bank, but it didn't seem to affect Markham's acquisition of accounts with Post Office Giro, the Bank of New South Wales and the Australia and New Zealand Banking Group.

Also on the 24th September, Markham wrote to the Bank of New South Wales saying he was going to Australia via the USA, and asking for a letter of introduction to the Melbourne branch, where £14,100 should be transferred. The next day he flew from Cyprus to Beirut where Stonehouse would try and finalise a trade deal, but this time he used the Markham passport. The alter ego identity was becoming increasingly real, and to make it more real still, between the 29th July and the 19th October, Stonehouse withdrew £62,912 from his personal accounts.

On the 10th October, my father again won his parliamentary seat in the general election with a large majority. Eleven days later, on the 21st, Mr Markham took a metal trunk to shipping agents in Binney Street, W1, and asked for it to be sent to Melbourne. The agent remembered the transaction because he was asked to help carry the trunk up the stairs. Mr Markham filled out the declaration and consignment note, took out insurance, and left the trunk to make its way by a series of impressively well-recorded steps into container No. INTU 241487, and to berth 39 at Tilbury Docks, where it was loaded onto vessel ACT 1. On arrival in Melbourne, it was examined by customs officer Robert Rowland Hill, who saw it contained only the clothing of a man.

On the 1st November my father flew to Zurich again and deposited £30,219 in the Markham Swiss Bank Corporation account. It was his own money and, try as they might, later on the DPP could find no charges to bring regarding these funds. On the 1st or 2nd November, he went to Management Business Services and paid in advance for the months of November and December, saying he was going to Australia, and gave instructions in writing for his mail to be forwarded to the Bank of New South Wales, 395 Little Collins Street, Melbourne, to take effect that day. Between the 6th and 11th November, my father took eleven flights crisscrossing America as his mind crisscrossed between Stonehouse and Markham, eventually returning to London. On the 15th November, *Private Eye* published their gratuitous and humourless character assassination 'Bungler Dashed'. By the 20th, he was gone.

Two years later my father would be on trial in London at the Old Bailey. Alongside him in the dock was his mistress, Sheila Buckley. In his summing up, Judge Eveleigh said to her 'I have no doubt that you were fully aware of what was going on.'[8] I only wish she had been. It was my father laying insane plans, nobody else. Sheila was never seen with him while he inhabited his new personas. 'Plan B' existed only inside my father's head, and as the months of July to November progressed, more planning and paperwork went into it. For months he went around central London alone, pretending to be Mr Markham or Mr Mildoon. He went in and out of the General Register Office, the Passport Office, embassies and numerous banks. He got a migrant visa for Australia, along with the required TB X-ray. Many times he'd respond to the call of his false name and go to various desks to collect the new paperwork. He could have been recognised as Stonehouse at any time. But people believed his new personas, and he enjoyed that. People responded to him as an ordinary person, rather than as a politician. There were no preconceived ideas about him coming from other people. He could walk down the street and conduct business without people having any opinion, good or bad, about him. Such anonymity is highly under-rated. And perhaps the most important element of this is that he himself could inhabit a 'normal person' space, because that's where he found the relief. Being Mr Markham was a safety-valve, a release, a lifesaver, and the more that persona became real, and the more the pressures of 1974 increased, the more Mr Stonehouse yearned to be Mr Markham, and escape. What began as a mad escape fantasy became the reality. He thought he had no choice. By the time he disappeared his debts included £40,000 to Rowe Rudd stockbrokers, following his rash gambling on the stock market, and £35,000 to Ambulant Finance, thanks to the nice young Kazi Ahmed, who'd suggested the BBT project in the first place. The DTI later raised serious questions about the date and authenticity of a letter written by Ahmed which led to my father being held responsible for this debt. It was all too much.

8

Man Gone!

On the 21st November 1974, my mother was having a good day. She was in a private viewing suite in Soho watching a promotional film she'd help produce and edit for a company she did public relations for. The clients were pleased with the film, and so was she. Then she went to the home she shared with my father at 21 Sancroft Street in Kennington, London, and made herself a cup of tea. About half an hour later the doorbell rang. It was my father's personal assistant, Philip Gay, and his wife, Caroline. My mother asked if they'd like some tea, and Philip said, 'we need something stronger'. A little surprised, my mother indicated with her hand towards the drinks cabinet and said to help themselves, but Philip only poured whiskey into a single glass and put it on the table in front of my mother. It was then she realised something was very wrong, and the Gays had come to tell her something – something bad. My mother drank that whiskey – the one and only time in her life that she ever drank spirits.

Apparently, my father and his business colleague Jim Charlton had flown to Miami on the 19th as planned on flight BA 661, dined at the hotel, and arranged that the next morning they'd have a swim before their 12pm appointment with the Southeast First National Bank of Miami. Around 9am, they headed for the beach, my father took off his outer clothes, rolled them into a neat package, and left them with Helen Fleming, the attendant at the cabana office where non-resident users of the beach paid for access. Jim didn't take a swim, but my father did, giving Jim cause for concern as he went out of sight, at least 180–200 yards from the beach. He landed back on shore some distance away, jogged back to Jim, collected his clothes, and they both went inside to change for the meeting, after which they had lunch as guests of the bank. Back at the hotel, at 4.30pm, my father said he was going to do some shopping and have another swim, and suggested they meet in the bar at 7pm for a drink before dinner. My father went back to the beach, leaving his clothes at the cabana again. Ms Fleming later said 'He seemed to be in a good mood.' A little after 8pm, Jim became worried because my father hadn't turned up, and asked the housekeeper for his room to be opened. All my father's belongings appeared to be in place, other than the beach clothes he'd worn earlier. Jim checked the hire car was still where they'd parked it, then alerted hotel security. It was now dark outside. Jim went with a hotel security guard to the cabana office and, with the aid of a torch, they could see through the glass that my father's clothing was placed on the shelf at the rear of the closed cabana office, as had been done in the morning. Now quite alarmed, Jim phoned the police, before searching the beach with the security guard. They couldn't find anything, so Jim went to the police station and reported my father missing. They told him nothing could be done until morning, and not to communicate with Mrs Stonehouse as missing persons frequently turned up shortly after disappearing. The next day, the 21st, Jim went back to the cabana office to confirm the clothes were still there, then accompanied a police officer as he searched my father's room and belongings, and itemised the contents of his briefcase. He phoned London and spoke to Philip Gay, my father's personal assistant, and asked for the family to be informed. Until my father was arrested in Melbourne, Jim was convinced my father had perished while swimming in the sea on the afternoon of the 20th November.

❖

My mother phoned her friend, Eric Blakemore, and asked him to drive to Somerset and collect my fourteen-year-old brother, Mathew, from school, and bring him to London. The last thing she wanted was for him to hear the news from reporters. Beatrice was at university and Jane and I were working, but we were all living in London at the time so, on receiving the news from our mother, we swiftly made our way to Sancroft Street. Philip Gay was still there, and repeated to us the events in Miami. Jane wrote in her diary how conflicted we all were: 'One second there's refusal to give up hope, next minute complete despair and such pain.' It was decided we'd go to Faulkners Down House, an isolated farmhouse my parents rented, adjacent to a farm just outside Andover, Hampshire. My mother and Jane would wait in London for Mathew to arrive, then drive down with Eric, while another of my father's associates, Philip Bingham, volunteered to drive Beatrice and myself. First we had to cross London and pick up some clothes. Philip used the handbrake at every traffic light and pedestrian crossing and I was soon feeling sicker than I was before, so I took over the driving and found myself quickly avoiding all traffic lights and congestion by using side roads I didn't even know I knew. When we got to the A316 and a straight road to Andover, Philip took back the driving. As I looked out of the window, I saw bodies of water I'd not noticed before. It's strange how stress can affect one's perceptions.

Our first thought as a family was that my father had gone swimming far out from shore and had either had a bad case of cramp, a heart attack, or been eaten by sharks. Those had been the visions I had while passing previously innocuous lakes and reservoirs on the drive. My father was an excellent swimmer, and his usual thing was to swim a very long way out from the shore, float around a bit, then swim back. One time in Dubrovnik, he and I had swum to Lokrum, an island about 650 yards away. I swam alongside until I got tired and then held on to his shoulder to rest a while. When we swam back, we saw my mother and an agitated group of people gesticulating on the shoreline. Apparently, there'd been a storm the night before and sharks had come into that area of water for protection. We knew from experience that when my father went swimming he wasn't interested in splashing around near the beach but in getting far away from it. In another life he would've made a good long-distance swimmer.

This was our first problem because the Florida Coastguard didn't believe us when we said he would have swum out such a long way. The current close to the shore went in one direction, while the Gulf Stream current further out went in the other direction, and we thought they were looking along the wrong part of the coast. When the Coastguard said they hadn't found a body, we weren't surprised and kept hoping he was stranded somewhere, still alive. A person could stay alive in those warm waters, we were told, for two days. We clutched at every straw that came our way. The phone call from my father on his earlier trip, saying he 'couldn't take it anymore', led my mother to wonder if he'd had a breakdown, or killed himself, or both. None of the options were good, but we still clung on to hope. My brother refused to accept he was dead for quite a while. On the 22nd, Jane wrote in her diary 'We are going to have to accept he is dead. I just hope they never find his body – then I can imagine him starting a new life with amnesia. But that's ridiculous.' Little did she know, ridiculous or not, that's exactly what he'd planned to do. On the 24th, Jim Charlton and his wife came to visit bringing, very disturbingly, my father's suitcase of clothes. It gave a sense of reality to the situation, and that reality looked and felt very bad. His briefcase had been retained by the Miami police who, we'd discover much later, would be asked by Interpol Washington to send it to Melbourne. The transport costs would be paid for with the currency inside the briefcase. On the 25th, Beatrice had to get back to London because she had university exams coming up. She was found 'shedding honest tears' at the buffet at Waterloo Station by a kind lady, who wrote to my mother sending 'prayers and hopes that your husband is safe'. Many more letters would be received from strangers over the next few years – some sympathetic and some not.

The next day the police came to the house and interviewed my mother. She had her grief and uncertainty to deal with, but there was worse to come because now the press started to get nasty, and my mother would find herself trying to bat away negative stories. Exactly one week after he'd gone missing, the front-page news in the *Daily Mirror* was saying the 'mystery deepens' and 'There has been a suggestion he has been kidnapped.' Nobody had suggested that, except the *Daily Mirror*, who added '– although no ransom demand has been received.'[1] On the 28th November, the *Daily Mail* said he was pompous and too wealthy; on the 29th my mother had to deny to *The Sun* that money was missing from the Bangladesh Fund; and on 1st December we read that a complaint had been lodged with a law firm that the 'fund had topped £1½ million' (as opposed to the £412,083 banked). That same day, the *Sunday Times'* Richard Milner – who'd caused so much trouble for the BBT, which led to a DTI inquiry, and a Scotland Yard Fraud Squad investigation, both of which proved nothing untoward – wrote another horrible piece: 'The strange legacy of the missing MP'. He was a press hound who wanted blood, and nothing was going to stop him. In the same paper, they ran 'The Price of Freedom' – an interview with Josef Frolik. He didn't mention my father's name – that was to come a couple of weeks later, but we could hear the knives being pulled from their sheaths.

On the 2nd, the BBC said that the FBI were reconciled to the fact he'd not drowned. That same day, my mother received a letter from a woman who said her uncle had disappeared in the same place years earlier and his body turned up seven days later in Jacksonville, over 300 miles north. Again, this revived our concern that the American authorities had been looking in the wrong area. Also on the 2nd, the *Daily Mail* expanded on so-called 'missing' money from the Bangladesh Fund, while several papers published the results of a press statement issued by a friend of my father, William Molloy MP. These included the *Guardian* story, 'Enemies may have killed Stonehouse', the *Daily Express*'s 'MP with foes everywhere', and *The Sun*'s 'Missing MP "may be a victim of a Mafia Plot"'. Molloy had said many good things about my father, and these had been reported, but it created the impression that he had enemies, and it whipped up the drama. On the 3rd, the damaging headline story was about my father's life insurances. We didn't take those stories at all seriously because, obviously, what's the point of having five- and seven-year short-term insurances when they can't be claimed for at least seven years if there's no body? We were naïve because my father would get sentenced to 30 years for those useless bits of paper.

On the 6th December, the *Daily Mail* said 'Mr Fixit' made 'at least £1,000,000' commission arranging big contracts in Bangladesh for British companies, while *The Observer* had: 'Why Stonehouse wanted to be rich'. On the 8th, the *Sunday Times* had another nasty piece about his businesses, but they did at least print some small respite in the form of a letter from Alan Rainbird, a former business associate, who said many positive things, including, 'John Stonehouse was a man of considerable ability and the highest principle. I appeal to the media to call off the vultures.'[2] No chance of that. A reporter was already on the phone, asking my mother about a flat my father rented at Vandon Court, Petty France, Westminster – about which she knew nothing. They said a girl lived there, and read her some potential names. One was Sheila Buckley. My mother spent the rest of the weekend phoning my father's friends, asking if they knew anything. They all said they didn't. Sheila was supposed to be staying in the country with friends, but couldn't be found. On Monday the 9th, the headline on the front page of *The Sun* was 'Riddle of Girl in Lost MP's flat'. The sub-heading was 'Stonehouse neighbour tells of a brunette', and the article explained that she thought a girl was living at the flat. The 'slightly built' girl was last seen on the 31st October, moving some belongings with Mr Stonehouse. I'd told *The Sun*: 'I just don't know who this girl could be.'

On Tuesday morning my mother finally caught up with Sheila and they arranged to meet at the flat of one of my mother's friends. Sheila was trying to behave normally, making polite small talk but, from the look in her eyes, she was terrified. My mother asked if she'd been having an affair with my father and Sheila broke down in sobs, saying 'Oh dear, oh dear', over and over again, with mascara running down her cheeks. My mother told Sheila that he'd had several affairs in the past but always came back to her, adding, 'He could have gone off with someone else entirely. If he reappears you're welcome to him. Then you'll find out how painful it is to live with an unfaithful man.' Sheila sat and cried for a while, then told my mother she'd been his mistress for a long time, that he loved her, and waited on her hand and foot. My mother drove Sheila to an underground station and when they pulled over Sheila said, 'You may as well know it all. I think I'm going to have his baby.' My mother felt sick. But she told Sheila, 'If John does turn up and you've got rid of it, it will make him very upset. He loves children.' Sheila left the car. What she hadn't told my mother was that she knew my father was alive, and that he knew she thought she was pregnant, because she'd just spent the weekend with him in Copenhagen.

It was humiliating for my mother to discover from the newspapers that my father rented a flat at 25 Vandon Court. The press wanted to know what she knew. She told them that his flat was no secret and that Sheila had lived there and, as Sheila had told her, she'd been paying the rent for two-and-a-half years. I've seen original documents that show Sheila paid the rent in June 1972, so that information could have been true. My father wrote to the landlords on the 30th September 1974 to relinquish the lease, giving a month's notice before vacating the property on the 31st October – when the neighbours saw him and Sheila moving belongings. This confluence of facts led the prosecution to assume Sheila was part of 'Plan B', but all it really says is that my father gave up the lease on the flat as part of his overall planning: he didn't want to leave his love nest to become a possible complication.

By Sheila's own account, she knew how painful it was to be married to an unfaithful man. She had met her future husband, Roger Buckley, when she was twenty and went to work at the same company of accountants. She ignored the warnings about his womanising and in 1966 they started a relationship. By the time Sheila switched jobs and started working for my father at the House of Commons, in May 1968, she was engaged to Roger. But soon after the wedding in 1969 she discovered he was having an affair. According to an article by Sheila in *Woman* magazine in October 1976, Roger was supposed to be going to night school, but came home at 1am. Sheila went to the school and found out he'd only attended a few lessons; then she checked his bank statement and found he'd been buying jewellery, but not for her. His firm took him to court over theft, and it was then Roger told Sheila he had a girlfriend and had been lying to her for a long time. At that point, Sheila moved out and the couple separated. She knew that my father rented a small pied-à-terre at Vandon Court; he said she could use it, and gave her his key. They started going to dinner, she fell in love with him, and the affair began.[3] Roger Buckley would be reported in the press as saying 'Stonehouse stole my wife', but it was likely his own infidelity that broke up that marriage.

❖

There were always press cars and random reporters outside the country house, and 21 Sancroft Street too. It took us a while to work out how to escape them at Faulkners Down House, which was reached by a half-mile lane from the main road: we had to walk through the wood at the back, over the field, and to the main road, where we walked along to a one-pump petrol station owned by a man who allowed us to park a car there. London was easier because of the street layout, and the support of good neighbours. Warren at number 23 wrote offering 'an escape route', and around the corner at 3 Stables Way, Pat and Caroline wrote to say 'We are quite horrified at the

John's parents, Rosina and
William Stonehouse.
© Julia Stonehouse

John and
Barbara
in 1947.
© Julia Stonehouse

Meeting
Ugandan
farmers in
1952.
© Julia Stonehouse

Members of the
Federation of
Partnerships of Uganda
African Farmers with
George Shepherd (L) and
John Stonehouse (R).
© Julia Stonehouse

Barbara working at
BICC, Kampala,
Uganda, 1953.
© Julia Stonehouse

Julia and Jane at Kampala Airport, 1954, after being photographed
by one photographer from the colonial government's Special
Branch and about to be photographed by another.
© Julia Stonehouse

Barbara looking out
of the window at
21 Alwyne Road with
a policeman outside
to protect against
further vandalism,
6th March 1959.
Photo by John Twine.
© ANL/Shutterstock

John arriving back from Rhodesia after being declared a prohibited immigrant, 13th March 1959.

© ANL/Shutterstock

Barbara at a demonstration in Whitehall to protest the killing of 52 Africans by colonial forces in Nyasaland (now Malawi), 1st April 1959.

Photo by Frank Apthorp. © ANL/Shutterstock

With fellow Labour and Co-operative MP Sydney Irving, to left, with constituents, 5th June 1958.

Photo by Gerald Pudsey. © Unknown

With Julius Nyerere, chief minister of Tanganyika, 5th September 1960.
The following year Nyerere would become the first president of an independent Tanganyika
(which became Tanzania in 1964).

In 1960, with Tom Mboya, Kenya's chief negotiator for independence from Britain and first
minister of justice and constitutional affairs following independence in December 1963.

In 1960, at the Botswana home of Seretse Khama, leader of the independence
movement from Britain, and first president of Botswana from 1966.

At a school fair in Wednesbury, 1959.

Start of a ten-mile Mayor Charity Walk with Peter Archer MP and the Mayor of West Bromwich, Mrs L. Peckover, September 1968.

Marching against the closure of T. I. Stainless Steel in Walsall, 8th July 1972.

Malta Labour Party demonstration demanding independence
from Britain, Valletta, 1st May 1961.

© Julia Stonehouse

With Dom
Mintoff, leader of
the independence
movement in Malta.

© Julia Stonehouse

Speaking at
independence rally,
Valletta, Malta,
1st May 1961.

© Julia Stonehouse

Outside a London Co-operative Society shop with staff and customers, 1963.
© Julia Stonehouse

With prime minister
Harold Wilson, 1965.
Photo by Brian Worth. © Julia Stonehouse

Clockwise: John, Julia, Barbara,
Mathew, Jane Stonehouse, 1965.
Photo by Godfrey Best. © Julia Stonehouse

European Airbus meeting with French and German representatives,
Jean Chamant (L) and Johann Schöllhorn (R), London, 25th July 1967.

Photo by Keystone. © Getty images

With Jean Chamant, the French minister of transport, to discuss Bristol Siddeley
(later Rolls Royce) Olympus 593 engines for Concorde, September 1967.

Photo by Maurice Tibbles. © Mirrorpix

After a test flight on the F-111 in Fort Worth, Texas, 13th October 1967.

Photo by Ferd Kaufman. © AP/Shutterstock

number of newsmen outside. If we can be of any help or provide an escape route to avoid them we would be only too pleased to do so.' We didn't actually need their kindly offered escape routes because the press never discovered we had one of our own. Sancroft Street had a back door leading to a private patio, and a triangular communal garden that was used by three streets, including ours, and could be accessed from the other streets via two gates. Instead of walking around the block and discovering this for themselves, the press took the milk off our doorstep, trying to force us to go into the street. One day I saw two reporters parked in a car outside waving our milk bottles back and forth and grinning. I grinned back, and went out the back door, through the garden, to the shop, and came back the same way. This is the way my mother left the house to meet Sheila on a second occasion, after my mother had returned from Australia in January. Her car was parked in the street on the far side of the garden and she picked Sheila up at the telephone box at Kennington Cross, yards from the omnipresent yet oblivious press. They drove around London and talked.

On the 12th December, things began to get gruesome with the *The Sun*'s story, 'Slab of Concrete Murder Clue to Lost MP'. It began: 'A Mafia-type "concrete overcoat" murder may solve the mystery of missing MP John Stonehouse police said yesterday' and said 'Fort Lauderdale police sergeant Jim Bock said the slab bears an imprint of a human body … police are working on the possibility that it was Mr Stonehouse's body.'[4] Bock was quoted as saying 'All the dates seem to fit.' Hair and fluid samples had been taken and were being examined by forensic experts. The connection seemed to be that my father was involved in international cement deals, but the Mafia liked to have a monopoly on the cement trade, and they operated out of Miami. On the 16th, the *Daily Mirror* introduced the concept of a 'Concrete Coffin Probe'. The British police were tasked with finding samples of my father's hair, and his blood type and dental records, and getting them to the Fort Lauderdale Police in Miami who, on

4th December, had found another blood-stained pile of concrete, containing hair once again. So now my mother was running around trying to locate samples of my father's hair, while his blood type proved quite difficult to ascertain, causing delay and annoyance to the Florida police.

It was around this time that stories began to appear about my father being connected in some way to the death of a 37-year-old Nigerian man called Sylvester Okereke, who was found floating in the Thames in November. The connection was that they'd both had some involvement in the sale of cement to Nigeria. The British soon established there was no association, but in Nigeria, in June 1975, two magazine articles weaved a connection, using faked corres- pondence addressed to my father at 'Vandon Court, Vandon Place'. Given that Vandon Place doesn't exist, and there was no reason for business mail to go to Vandon Court, this whole story seems a figment of someone's imagination. Nevertheless, it came to the attention of D.E.R. Moore of the West African Department of the Foreign and Commonwealth Office, who wrote on the 29th August 1975 to the Solicitor's Branch of the Department of Trade, with a longer draft letter for the attention of the Home Office. It ended up on the desk of Brian Bubbear at the Directorate of Custody: 'So far the Nigerian Government have not raised the issue with us; nor do we expect them to. They will probably shed no tears over the demise abroad of a man alleged to be a former Biafran intelligence officer. But if the press attention turned to Stonehouse's alleged (and denied) espionage background, their interest might increase.'[5] The Biafrans, in the south east of Nigeria, attempted to break away from Nigeria in 1967, leading to the Biafran war which lasted until 1970.

Aside from the usual background noise of negativity, such as in the *Daily Mirror* on the 13th December – 'The Jinx that Haunted John Stonehouse' and 'A man hungry for big money' – the press focus over the 12th, 13th, 14th and 15th was on life insurance. A massive banner headline on the front page of the *Daily Mirror* on the 13th said: 'Lost MP insured his life for £119,000'. On the 14th, my mother told the *Daily Express*, 'Cannot people understand that if his death was merely to raise money it was a pointless exercise? If this was my husband's intention, he was very remiss in not leaving his body.' And she told the *Daily Mail*, 'It is going to be a great struggle to get any money unless a body is found.' One of the insurances was with the Royal Insurance Company, £30,000 for a seven-year period, taken out in early August. It would have run out of term by the time seven years without a body had passed. On the 15th December the *Sunday Express* quoted the chairman of the Royal, Mr Daniel Meinertzhagen: 'I should imagine that if no body can be found there would be some difficulty establishing a claim. Certain legal actions would have to be taken by the claimant.'[6] The police arrived to question my mother: a woman and a man. They sat on the sofa, and my mother showed them the policies. The woman looked first, then handed them to the man. He mumbled something, and the woman handed them back to my mother who told them that the trigger that led to the life insurances had been the demolition of my father's car by an IRA bomb on the 19th May. My mother arranged the policies, and my father organised when he should go for the medical checks. The policeman asked: 'why so many?' She told him they were short-term, and in smaller amounts, so that gave flexibility. One or two could be stopped, or changed easily. Apparently satisfied, the police left. Not long after, a reporter arrived and asked about the policies. She showed them to him too. There was never any secrecy about the life insurances, and once people grasped that they were short-term and simply couldn't be claimed without a body, they accepted that. Until the director of public prosecutions came along, that is.

We'd been waiting for Frolik to cash in on the Stonehouse disappearance, and that body blow came in the *Daily Mirror* on the 16th and 17th December. On the 16th, under the large front-page headline, 'Stonehouse Security Sensation', we read: 'Missing MP John Stonehouse was under constant security watch before he disappeared. Secret Service officers built up a five-year dossier on him following certain allegations made when he was Minister of Posts and Telecommunications.'[7] On the 17th, under the front-page headline 'MP was named as Spy Contact', it said: 'Missing MP John Stonehouse was a contact for a communist spy ring, according to a high-ranking Czech intelligence agent.'[8] And there was a picture of Frolik staring out at us. At that time, it was assumed my father was dead, so Frolik didn't think he'd have to worry about libel laws as anything can be said about a dead person with no legal comeback (Frolik didn't mention my father by name in his book, when it was published in July 1975).

The prime minister, Harold Wilson, immediately consulted the head of MI5, Sir Michael Hanley, and by 3.15pm he was on his feet telling the House of Commons that the allegations had been made in 1969, investigated by the Security Service who questioned Frolik and Stonehouse, and came to the conclusion there was no evidence. He added that he had, today, been told no evidence had come to light since then, and there was no truth in the reports that Stonehouse was under investigation or surveillance by the Security Service at the time of his disappearance. The former prime minister, Edward Heath, replied, saying that the very fact a statement is being made in response to press reports 'opens up a situation in which all sorts of stories can circulate in the press and allegations can be made, and if they are not then denied in Parliament credence is given to them'. Harold Wilson then reminded Heath that he himself had made a statement in the House following the disappearance of high-ranking MI6 officer and KGB spy, Kim Philby: 'considerable surprise was caused when he volunteered the statement that Philby was the third man involved on a famous occasion.' Wilson then added the comment which would add insult to Frolik's injury: 'One must always face the possibility that defectors, when leaving a country where they previously were and finding their capital – intellectual capital, of course – diminishing, try to revive their memories of these matters.' He said it had been ascertained that my father 'was not in any sense a security risk', and that it was only 'fair and right' that he make a statement 'since so many newspapers have published top front-page headlines on this matter'. Because, that same day, the *Daily Mail*'s front page had been 'Was Stonehouse working for CIA?' Wilson further added, 'He was not an agent of the CIA.'

We appreciated the comments of Mr Molloy: 'Would the Prime Minister agree that the media should respond to his statement, in that the tarnishing rumours and innuendoes should cease and that the Stonehouse family should now be released from the distressing pressures causing unnecessary pain and anguish to them?' The prime minister replied: 'Great distress has been caused. I understand that the mother of my right hon. Friend has suffered a serious heart attack because of the anxiety and pressure. Some members of the press are hounding them in their homes – the children, their domestic staff and other persons connected with the family – to ask them far-fetched questions about matters which at the end of the day must be settled by the police authorities in another country.' The prime minister was referring to America when he said 'another country', but on this same day, the 17th December, it was the Australian Victoria State Police who were trying to settle questions by messaging Interpol and asking what they knew about Mr Joseph Markham.

The following day the *Daily Mirror*'s banner headline read: 'Wilson: Defector Did Name Lost MP', reporting that Wilson had said that security services had 'found no evidence to support these allegations or that Mr Stonehouse was a security risk'.[9] Also that day, the *Daily Mail* broadened the subject under the heading 'The spy and Mr Stonehouse', saying 'People have a right to be reassured that he was no Czech spy. But also what he was up to in business dealings.'[10] The *Daily Express* also ran the Wilson denial, but linked it with a story headed 'The MP who loved money'. Not a day could pass without the press making my father look bad: if not a spy, then *greedy*. *The Sun* had a small front-page panel, 'Missing MP was quizzed by MI5 says Wilson', with most of the page reporting on the three IRA bombs in London. Two Irish women were seen running away from one scene in Bloomsbury, where a post office worker was killed. It reminded us, as if we needed it, that taking out life insurance in 1974 wasn't strange, it was sensible. There was a two-page spread, 'The Stonehouse File', on pages four to five which included the tantalising question: 'Was he being blackmailed by the Czechs?' Christopher Sweeney of *The Times*, who'd published an interview with Frolik in January, had told LBC radio that 'according to Frolik, Mr Stonehouse was being blackmailed'. This story wasn't going away. There was speculation that he'd defected by swimming to a submarine off the coast of Miami, been taken the 200 miles to communist Cuba, and put on a ship to Russia. On the other hand, was he the man spotted dancing in a Florida nightclub? The speculation and negative press reports kept coming. As did the reporters at the door. In the country, when it was raining and we didn't want to walk through the wood and across the field to get to the shops, we adopted a siege mentality – trying unsuccessfully to make bread from the contents of an increasingly bare cupboard.

On the 19th December *The Times* announced that my father's phone had been bugged on the orders of the prime minister, Harold Wilson. On the front page of the *Daily Mail* there was a photo of Sheila in her wedding dress under the headings: 'Woman who moved into Stonehouse's bachelor flat' and 'Secretary knew secrets of missing MP'. The financial losses in the property market had badly affected the Crown Agents and on the 20th the *Daily Mail* ran a story saying some of their losses were because of an investment they'd made in my father's BBT, which in June had been renamed the London Capital Group. On the same day, the *Daily Mail* ran a piece titled 'Missing MP ran his empire on borrowed cash'. On the 22nd, the *Sunday Times* ran two stories: on the front page we read 'Did Mafia cut in on Stonehouse's £6½ million deal'; on page thirteen, 'The Demise of a Super-Salesman'. The only good news was that the Miami police had checked my father's blood group against samples from the 'concrete coffin', and they didn't match. The whole family were emotionally and mentally exhausted by the time we again retreated to Faulkners Down House to prepare for Christmas. My poor mother was close to collapse. At this point there'd been so much negative publicity, people didn't know whether my father was a communist spy, a CIA spy, involved with the Mafia, a greedy fraud, a thief or an adulterer. But they'd learned one thing from the newspapers – he was bad!

On Christmas Eve we were wrapping presents in my father's study and remembering him. He always left Christmas until the afternoon of Christmas Eve, when he went shopping. I went with him once to the Army and Navy department store in Victoria and watched him buy a dozen presents in half an hour. It was amazing. At the perfume counter he stood behind and above the crowd, holding up two fingers, until he caught the eye of the saleswoman, when he confirmed 'two' and pointed to a perfume, then put up one finger and pointed to another. The woman put the three bottles of perfume in a bag, took his payment, and we moved on. In this way we went from department to department, quickly collecting presents. When he got home, he'd always wrap them himself using unusual and amusing paper he found around the house and making his own gift-tags with funny little drawings on them. We missed him.

At about 1am, Beatrice had gone to bed but my mother, brother, sister Jane and I were still in the study when the phone rang. It was a *Daily Mirror* reporter saying they were 99 per cent certain my father had been found in Melbourne. He rang back at 2am and confirmed the news, saying the Melbourne police were going to make a statement at 4am our time. From then on, the phone rang continuously with journalists wanting to know what was going on, so we decided to take the phone off the hook until 4am, when we might have some answers. It then occurred to my mother that the man they'd found was likely to be Bill Stonehouse, my father's pilot brother, who'd gone to Singapore a few years earlier and had actually lived in Australia previously. From elation, we fell back to despair.

As soon as Jane put the phone back on the handset at 4am, it rang. We saw the utter amazement on her face and heard her say 'Daddy, Daddy, is it really you?'. Jane wrote in her diary: 'I went weak, cold, hot, shaky. He sounded as if all his nerves were being stretched right to their limit, ready to snap. His voice was high and he was definitely not himself. All he could say was that he was sorry, sorry, sorry.' The front door was banging furiously. Jane handed the phone to my mother, who was visibly shaking. She fell into a chair. 'John?' she asked, unbelieving. 'Yes, darling, it's so good to hear your voice,' he said. My mother's questions came in quick succession: 'What's happened? Where are you? What have you been doing?' He replied, 'I'm sorry I've given you so much trouble, darling. It didn't work out. I tried to make it easier for you all, but it didn't work out. I'm here at the Melbourne Police Station with my very good friends John Coffey and Bob Gillespie.'

The door was still banging loudly, and Jane went to answer it. It was three *Daily Express* reporters holding air tickets to Melbourne in their hands. She wrote a note: '*Daily Express* at front door. Have tickets first plane out to Australia. Do you want to go?' and thrust it into my mother's hand. She told my father what the note said and asked if he wanted her to come. 'Yes, come as soon as you can,' he said, and then came the kicker: 'and bring Sheila with you.' This came as a shock because we had no idea that Sheila was so important to him. She was 28, Jane was 25, and I was just about to turn 24. Sheila was of our generation, not his. Jane wrote in her diary: 'What a nerve – he's flipped his lid.'

We were all crying, and laughing, and hugging each other and trying to analyse what he meant by 'it didn't work out' and 'make it easier for you all'. We were baffled, but thrilled. By now it was about 4.30am and the three *Daily Express* men were waiting in the sitting room. They were keen to get away as soon as possible to avoid the rest of the press who would surely be on their way. One of them, Jack Hill, said they'd cover my mother's flight and expenses and pay £4,000 cash in return for the first story of their reunion, plus pictures. As my mother had no other funds at the time, she accepted the offer, and went to get ready. Paul Hopkins, the chief investigative reporter of the *Daily Express* then arrived; she'd travel with him and Bill Lovelace, their photographer. Before she packed, my mother phoned Sheila with the news my father was alive. It sounded as if she already knew. My mother asked her not to go out to Australia, at least for the present, and Sheila agreed. By 5.30am a three-car cavalcade was heading for Gatwick Airport.

Half an hour later, the rest of the press started to arrive. It was important not to let them know my mother wasn't in the house. We didn't want them chasing her down at the airport. In fact, the *Daily Express* had laid good plans. They figured that the press would expect my mother to travel through Heathrow, so they'd booked flights from Gatwick to Paris, with a connection in the afternoon to Melbourne. They went to the ticket desk and Paul Hopkins asked the woman: 'I think you have tickets for me.' The woman asked: 'What name?' 'I don't know,' he said, 'what names have you got?' She looked at him quizzically. 'How many tickets should you have?' she asked. 'Three to Paris,' said Hopkins. 'Well, I've got one for a Mrs Church, one for a Mr Poulson and one for a Mr Hanlon,' the woman said. Hopkins knew they were the right names because he'd worked on the John Poulson fraud story, and these were the aliases his office had jokingly adopted for their incognito travel. After a couple of hours at the new, futuristic Charles de Gaulle airport, they were on their long flight to Melbourne.

We found out that the CIA had been bugging the phones at Faulkners Down House when my friend Derek arrived. From America, a 'friend of a friend' had played down his phone a recording of Derek on our phone at Faulkners Down, taken when he'd been there a week or so earlier fielding calls from the press. He got his electronics kit out and played us recordings of our own telephone calls on the F.M. radio. 'It's the CIA', he said, as he de-bugged the phones. Derek wasn't just an electronics expert; he was the go-to computer and security guy used by three royal families that I know of. He was in a class of his own. We weren't outraged that the CIA had been bugging us, we were used to the phones being tapped: them or someone else, did it matter?

It was a strange Christmas Day. The phone never stopped ringing and the door never stopped banging. We were besieged. By late morning, the owner of the house and farm arrived to say the farm vehicles couldn't get up the lane and we'd have to move out – permanently. But Jane, Beatrice, Mathew and I weren't bothered; he was alive, and that was all we cared about. And the woman did have a point: there were 25 press cars parked down the tiny lane and none of us could move. We heard that our father could be deported and that our mother might not be allowed into Australia. Everything was uncertain – literally everything. At least we had food, which is more than can be said for the dozens of reporters and photographers barking around the house like a pack of hounds with the scent of blood in their nostrils. They should've been with their families and probably resented having to be there, out in the cold, in Hampshire. Some would soon be on their way to Australia. I bet their wives and children weren't too pleased with the timing. Either way, if we thought the press had been bad up to this point, it was about to get a whole lot worse.

On the 27th December 1974 the *Daily Mail* proudly announced it had 25 people working on 'the Stonehouse file' and they named their seventeen reporters in London, two in Melbourne, two in New

York, three photographers in London plus one in Australia. The *Daily Express* put 22 reporters on the job, including their cricket correspondent, while *The Times* added their Sydney-based opera writer to their team. The *News of the World* equipped their nine reporters with £15,000 in cash, ready to pay random people for whatever they could get. The press invested heavily in the story and they wanted spies, sex and scandal. We felt hunted, a commodity, and that the last people the press cared about was us.

9

Man Drowning

While the coastguard were looking for John Stonehouse or his body, Mr Markham was on a non-stop flight to San Francisco. He caught a taxi into the city and asked the driver to take him to a good hotel. They arrived at the vast and magnificent Fairmont, high on a hill overlooking the city and North Beach. He asked for a single room, but they didn't have one so accommodated him for the same price in their best suite, the largest my father had ever seen. It seemed as if luck was on Markham's side.

The next day, the 21st November, he flew to Honolulu and booked into room 1706 at the Sheraton Waikiki Hotel. Mr Markham would make two calls from the Sheraton, both of five minutes duration, to the Highfield House Hotel in Hampstead, the first on the 22nd November, and the second on the 25th. Residents at the Highfield House Hotel didn't have phones in their rooms. All calls to them went through reception, who buzzed individual rooms, alerting the occupant that they should take a call at the communal phone on the landing. At the trial at the Old Bailey, which began in April 1976, Sheila said she was completely bowled over to receive that first call from my father, that he was completely distraught, incoherent, and she thought he sounded suicidal. She asked whether she should let the family know, and he said 'no'. She thought it would be danger-ous to tell anyone he was alive because of a possible suicide attempt by him. Three days later, he phoned her again. She said the calls were confusing because he was speaking about himself in the third person, saying 'John' had to get away from the pressures in England. She said that at no time did he use the first person – 'I' – it was always 'he' or 'him'. He seemed confused about who he was.

On the 22nd November, my father went to the Bank of Hawaii and, using the name 'Lewis Jones', purchased two bank drafts of $8,977 and $4,200, issued in the name of Joseph Markham. On the 25th November, Markham booked out of the Sheraton Waikiki Hotel, paying $308.76 on his American Express card. Now he faced his greatest challenge – entering Australia and having his new migrant status accepted. It turned out to be easier than he expected. The flight to Sydney had a stop-over in Nouméa, New Caledonia, a French territory, and from Sydney he flew to Melbourne and, on the 27th November, arrived at the portentous desk of freedom. The immigration officer took his passport, and the large manila envelope he'd taken with him containing the X-ray negative and certificate confirming he didn't have TB, stamped his passport with a big round print saying 'Permitted to Enter' and said, 'You are one of us now.' He also mentioned that entry wouldn't be so simple after 31st December, when a visa would be required.

Markham booked into the Sheraton Hotel on Spring Street and at 2pm headed for the Stock Exchange branch of the Bank of New South Wales (BNSW) at 395 Little Collins Street, where his account was supposed to be. He found that the building had been demolished so he went to the bank's HQ at 425 Collins Street and found his documentation was there. Mr Mulcahy had the letter of introduction from their London branch, and ascertained that the £14,100 (A$24,982.38 in Australian dollars) Markham had asked to be transferred from London to a deposit account was there. He withdrew A$3,000, which was used to open a current account, and Mr Markham was given a temporary book of five cheques, pending the printing of a personalised cheque book. Mr Markham told Mr Mulcahy that he was an export consultant and he'd like to convert two Bank of Hawaii bank drafts into one BNSW draft for

US$13,177. Mr Mulcahy took him to see Mr White in the Overseas Exchange Section, who prepared the draft – which would later be credited to Markham's Swiss Bank Corporation account in Zurich. Then Mr Markham went back to Mr Mulcahy and, using his temporary cheque book, withdrew A$500 in cash.

The next day, the 28th, Mr Markham went back to the BNSW at 425 Collins Street and asked Ms O'Bree if he could withdraw A$21,500 from his savings account. After taking twenty minutes to arrange the cash, Ms O'Bree handed it to him. At 11.30am, this same man walked into the Bank of New Zealand (BNZ) at 347 Collins Street and asked the female teller about savings investment account interest rates and removed a large amount of cash from the satchel he was carrying, and placed it on the counter. Watching nearby was the ever-observant Mr King, who went over and directed the man to the teller's box so he could count the cash. It came to A$22,000, and Mr King put it in the safe before introducing the man to the bank's accountant, Mr Rowland. The man introduced himself as Donald Clive Mildoon and told Mr Rowland that he was an insurance broker, and that after about twelve months he'd be moving to New Zealand. Mr Rowland asked Mr Mildoon for a passport as identification but Mr Mildoon said he didn't have it on him but he'd bring it on a later visit. Without ID, Mr Rowland couldn't open a current account, but he could open an investment saving account, and did so. At 12.30pm, Mr King had finished his lunch in the staff room and had gone for his customary lunchtime stroll along Collins Street. That's when he saw the man whose cash he'd counted earlier come out of the BNSW at 425 Collins Street, and return to his bank, the BNZ at 347 Collins Street, where the man deposited a further A$2,200. Mr King told Mr Rowland what he'd seen and Mr Rowland made a note on the bank's Master File Card, indicating that this customer should be treated with extreme caution and that no cheque account should be opened without certain identification. Meanwhile, back at the BNSW, Mr Street was thinking it unusual for a person to withdraw A$21,500 in cash and he telexed London asking for a copy of certain correspondence. Although everything seemed to be in order, Mr Street now joined Mr Rowland and Mr King in thinking there was something odd, and possibly fraudulent, about this man. My father had been in Melbourne less than two days, and through his own careless behaviour had already managed to raise the alarm. The banking community of Collins Street would put their heads together and ensure that by the time he turned up again, Mr Markham/Mildoon would be under police surveillance.

Oblivious to this, Markham transferred his suitcase to a cheaper hotel, The Regal on Fitzroy Street, in the district of St Kilda, and headed straight for the airport. This time he was going to Copenhagen, via Perth, Singapore and Bangkok, with a short stopover in Tashkent, Uzbekistan. On the 29th November he arrived in Copenhagen, booking into single room number 357 at the Grand Hotel around 9.30pm, where he stayed for one night. He made no calls. On Saturday the 30th, he booked into a cheaper – and warmer – hotel. All alone, he wandered around the cold streets of Copenhagen on that Saturday, and Sunday, and Monday and Tuesday, looking for English newspapers to find out what was going on back in the UK. 'Ghostly memories' were haunting him, and he wanted them put to rest. But there was to be no rest. He wrote: 'From the newspaper accounts it was evident that some people – and certain sections of the press themselves – were not only dancing on the grave of the missing man, they were trying to dig up the corpse to tear it limb from limb so it would get no peace. The allegations were fantastic.'[1]

Early on the morning of Wednesday the 4th, he finally phoned Sheila at the Highfield House Hotel and lamented 'They won't let him die, why won't they let him die?' She was frantic and, on top of that, thought she might be pregnant. He said he wanted to see her. She was concerned that she wouldn't be able to get to Copenhagen without half the British press finding out. He said if she didn't come to him, he would come to London. As he sounded far too unstable for that, Sheila agreed to go to him and went to the Hampstead Travel Agency in Heath Street and bought a one-way ticket to Copenhagen, for Friday 6th December, departing Heathrow Airport at 2.30pm. Sheila had asked for a later time, but the 4.30pm flight with Scandinavian Airlines was fully booked. She paid with her own credit card but had the ticket issued in the name of Mrs E. Morgan. Later that day my father phoned back to find out her plans: she'd be arriving on Friday evening.

On the afternoon before going to Copenhagen, Sheila went to see her doctor to get tranquillisers, and broke down in tears. The doctor warned her about the dangers of taking an overdose. She headed for the airport, all the while worried about being followed by the press. This was the weekend they, and my mother, wanted to ask her questions about the flat in Vandon Court. At Copenhagen Airport, she found my father sitting in the middle of the arrival lounge, with his head resting in his cupped hands. He looked pale and thin; he was distraught and nervous. Many British people had arrived on the same plane, and it was a miracle nobody recognised him.

Over the next day-and-a-half, he told Sheila that he'd been travelling under the name of Markham and planned to settle in Australia. He asked Sheila to write to him in the name of Mildoon, care of the Bank of New Zealand. At the trial Sheila said: 'It was then that he told me that he was also Mr Mildoon, which had the result of leaving me totally confused, but my own confusion was the least of my worries.'[2] What they talked about, nobody knows. Personally, I think that when he phoned her from Hawaii he told her he was going to Australia because when she went to dinner with Caroline Gay, Philip's wife, on the 25th or 26th November Sheila said she intended to work abroad and might go to Australia as she had friends over there. She did have friends there, but now she had a special friend there as well. Caroline told the police later that Sheila 'kept insisting that everyone should accept that John Stonehouse was dead', implying he'd had a heart attack because he'd 'had difficulty in using one of his arms or hands'.[3] At that point, of course, she knew he was alive. It wouldn't surprise me if, on learning he was alive when he phoned from Hawaii, she determined to heal him, save him and start a new life with him. He was all she cared about. She loved him, was devoted to him, stood in the dock at the Old Bailey with him, waited three years for him to get out of jail, married him, had a son with him, and my father died in her arms. However, 'saving' a man is a very different thing to being involved in his madcap idea in the first place. That's where the Old Bailey judge and I differ in opinion. On Saturday 7th December, my father bought Sheila's return ticket on flight SK 503 to London, leaving at 4.15pm on Sunday 8th, when he would fly to Singapore, with stops in Moscow, Delhi and Bangkok. From there he went to Perth, to acquire the precious immigration stamp, and spent the night of the 9th in a motel before flying on to Melbourne.

I've lost count of the number of flights my father took between 20th November and 10th December. If they'd had frequent flyer points in those days, he would have been given a platinum card. What they did have was a selection of British and other newspapers which they gave to passengers, and his face was all over them, next to the words 'Missing MP'. Any passenger on any flight could have recognised him. My father was a trained RAF pilot, he'd been a minister of aviation, worked on the development of Concorde, and negotiated the sales of Rolls Royce engines that powered the very planes he was flying around in. He knew pilots, airport staff and airline executives. Any one of them could have recognised him from former professional contact as he walked through the many airport lounges. When Sheila met him in Copenhagen, he was not wearing any kind of disguise. If he was trying to keep a low profile, this was no way to go about it. If he wanted to escape the British authorities, why not go to Brazil where they had no extradition treaty? He'd already made basic, stupid mistakes that would ensure he'd soon be under police surveillance, and booked into the Regal Hotel in St Kilda using two names, confusing Steve Erdos on reception. He'd soon use two names when renting an apartment from Mr and Mrs Wilcocks. He confused people because he was himself confused. This wasn't the behaviour of an arch criminal, and he wasn't stupid. He simply wasn't thinking straight.

On the 10th December my father arrived at Melbourne airport, bought a newspaper and caught a taxi into town. There was an advert in the paper for 'Executive Apartments to Let', and he diverted the taxi to check them out. The proprietors, Bob and Joan Wilcocks, were charming, there was a pool, and the small apartment was cheaper than his cheap hotel. Mrs Wilcocks gave him a card and asked his name. 'Markham,' he said. Mrs Wilcocks later said: 'Within the next few days I was aware he had taken a flat on a three-months lease. However, as a result of what my husband told me I subsequently addressed the man as Mr Mildoon.' He paid the A\$150 bond, and a month's rent, and moved into 411 City Centre Flats at 500 Flinders Street.

On the 11th December there was more crazy banking to do. He went to the Australia and New Zealand Banking Group at 66 Elizabeth Street and, introducing himself as Mr Markham, an export consultant who was going to be married shortly, spoke with Mr Joynt of the Migrant Advisory Centre. Here he opened a current and a deposit account with A\$100 each. Also on the 11th, Mr Mildoon went back to the Bank of New Zealand and asked Mr Davenport if he could open a current account. But Mr Rowland had told Mr Mildoon on the 28th November that it couldn't be done without a passport, and he didn't have a passport. Mr Davenport referred to Mr Rowland's notes on the account, written after Mr King's lunchtime observations, and declined the request because 'certain comments on our records decided me to treat Mildoon with caution'. Also treating him with caution was Detective Sergeant John Coffey of the Victoria Police who, on this same day, went to the Bank of New South Wales, and the Bank of New Zealand, and then to City Centre Flats at 500 Flinders Street, where he took possession of a tenancy application form.

At 10.15am the next morning DS Coffey was undercover and had taken up position outside the Bank of New South Wales on Collins Street. When he saw my father come out, he followed him around Melbourne. At this early stage the police weren't sure about what they were watching. They thought he might have committed a fraud, or was about to, or was simply a runaway husband using two names. They followed him for a couple of hours a day to begin with, usually in the morning, so they may not have seen that on the afternoon of Friday the 13th Mr Mildoon opened another bank account, this time at the Commonwealth Banking Corporation at 227 Bourke Street. Here he spoke to Mr West of the Migrant Information Service, telling him that he was an insurance broker, had substantial funds owing to him in Switzerland, and was hoping his fiancée would join him in March 1975. Even without a passport, Mr Mildoon was allowed to open a current account with A$100, plus a deposit account with the same amount. Mr West then took him to the branch next door at 225 Bourke Street, where a temporary cheque book was issued. Now he had seven accounts at four banks: Markham had a current and deposit account at two banks; and Mildoon had a current and deposit account at one, plus an investment savings account at another. He was giving himself options and hedging his identity bets. Mr Mildoon must have felt pleased that he'd managed to acquire a current checking account without a passport for ID, and had a nice place to live. He was getting somewhere. His aim was to ultimately disentangle himself from Mr Markham, who was too close to Stonehouse, and become Mr Mildoon, but he knew he couldn't entirely break the link with Markham because Mildoon didn't have a passport and couldn't risk getting one because he might have to explain what happened to the one issued to the real Mr Mildoon.

Nevertheless, a new, uncluttered, life seemed in reach. But eight police officers were now taking turns to follow him, and they were so intrigued that they went to his apartment when he was out on the 17th or 18th and, without a warrant, searched it. Detective Senior Sergeant Hugh Morris said: 'We saw nothing during the course of that entry that helped us in any way. I saw a box of matches from the Fontainebleau Hotel.' The significance of the matches would not become clear until a week or so later, when they realised who he was. Morris confirmed they were taking the enquiry fairly seriously. 'We thought we might have a big international criminal on our hands. We did not want to lose him. We did not want him committing any offences in Melbourne. At one stage it was thought that it might have been Lord Lucan.'[4] He was the other big character the world was looking for at the time. Lucan had gone missing from London on the 8th November after allegedly killing Sandra Rivett, his children's nanny, in the basement of his wife Veronica's house in Mayfair, mistaking Sandra for his wife. Lucan has never been found.

By the 19th December, the police were still confused about who their suspect was. At the trial, Coffey said: 'At that stage we were not certain which was his true identity, Markham or Mildoon. We were concerned that two persons had allegedly been booked into a hotel in St Kilda but only one had been seen.' Coffey believed 'he was contemplating something. I suspected he was up to no good. I did not know the how, the why or the when.' He didn't have a lot to go on: 'As far as I could tell Mr Stonehouse led a very modest life during the time I observed him. The flesh spots of St Kilda held no attraction for him. As far as I was able to see he was not living it up. He was living comfortably, he was never in the company of any other person. Apart from his bank accounts, I am not aware of any other attempt to establish any other operation in Melbourne. Apart from the bank accounts he never sought to establish any commercial roots in Melbourne. He had spoken to others but he had taken no steps towards it. He was never without his dark glasses and never without his hat. He was watching television with his hat and his glasses on inside which made me suspicious.'[5] This conflicts with what DSS Morris said at the trial: 'Certain photographs were taken of Mr Stonehouse before he was arrested. In those photographs he quite often appears not wearing a hat. From my observations of him quite often he did not wear a hat.'[6] He also wasn't trying to be incognito at the apartments where he was staying. One of the owners, Bob Wilcocks, said: 'He spent a lot of time in his room and I remember he was very fond of classical music. He used to play a lot of Beethoven on a cassette recorder. He had a set of photographs in his room. I didn't look at them closely, but I suppose they were his wife and daughter. He mixed very easily with other guests and was always most polite and friendly. He did not seem at all a man who was hiding out. He was always very natural.'[7]

Mr Mildoon joined the Victorian Jazz Club where he met some friendly people who invited him to barbecues at their homes, and on some evenings he went to the Melbourne Chess Club in Elizabeth Street. He applied for a driving licence, and started looking for a job. He walked everywhere, exhausting the police who were following him. DS Coffey reported on his routine: 'The first thing he did was to go and buy a copy of *The Times* and sit in the sun and read it.'[8] My father was still trying to find out what was going on back in the UK. Then the Australian newspapers picked up on the UK *Daily Mirror* interview with Frolik on the 17th, saying he was an StB spy. My father wrote it was the 'horror of horrors'[9] when he saw that one of the Australian newspapers had a large photo of him. On the radio news he heard that Harold Wilson was going to make a statement in the House of Commons, and was later relieved to hear he had been publicly exonerated.

On the 19th December, Mr Davenport at the Bank of New Zealand informed the police that a letter had arrived for Mr Mildoon. This was the first of four letters that Sheila would send. DS Coffey and DS Thomas went to the bank to collect it and Coffey steamed

the letter open. He said, 'I took it to the forensic science labora-
tory, opened it myself, caused the contents to be photostatted and
returned it to Mr Davenport personally.'[10] Mr Davenport objected to
there being no search warrant, but that wouldn't stop him handing
over a further three letters. 'At the time I obtained the letters I didn't
have sufficient information to go before a magistrate for anything,'[11]
Coffey said in court. Sheila wrote the letters in Chippenham where
she'd gone to avoid the press who, by this time, were keen to talk
to her. She wrote in a code of her own making, in case a bank teller
would read it; it wasn't a prearranged code between her and my father
when they'd met in Copenhagen. 'The rags are hounding,' she wrote,
by which she meant 'the newspapers won't leave me alone', and 'My
boyfriend is away at the moment and I have heard the most dreadful things about him from his former wife.' Sheila is referring here
to the meeting she'd had with my mother on the Tuesday following
her return from Copenhagen about the press stories of the 'brunette'
who lived at Vandon Court. My mother had told Sheila that he'd had
affairs, but that he always returned to her. This spooked Sheila and
at the trial she said she was very upset and felt lonely and isolated.
She was the only one who knew he was alive and what she'd heard
challenged the whole basis of their relationship. The letter said: 'At
the moment, (saw her yesterday) she is questioned re self-service
project. He lied about insurances to me. There's been a Mafia type
murder in some place and they're tracing blood groups etc. They
suspect B. of murder because of insurances. S. has had to promise
to retrieve if she's accused.' Sheila later explained to Detective Chief
Superintendent Kenneth Etheridge of Scotland Yard what all this
was meant to convey. She said the 'self-service project' referred to
'secret service enquiries'. On the insurances she said, 'I mention that
Mrs Stonehouse was being suspected of murder because of the insurances, and this had all arisen because of the stupidity of taking out so
many policies.' When asked by the police what she meant by 'S. has
had to promise to retrieve if she's accused', Sheila said: 'I would like

to say that that is a misleading sentence. What I meant to say is that I had to promise myself to do something about that, in other words, knowing that he was alive, I would have to disclose it if there was a possibility of Mrs Stonehouse becoming implicated.'[12]

Detective Sergeant John Coffey of the Victoria Police said: 'We thought he might have been Lord Lucan only because of the first letter' – with its talk of 'murder'. At this point, everyone was confused, including Sheila. In this first letter, she'd written, 'I do not recognise him as the same man at all. Two entirely different personalities, and I'm frightened to death. Like a szchitsophrenic (can't spell that).' She later explained to Etheridge what this meant: 'In view of his behaviour, I did not recognise it as that of the conduct of John Stonehouse. The John Stonehouse I knew was a man of positive and brilliant thinking with a first-class brain, but the man I now heard about was a completely different man, totally unlike the man I know. I really believed at that time that something had happened to him mentally. He had turned from a totally rational politician and businessman into an irrational, illogical man.'[13]

On the 20th December Coffey picked up the second letter from the bank, written by Sheila on the 13th. In this, she'd written, 'My biggest problem apart from Industry – like flies – is insurance. The only one the female persisted about was the first, – subsequents were forced by male who was never terribly intelligent, and this is front rag stuff now.' Sheila told Etheridge it meant: 'The insurances were still the problem and really that is all I mean by that. My reference to "Industry" does in fact refer to the Department of Trade and Industry which was now becoming actively involved in the investigation.'[14] In relation to the insurances, Sheila's problem was that all she had to go on was what she read in the newspapers, and they had the facts wrong.

In the third letter, dated 17th December and collected from the bank and copied by Coffey on the 23rd, Sheila wrote: 'There's a defect in the material I had. George has joined the co-operation

India Association' – by which she meant he'd been accused of being a spy for the CIA. She reassures him that his Markham cover is not blown by saying 'the projects on the ports thing is still OK', and lets him know that Scotland Yard are no closer to finding him, with 'the Scottish thing is still at it, barking up all the wrong trees'. She also made it clear that she was prepared to join him, with 'I long to go to work in Africa, or anywhere else for that matter.' This letter was written on the day Harold Wilson spoke in the House of Commons about the Frolik spy allegation that had been front-page news that day: 'Uncle Harry is speaking about this to his big family this after-noon,' and reports later in the letter 'marvellous news, is standing by George completely.' 'George' was her code name for my father. She then drops a bombshell: 'He told me and all of us everywhere that G's mother had had a heart attack and he blamed the R's entirely for that.' 'R's' meant rags or newspapers. Sheila continues, 'I am so upset over his mother. She was getting on OK until Friday when all this broke re the insurance project, so without wishing to be cruel, you can guess who is responsible. I cry all the time about her but cannot get in touch. George must not do anything as she is very elderly and it has to come anyway. She is in hospital and is being well taken care of. I pray for her every night so I will tell him (George) not to worry. Those bloody insurances.' Sheila told Etheridge, 'I blamed the press comments on the insurances for his mother's earlier heart attack. It looked so bad. I am also telling him not to come back, because she is so old.'[15]

Although the press and prosecution would find Sheila's let-ters so damning, indicative of a great conspiracy, they were utterly perplexing to the police and, more importantly, to my father. The unarranged 'code' Sheila decided to use was confusing and made the information in the letters open to interpretation. She didn't have any insight into what was really going on and could only relay press reports, which were invariably factually incorrect. Also, she was send-ing mixed messages about what she wanted from him: in one letter she told him not to come back to the UK even though his mother was ill, and in another she says she needs him back. A couple of months after the end of the trial, Sheila wrote: 'I'll confess that in my letters I rather emphasised that there was a baby and I did this deliberately. I know this was rather cruel but I thought that if he thought everything at home was hunky-dory he needn't come home, but could go on in his make-believe world for ever. But if he realised I was in dreadful trouble, as indeed I was, and desperately needed his help, then he might do something about it. In fact, I deliberately suggested that I was considering an abortion. I knew this would get him, and he would think, "Oh no, she's not going to get rid of my baby," and come rushing home.'[16]

By the time the Melbourne police had the third letter in their hands, they'd already contacted Interpol to ask them what they knew about Mr Markham and on the 21st December they heard back that Interpol weren't looking for a Mr Markham but they did want to know the whereabouts of John Stonehouse. The Melbourne police messaged Interpol for a full description, and received a photograph back. This was the first inkling they had that they'd been following the runaway MP. Two policemen moved into the flat facing my father's at the City Centre Flats at 500 Flinders Street and, with the aid of walkie-talkies, followed his every move. The proprietors had been told and continued being friendly with my father, introducing him to fellow residents at an opening celebration cocktail party. To my father, all seemed well, but by the 23rd he was under 24-hour surveillance.

That same day, back in the UK, Sheila was being interviewed at the offices in Dover Street by Detective Chief Inspector Barbara Tilley and Detective Sergeant Crock of New Scotland Yard. Sheila told them that although a very good swimmer, Mr Stonehouse had got a bit 'paunchy' recently and 'on one occasion she had found him lying down resting and this was something he never did in the ordinary way. He also complained of pain in his right arm.' Both police officers were struck by Sheila's unprompted remark that 'he was dead', and Tilley noted, 'Throughout the interview she did not appear to be upset or distressed at the apparent death of Mr Stonehouse.'[17] What Sheila didn't tell the police was that three days earlier she'd posted her fourth letter to Mr Mildoon, tucked inside a Christmas card; and what the police didn't tell Sheila was that Interpol and the Melbourne police were already closing in on Mr Stonehouse.

On the morning of the 24th December, my father went to a bank to collect a new cheque book, and then to the Regal Hotel in St Kilda to see if any post had been forwarded there. Meanwhile, police officers Coffey, Morris and Clarkson were preparing to make the arrest. They'd be armed. Coffey said: 'Officers of the Fraud Squad don't usually carry guns but this was an unusual enquiry.'[18] At 10.40am my father headed for the station where he bought a ticket and ran to catch the waiting train. Once on the train he was approached by three men. He didn't at first know who they were. Morris was the first to grab him and showed him his warrant card. The three quickly ushered him off the train, which was about to depart. In the deserted booking hall they searched him and asked: 'Are you Mr Markham?' He said nothing. They sat him on a bench. He was in shock. They cautioned him. The three policemen stood over him, holding back his arms. One of them said, 'Don't worry, it's all over.'

In the car on the way to the police station the police said they suspected he was an illegal immigrant. He said nothing. DSS Morris lifted his trouser leg, looking for a scar. They'd had a telex from London about a scar on Lord Lucan's leg. As Coffey said, 'We were still rather confused about his identity until he admitted his identity 51 minutes later.'[19] At the police station they started interviewing him and half-way through told him it was being recorded. He said he didn't mind. Morris reported that, 'He told us of tensions and pressures which caused him to do what he did. We listened to him

sympathetically and encouraged him to talk.'[20] He mentioned
blackmail, and general disillusionment and about the *Sunday Times*
article that had started all the problems. At 1pm Coffey went to the
apartment in Flinders Street and collected up all my father's possessions, which he handed over to acting Superintendent Gillespie of
the Commonwealth Police – the Federal branch of the Australian
police – who now took over. They went with my father to their own
offices where Detective Inspector Sullivan questioned him all over
again, cautioned him again, and suggested a couple of lawyers. By
luck my father chose a man who would become a great ally, Jim
Patterson. Then he phoned my mother at Faulkners Down House
and asked her to come to Melbourne, and to bring Sheila with her.

10

The Reunion

My mother had plenty to think about on the 37-hour flight to Melbourne. When the journey started she was focused on a joyful reunion, but as time went on and she thought about the situation, the emotions turned into anxiety and trepidation. What had happened to her husband? She'd heard nothing from him for five gruelling weeks, other than what he'd said on the phone on Christmas Eve. She didn't yet realise he'd had a breakdown. Her mind was turning over and over: if it was about Sheila, he could have asked for a divorce; if it was financial, it could have been resolved. The words my father had said on the phone during his first trip to Miami had been ringing in her ears ever since his disappearance: 'I can't take it anymore.' What was the 'it' that had brought them to this bizarre turn of events?

In her rush to get out of the house and onto a plane, my mother had forgotten to pack comfortable shoes for the journey, and now her legs were swelling inside the knee-high boots she was wearing. She couldn't take the boots off because she'd never get them on again. It was an uncomfortable journey all round. She was travelling with Paul Hopkins and Bill Lovelace of the *Daily Express*, whose offer she had no choice but to accept because my father had wiped out their joint bank account. She ran a public relations business from home with the help of her fantastic secretary, Margaret Picco, but there wasn't enough money in that account to pay for her expenses now. People would criticise her for accepting financial help from the press, but she had household expenses and a fourteen-year-old son to think about. She was exhausted by the time the plane touched down at Tullamarine Airport. Much to her relief, the only reporter there was the local 'stringer' for the *Daily Express*, Peter Game. He was with his wife, Betty, and mother-in-law, and the British Vice-Consul, Ivor Vincent, was there too, with his wife. The three ladies hugged my mother, which was a welcome display of warmth and comfort, although it made my mother weepy. Nobody seemed to notice she could hardly walk on her swollen legs inside the tight boots. The Vincents and Games both offered to put my mother up in their homes, but she opted for the motel Peter had arranged, as the next few days were going to be difficult for her emotionally, and an impersonal hotel room would at least give her a chance to relax from time to time. She and the reporters booked into the motel under their assumed names, and almost as soon as she'd unpacked the phone rang. It was Bob Gillespie of the Australian police, offering to pick her up and take her to the detention centre. My mother was surprised. 'You mean I can actually see him today?' she asked. 'Yes, of course,' said Bob. My mother said she needed a bath and a couple of hours sleep, after which they'd go and meet my father.

He'd spent Christmas Day in a sparsely furnished cell behind a security fence and barbed wire at the Maribyrnong Detention Centre, waiting for the courts to open on Boxing Day, when he'd face the charge of illegal immigration. Although his possessions had been taken away, including his washbag – so he couldn't comb his hair or shave, he'd been allowed to keep his radio. He listened to music and waited for the news to come on. Ironically, one of his guards was a Mauritian who'd immigrated to Australia and remembered, when he was a sergeant in the Mauritius Police Force, guarding my father at Le Reduit, the Government House, when my father was under-secretary of state for the colonies.*

---

* Mauritius is isolated in the Indian Ocean between Africa and India, and on the trade route from China, and had been settled by many diverse racial groups.

My mother was driven past a large group of waiting reporters, photographers and TV crews and through the entrance gates of the detention centre. A chill went down her spine. It was just like a prison, with guards all around, and the last place she'd imagined meeting her husband. 'But it was better than a morgue,' she told herself, 'and he won't want you looking glum so you'd better cheer up.' She had one overriding thought in her mind – how would she be greeted by the man who apparently wanted her to believe he was dead? She found the situation horrifying, and for every step she took forward she wanted to take two back. It was only because Bob Gillespie was guiding her along by the arm that she moved forward. On the journey there she'd been reassured that he was 'tanned and well' but the police didn't know the old John Stonehouse, only this new one, so when she saw him she was shocked. He looked dreadful. His complexion was ashen and his eyes glazed but wild. He'd lost a stone, aged years, his hair was turning grey, and his voice was strangely high-pitched. His demeanour was confused and deflated, almost sheepish, and quite unlike the confident, self-assured man she knew. She was facing a broken man, but he looked pleased to see her, and they kissed warmly in the reception area under the full gaze of the prison officers and policemen.

They were becoming independent from Britain and nobody wanted to see strife, but the political leaders couldn't agree on an electoral system. My father had been there a couple of times and knew many of the leaders involved. He met them again in his official capacity during June/July 1966 and devised an amendment that satisfied all parties: the legislative assembly would have 70 members including eight 'Best Loser' specially elected seats, allocated to the Best Loser candidates of communities that would otherwise be underrepresented. I've been told by Mauritians that this amendment gave elasticity to the system and is responsible for the fact that Mauritius has largely avoided racial tension since independence – because people feel their system of representation is essentially fair. (Ref: 'Agreement reached in Mauritius on the Future Electoral System on the Occasion of the Visit of Mr John Stonehouse, MP, Parliamentary Under-Secretary of State for the Colonies.' Sessional Paper No. 8 of 1966 [Port Louis, 1966].)

Her first words to him were, 'what *have* you been up to?' He put his arm around her shoulder and replied, 'It's a long story, I'll explain.' She was introduced to his lawyer, James (Jim) Patterson, and his assistant, Fran, and they were ushered into a bleak interview room, sparsely furnished with one table and a few chairs. My parents just looked at each other for a while, my mother's head spinning with questions. They were both nervous, and at pains not to upset each other on this first meeting. Too much pain and agony had been suffered on both sides and it was as if they were both treading on ice – at any moment it could crack and they'd be drowned in their own grief. But my mother had things to say. He'd allowed her and the family to think he was dead for five weeks, and then had the audacity to ask her to bring his mistress with her. She'd told him before that another affair would be the end of their marriage. For five minutes she told him how cruel he'd been to casually abandon four children, allowing us and her to suffer the grief of believing him to be dead when he was very much alive, plus leaving her to deal with all the problems he'd left behind. He'd just expected us to get on without him as if that were a perfectly normal thing to do to a close and loving family. Then he just broke down and cried and cried. My mother had to hug him and try to comfort him as he sobbed his heart out. As she tried to soothe him, my mother realised for the first time that he must be really ill – she had never seen him react to any situation in anything close to this manner. At that point she realised she was dealing with a nervous breakdown and would have to stop thinking about herself and start thinking about him. As they talked, she came to see that he was in a state of shock. He'd been living in another persona and was finding it hard to readjust to being John Stonehouse again. My mother hugged him and kissed him and told him we were all so happy he was alive.

My mother turned to Jim Patterson and said, 'You may think that John is well and healthy, but this is not the John I know. He has clearly had some kind of breakdown and needs psychiatric help.'

There was a knock on the door, and the meeting was brought to an end. My mother would be in Australia for three weeks before returning to London, and then returning to Melbourne again for a second time. My brother Mathew would spend months there, as would my sister Jane, and they would all have hands-on experience of my father's ongoing breakdown. He'd be listless and wouldn't want to do anything, sitting around in his dressing gown all day. They never knew what to expect. One minute he'd be curled up in a ball on the sofa and the next, in a fighting mood. My father's mental state became the family's priority, the entire focus was to get him through this experience without additional pressure. The fear within the family was that he'd commit suicide. His mental state needed gentle care and attention now, everything else could wait. In public, his pride forced him to appear compos mentis, but in private he was a wreck.

On Boxing Day my father appeared in court, where a transcript of the police interview taken immediately after his arrest was read out. Much of it described the problems with the BBT and the financial difficulties my father had got into trying to prop it up. In the witness box he said: 'I was being blackmailed and felt I had no escape,' and 'I don't want to say anything here or apportion blame. Some of the responsibility was my own.' He wanted to stay in Australia, he said, and start a new life, adding, 'I can only say in the past two days I have received more consideration, understanding and support than in the past two years in England.' There were no charges against him in the UK but while the Australian labour and immigration minister, Clyde Cameron, decided whether he was to be deported as an illegal immigrant or not, my father was sent back to the detention centre.

On the 27th December a photo of my parents kissing at the door of the Maribyrnong Detention Centre was on the front page of the *Daily Express*, with a large caption: 'The kiss of forgiveness'. The banner headline read: 'Exclusive: John Stonehouse tells the *Express*

"WHY I CAME TO HATE ENGLAND"'. I doubt anyone back in England had sympathy with that, coming from a man who'd faked his own death, abandoned his wife and children, had an affair with his secretary, stolen lots of money from who-knew-who but *someone*, was a spy for the commies, or the CIA, had left his constituents to fend for themselves while taking his salary, and had something to do with the Mafia. It didn't really matter that he said, 'I was being blackmailed by men who threatened to use my political career to squeeze me dry.'[1] Nobody was interested. They just wanted to know about the affair, which Sheila was still denying. That same day, on page two of the *Daily Mail*, a headline read, 'I'll fly out if he wants', with Sheila reportedly saying: 'At the moment I am continuing to look after his parliamentary work. I will remain totally loyal to him.'[2]

But the big headline on the front page of that *Daily Mail* was the real breaking story, possibly the most damaging in this entire saga: 'CAPTURED IN A DEAD MAN'S SHOES'. When Mrs Mildoon and Mrs Markham discovered their husbands' identities had been used by my father, the whole country took a sharp intake of breath: this was the final straw. From that point, I doubt there was a person in the country who had a good word to say about him, and trying to recover any semblance of understanding was going to be a long uphill struggle for my father, towards a summit he would never reach.

In London, my sisters, brother and I were shocked by what we were reading in the papers. The *Daily Mail* had five pages of coverage that day, plus an editorial, headed: 'Surprise! Surprise! John Stonehouse Lives', in which they congratulated themselves on being dogged in their pursuit of dirt: 'Some lines of inquiry caused undoubted distress to the relatives of Mr Stonehouse. But the instincts of the press have from first to last in this affair been sound. We believed that, for his own bizarre reasons, John Stonehouse had contrived to vanish. And we were right.'[3] On page three, there was a map of the world with arrows showing little aeroplanes flying from London to Miami, to Hawaii, to Australia, to Singapore, to

Denmark and back to Australia. From this graphic, complete with a
man swimming off the coast of Miami, and a passport in the name
of Markham, we learned some of what had been going on. One mystery was that he'd been receiving mail. The press had certainly been
doing their homework or, more likely, the police had been handing
the press a lot of information.

By the 28th December, four days after his arrest, the British were
baying for blood and parliament needed to look as if it was 'doing
something'. On the front page, the *Daily Mail* headline ran 'YARD
READY TO FLY STONEHOUSE HOME': 'It is believed that he
can be brought back for obtaining the forged passport in Markham's
name – an offence he has already clearly admitted and which carries
a maximum penalty of two years' jail.' The police had already been
making enquiries at my father's offices during December and no
criminal charges had been brought. But now they had the Markham
bank accounts to look into, and they were gearing themselves up for
a heroic extraction of the fugitive. The *Daily Mail* reported: 'Two
officers are to be briefed to stand by ready to fly to Australia at short
notice if he is not deported and extradition becomes necessary.'[4]
Alongside the story, in case we'd forgotten the love triangle, they
had a picture of a smiling Sheila with the heading 'Blackmail? Well,
massive pressure'. She is reported as saying 'massive, unfair pressure
was being put on him. I know who was doing it. There were several
of them. But I won't go into details until I have spoken to John.' My
mother was quoted as saying, 'It's the problems of a man in public life
who goes into business, comes up against lots of pressure in business,
and then people put pressure on him because of his political career.'[5]

At 2am on the 29th December my father was suddenly released
from detention and told he could report weekly to the Melbourne
authorities while the Australian government decided on their course
of action. Away from the eyes of the press, the police took him
40 miles east to Yellingbo, and the home of his old school friend from
Southampton, Griff Bartlett, who'd come forward and volunteered

to look after him. As teenagers, they'd both been involved in an idealistic organisation called 'Citizens of Tomorrow'. Now Griff was living with his partner, Lettie Doolan, in a huge ramshackle house set in ten acres of a fauna reserve. The next day he phoned my mother and arranged to meet her in the Mentone district of Melbourne. My mother was taken there by the two *Daily Express* reporters she'd travelled to Australia with and who, for their own advantage as well as hers, had been helping her avoid the rest of the press pack. Dusk was falling by the time my father arrived at the rendezvous, an hour late, and reluctantly agreed to have his photo taken – part of the deal my mother had struck with the *Express* for getting her to Australia on Christmas Day. With the help of a flash, Bill took a photo of them on a nearby beach, with their arms around each other and looking out to the sea. The reporters promised not to follow my parents, and my mother got into the front of a car driven by Lettie, with my father in the back. Even though it was an awkward position, my mother bent her hand backwards over the seat and my father held it all the way.

When they arrived at Griff and Lettie's house, my mother was very surprised to walk through the front door and into a huge ball-room, large enough for several hundred people, with a grand staircase at the end leading to a stage, with a modern organ on it. But the grandeur was faded, and in stark contrast to the amenities of the house which were bare and minimal – no running water or internal sewerage system. Griff and Lettie were great friends to my parents during the next six months' ordeal, helping in any way they could in between looking after several children, many animals, Lettie's full-time job in Melbourne as a printer and union rep, Griff's job as an architect, and them both being volunteer firefighters. In the early morning, my mother heard the sound of bells and was told those were bellbirds which, along with the cockatoos and parakeets, and a wonderful environment of tall blue gum trees, provided my parents with welcome distractions on the long walks they now had the opportunity to share together.

Finally, they could talk. My father said, 'I thought it would be better for all of you if I were dead. The companies would have received the sympathy of the banks and others and would've been able to carry on and all the staff safeguarded. I couldn't bear the thought of the family seeing me go through the public humiliation of failure. In time you would have forgotten me and rebuilt your lives. I wanted to be rid of the sham of that VIP nonsense and be treated like anyone else. I've been blackmailed, abused and beleaguered financially just because I am who I am. I can't go on like that any longer.' To my mother, who was sane, the answer to his problems seemed simple enough: wind down the businesses and get out of politics. But to my father, who was insane, faking his death, or suicide, seemed rational solutions. I wonder how many men have killed themselves thinking 'it would be better' for their family and colleagues if they were dead? Irrationality leads to dangerous fantasies and wild expedients. As my parents walked and talked, my father broke into tears, and my mother became desperately miserable. By far the worst thing for her was realising that despite their tremendous relationship he'd felt unable to confide in her in London. When she asked about Sheila, all he could say was, 'Barbara, I love you and I love the children and I don't want to do anything to hurt you.'

He talked about his time in Melbourne, but couldn't yet talk about the days he spent in Copenhagen. That would have to wait until he'd seen the psychiatrist a few times, when the internal power struggle between the old personality of John Stonehouse and the new one of Joseph Markham was explored. The five days he spent alone in Copenhagen had been agonising as he tried to sort himself out, separating one identity from the other. On day six, he'd reached out for help and phoned Sheila. It was good that my mother had Griff Bartlett in Melbourne, because he was the only person there who'd known my father before the breakdown and could see how different he was. Other people thought my father was behaving normally, and that was a large part of his problem – they couldn't recognise the degree of his mental collapse.

As 1974 drew to a close, the Stonehouse story provided more twists and turns. Everyone wanted to know who had been sending my father letters in Melbourne. Sheila was the chief suspect, but wasn't named. On the 30th December the *Daily Mail* had a story headed 'Yard hunts for a fellow plotter', while the front page of the *Daily Mirror* was taken with 'RIDDLE OF CALLS BY STONEHOUSE'. The very fact that my father had been in communication with someone led the entire nation, whipped up by the press, to believe the whole scenario – the disappearance – was a contrived plot. It didn't occur to anyone that he was, in his desperate mental state, reaching out for help. That would have been the generous route to take but, as we were to learn, Britain was in no mood for generosity. On the last day of a horrible year, the newspapers were focused on the letters and phone calls, the life insurance, and the fact that Peter Shore, the secretary for trade, had ordered an inquiry into my father's business affairs.

In Melbourne on the 31st December, my father took my mother to the Bank of New Zealand at 347 Collins Street and Mr Davenport gave him A$100 cash from the current account of Clive Mildoon. Davenport said: 'He told me that his correct name was Stonehouse and introduced his wife who was with him … I informed him that under the terms of the Investment Account those funds would not be released without a month's notice. He then made out in my presence a written request to draw the Investment Account funds as soon as possible.'[6] Apparently, in Australia at that time a bank account could legally be opened in any name a person chose, so when my father returned to the banks to get his money, they accommodated him. On the 28th January he went back to the Bank of New South Wales at 425 Collins Street where he had an account in the name of Markham, and Mr Street arranged for the funds to be transferred to account number 872205 in the name of Stonehouse. Of course, all the bankers now knew exactly who he was. On the 5th February, the balance in Markham's deposit account was transferred to the new current account. Mr Mulcahy explained how the 'Markham' funds in London came into the new Stonehouse account: 'Mr Markham then gave me written instructions by way of a letter dated 3rd March, 1975 to close his account in the name of Markham at our London office ... I made arrangements for this to be done and the balance was transferred to this Branch by way of telegraphic transfer. I identify the credit slip dated 5th March, 1975 which evidences the credit to his account of $5,754.90 ... Following this, the Current Account in the name of Markham at this Branch was closed on 11th March 1975 and the balance of the account, A$5,961.62 was transferred to the John Thomson Stonehouse Current Account, this is evidenced by a cheque payable to J.T. Stonehouse, signed J.A. Markham dated 10th March, 1975.'[7] This must rank as one of the strangest events in banking history: Mr Stonehouse signs a cheque in the name of Mr Markham, to the credit of Mr Stonehouse.

On the 1st January 1975, my father had his first consultation with psychiatrist Dr Gerard Gibney. This was an immense relief to my mother, who hoped he could now, finally, get some help with his mental turmoil. Dr Gibney recognised at once the severe depression my father had been suffering. Partly, he deduced, this was because although it cost him socially, politically and financially, my father had persisted in following causes for oppressed peoples around the world. He was spent. On the second visit, Dr Gibney took my mother aside and told her he was concerned she was heading for a breakdown too, and needed to take some protective steps. He told her not to try to think too far ahead. Not even day to day. He said break your life up into small sections, like bricks in a wall, and try to get through each half hour, building up each half-hour section bit by bit. Soon, he advised, she'd be able to tackle a whole hour, or even half a day, at a time.

The world will still go on whatever happened to them, he said, and her job was to keep sane and adjusted so she could join it in due course. It was helpful advice, which my mother took on board.

It was now that the letters started arriving from people who'd gone through similar experiences – either mental health issues, or being abandoned by a husband for a younger woman. They'd be addressed 'Mrs Stonehouse, Australia', and were like a wave of love coming from all directions, giving my mother terrific support. She felt alone on the other side of the world, dealing with a broken man, but the empathy of strangers kept her company. Meanwhile, reliving the events of 1973 and 1974 sent my father into a tailspin, and by the middle of January he had to be admitted to Trentford Private Hospital for a few days because Dr Gibney was concerned he might attempt suicide.

That my father had adopted the Markham persona for five months before he disappeared was proving to be a huge problem to him. People thought this was proof of his devious long-term planning. What they couldn't appreciate was the relief my father had felt in adopting a parallel persona, and imagining an alternative life as that different person. But there was no safety valve now and Stonehouse lay in mental tatters. There were no criminal charges, so the press didn't have to worry about *sub judice* and could go to town. My parents were like rabbits being chased by a pack of hounds and the dogs were panting, waiting for a kill. They expected that to come from Scotland Yard's Detective Chief Superintendent Kenneth Etheridge, and Detective Chief Inspector David Bretton, who arrived in Melbourne on the 3rd of January. They didn't have arrest warrants, and didn't question my father. Instead, they lurked around for three weeks like spectres of impending doom.

Back in London, my father's associates were unhappy they'd been left in the lurch. They requested his resignation as director from the London Capital Group, EPACS and Global Imex, and he'd been happy to comply first thing in January. But the offices at

26 and 27 Dover Street, W1, were hardly quiet. Detective Inspector Townley of Scotland Yard's Fraud Squad visited on January 3rd, 6th, 7th, 10th, 15th, 17th, 24th, 28th and the 29th, and on February 3rd, 4th, 6th, 7th and 19th. At the trial over a year later it became clear that Townley had been so haphazard in his searches that he was even unclear where my father's desk was – which seems incomprehensible given he had only one desk in his one office. Townley also seems to have been unaware of the safe. This is important because when my father was questioned by DTI inspectors in February, he told them that the papers they needed to explain his actions were in his desk and in the safe, but in Townley's statement for the trial he said: 'There came a time when I did take possession of documents from the EPACS office. They were not taken from a safe at 26 Dover Street. I don't know which is Mr Stonehouse's desk … There were certainly documents on the premises that I did not see. I certainly did not specifically go and look in Mr Stonehouse's desk. I cannot say whether the papers said to have been in Mr Stonehouse's desk existed or not.'[8] My father was unaware in January and February what was, or was not, happening at the office in London, and after he was arrested in March he was not allowed to speak to work colleagues as they were now classed as witnesses. Some time after he was extradited to the UK and had been bailed, he happened to be driving down Dover Street with his solicitor Michael O'Dell when they saw bags of rubbish outside the offices. He opened them up and found they contained paperwork that was helpful to his defence. Who put them there remains a mystery, as does what the police were actually doing in Dover Street on those fourteen occasions. Certainly they weren't looking for anything that could help my father's defence, which became disadvantaged by his lack of access to paperwork.

The idyllic hideout in Yellingbo was soon discovered by the press, and the house was besieged by 3rd January. My parents had to flit from one place to another, helped by Peter Game, the local *Daily Express* 'stringer'. Constantly having to pack and unpack, find new accommodation, and dip and dive to avoid the press pack was an added burden to my parents. There seemed to be no peace. Eventually they found a tiny flat, and moved in, but every day there was a new drama to deal with – either a bad newspaper report, or the immigration proceedings, or news about the business in the UK. The response from parliamentarians at the House of Commons was universally hostile, and it became clearer by the day that returning there would just be a destabilising nightmare. But my mother, at least, could return. She had a business to attend to, a flat near the constituency to sell, a rented house in the country to pack up, four children who needed to know what was going on, and a publisher to find for the book my father had started to write as a form of therapy, on the advice of his psychiatrist. She returned to London early on the morning of the 16th January. She only had a small case of luggage because she was planning to return to Melbourne on the 6th February. The press asked her how she felt towards my father and she said, 'As I have always done.' She still loved him, and would stay loyal. The next day the *Daily Mail* took up a page with photos of the love triangle: my mother arriving at London Heathrow airport; Sheila's 'hideout' in Cornwall; and my father's 'hideout' in Melbourne. The public apparently loved this angle of the story, and that hunger was to prove very costly to my father's case.

11

So Much for Comrades

On 24th November 1974, four days after my father disappeared and was generally presumed drowned, Tony Benn wrote in his diary: 'Bob Mellish had dug out a Hansard text of the last written question John Stonehouse asked before he disappeared, requesting the statistics on death by drowning. It was a most extraordinary coincidence – or else very mysterious.'[1] In fact, 'the last written question' was about the M6 motorway in his constituency of Walsall. The last reference to drowning in Hansard was six months earlier, on 24th May, during a debate on 'Canals, West Midlands'. Part of my father's speech went: 'There are about 2,000 miles of canals in the United Kingdom ... I am concerned about the 200 miles or so of canals in the West Midlands and the Black Country in particular. I understand that there are more canals in the Black Country than there are in Venice. ... There are three aspects to which I wish to refer: first, safety; second, amenity; third, economic viability. In recent years many young children have died from drowning because they have been able to gain access to unprotected and overgrown canals. That is deplorable. Last year alone five young children died from drowning in Walsall. Those young lives could have been saved if the canals that are unsupervised had had sufficient fencing.' He then talks about the potential of canals as a public amenity, including cleaning them up so anglers could use them, and says, 'If we were able to improve our canal system and make better use of it for transport, it could be linked with the European system, thus saving costs as well as bringing us in touch in transport terms with a valuable network in Europe.' Two other local MPs had joined in the plea for something to be done, Geoff Edge and Bruce George, who made the point that, 'In one small stretch of canal twelve children have been drowned, and our local coroner has a file which grows annually.' Bob Mellish was mischievous in his suggestion my father's last question was on drowning statistics, especially given that he says he had 'dug' it out, and Tony Benn was too quick to lap it up and publish it in his diary. The last words my father actually said in the House of Commons before he faked his death on 20th November, were these on the 14th: 'As the most serious danger facing the world is a world food shortage, with a dangerous threat of widespread famine, especially in Third World countries, may we not have a debate on the subject to discuss what contribution this country can make towards helping improve the position?'

Bob Mellish was the Chief Whip of the Labour Party and furious that my father was absent from the House of Commons because the government had a majority of just three. Reducing the available number of Labour MPs from three to two made it even harder for the government to pass their agenda through parliament and, if a general election had to be called, any MP could lose their job. They were all angry that my father had put them one step closer to that risk.

They also weren't too pleased with what he'd said in the House of Commons on the 4th November, two days before his first attempt to escape his life. In a debate on 'Industry' he said this: 'In West Germany there is a degree of worker participation in the management of industry which might be an example we should follow. Another significant point is the fact that the trade union movement in Germany participates constructively in industry. I would like to see that being done here, where trade unions tend to be more disruptive than constructive.' Later, he says: 'If the TUC and the trade union movement generally cannot keep their side of the bargain of the social contract, we shall undoubtedly have to have a wages freeze in 1975. I hope that we can break away from the depressing cycle of stoppages and strikes which handicap industry and sap the country's morale. I regard a strike as the last refuge of a bankrupt negotiator facing an inept employer, both operating within a flimsy structure which provides no real rules of conduct. The TUC and the Secretary of State for Employment must aim for the abolition of all strikes, unofficial and official. We should apply a little civilisation to this area of our affairs and stop inflicting terrible wounds on ourselves to prove our manliness.'

My father's animosity towards the trade union leadership was well known within the Labour Party, which was funded by the unions, and Labour parliamentarians didn't look kindly on anyone who challenged that mutually beneficial relationship. But my father's criticism was not reserved for the Labour Party, it applied to the whole of British politics: 'For too long Britain has allowed itself indulgences which a successful and expanding country would hesitate to allow itself. Our problem is deep-seated, and can be best summed-up as 'the end of Empire syndrome'. It is a failure to adjust to our new situation in the world, which does not owe us a living and is making it extremely difficult for us to earn one.'

Labour Party infighting during the 1960s and 1970s had a negative impact on all they tried to do. I've found reading the biographies of the main characters in this drama depressing, and the more of them I read, the more depressed I become, as the breadth and depth of their criticism of each other emerges. The whip's office was a source of poisonous rumours while the National Executive Committee of the Labour Party, the unions, the constituency parties, the backbenchers, the ministers, cabinet and prime minister, all seemed to be working against each other. Respect of colleagues was conspicuous by its absence. By 1974 my father was thoroughly disenchanted with the whole thing.

When he was arrested on the 24th December, my father sent a telegram to the prime minister saying he 'regrets that I have created this problem', that he'd had a 'mental breakdown', adding 'I can only apologise to you and all the others who have been troubled by this business.' The PM didn't have the time or inclination to reply. By this time, the government were trying to deal with a financial crisis of 26 per cent inflation, unemployment at a 30-year high, and an International Monetary Fund that was threatening to abandon the country. The last thing Harold Wilson needed was a runaway MP.

By this time, there'd been so much bad publicity, Labour politicians were keen to disassociate themselves from my father. My mother too would face years of total silence from former colleagues. Being involved in the Party as an MP and MP's wife for seventeen years meant nothing. There was no sympathy or understanding, they didn't acknowledge my father had had a mental breakdown and all thought the worst. So much for 'comrades'.

The Labour Party knives were quick to come out. On the 28th December, Labour Party MP Maurice Edelman wrote a commentary for the *Daily Mail* which is typical in that he wanted to appear understanding of mental health issues, but at the same time didn't accept the role mental health issues had actually played. He wrote: 'There will be considerable sympathy with anyone who breaks down under stress. But with his particular enterprise, Mr Stonehouse entered into a whole series of plots. He allowed his mother to endure an extremity of grief. His deception about his disappearance at sea was a lie to his constituents.'[2] While wanting to appear sensitive to breaking under stress, he's saying there's a particular way to break. On no account have any 'plots', and don't upset your mother. And before you go mad, consider how your constituents are going to feel. It's like saying if you're going to throw yourself in front of an oncoming train, think about the driver and how he or she is going to feel. And what about the passengers who are going to be delayed? This kind of conflicted thinking, born of a disbelief that the man had mental health issues, was going to underlie all that came afterwards.

The self-serving Edelman couldn't help revealing what many other Labour MPs felt: 'He was born into the Labour movement and yet he couldn't wait to get out into the exciting, capitalist embrace.' My father worked tirelessly for the cause of socialism for fourteen years before he even thought about entering business. That's not 'couldn't wait'. And while he saw promoting British industry as a good thing for the country, Edelman saw it as defecting into the 'capitalist embrace'. This tribalism in British politics is what drove my father to distraction. Edelman got bitchy: 'I see him in my mind's eye, moving through the lobbies, reserved and aloof, occasionally exchanging some trivial pleasantry with one of his contemporaries, a good-looking man who would enhance any party and yet one who always seemed to be waiting for the right person to talk to.'[3] My father was not reserved or aloof. What Edelman means is that he didn't spend time drinking pints at the bar frequented by the Labour clan hatching divisive schemes and instead took himself off to the chess room with fellow enthusiasts, including Conservative Party MPs, while passing time waiting for votes. The 'good-looking' comment is revealing; perhaps Edelman was aware that many wives of MPs and female House of Commons staff found my father attractive. Jealousy all too easily turns into hate.

The MPs were worried that the bad behaviour of Stonehouse would reflect badly on them, and the country was getting angry. 'Come Home Stonehouse', yelled the *Daily Mail* on 2nd January, saying 'Yard men fly out to "invite" runaway MP to return.'[4] The policemen didn't actually talk to my father, yet alone 'invite' him to return, and the Government were silent too. It was, of course, the calm before the storm. Meanwhile, the press were having a heyday, with so many stories to reveal, including the mysterious phone calls and letters. On the 4th, the *Daily Mail* called Sheila the 'Beautiful enigma', and on the 6th, their front-page headline was 'What "S" Wrote to Stonehouse', with a few quotes including, 'kind words from uncle Harold', and 'lots of questions from the fuzz'. The *Daily*

Mail did not say where they obtained the letters, but the only possible source was the police. They asked: 'Who is the accomplice who fed Stonehouse with information since his disappearance? And who received phone calls from him at the Highfield House Hotel in Hampstead? There have been widespread reports that the mystery figure was, in fact, his secretary Mrs. Sheila Buckley.' Sherlock Holmes was now joined by James Bond: 'The letters will be studied by MI5, Britain's internal security force, and Scotland Yard will check all typewriters which could have been used in London by Stonehouse's secret correspondent.' The letters, according to the *Mail*, 'make nonsense of his claim that he went to Denmark to find out about British reaction to his faked drowning'. What the *Mail* didn't say is that the letters were so highly coded they were largely incomprehensible. And while they were right that 'a secret meeting with his contact'[5] took place in Copenhagen, they didn't know that my father spent five days there alone before phoning Sheila and telling her where he was – and that delay indicates they were not co-conspirators.

Sheila was in hiding at her aunt's house in Cornwall and must have been perturbed by what she read on the front page of the *Daily Express* that day, alongside photos of my parents smiling and looking into each other's eyes with the caption 'Together', and one of her with the caption 'Alone'. In this exclusive interview, the top headlines read: '*The wife*: He says there is no other woman' and '*The secretary*: He admits she helped his plan'. This last line was a classic journalistic twist on what had actually been said in the interview. The reporter, Paul Hopkins, had asked my father two questions, one after the other: if he'd phoned Sheila twice from Honolulu, and 'It appears obvious that she was assisting you in your escape plan?', and reported 'He nodded in agreement to both questions.' The word 'appears' replaces what Hopkins writes elsewhere in the text: 'And he nodded in agreement when asked if it seemed obvious she helped him in his getaway plan.'[6] Here's where the twist happens: Hopkins asks whether it *appears* or *seems* obvious, and it well might *seem* so, but that is not the same as the headline: 'He admits she helped his plan'. What my father was agreeing to was that it looked bad. However, the headline is what people remember – 'she helped'. That's conspiracy, and an admission of conspiracy, no less. This twist would cause the nation to dismiss the notion of a breakdown, and see the 'plan' as collusion. These two things are mutually exclusive: there's either one person having a breakdown, or two people involved in a conspiracy. This is why journalists had such a negative role in my father's story – they twisted things.

MPs were as much influenced by this reporting as anyone else. The largest headline on this page was 'MY DIRTY TRICK, BY STONEHOUSE'. Hopkins had put it to my father that either my mother had colluded, or he'd 'caused her great pain by putting her under suspicion – in addition to her initial shock of believing him dead'. My father answered, 'That is my greatest regret in this whole business. It was a dirty trick.'[7] So, altogether, by the 6th January, Stonehouse had – in an interview – admitted he'd done a 'dirty trick', and conspired in a 'plan' with his secretary/mistress. The emerging picture was downright embarrassing to the government, and MPs of all parties wanted to distance themselves as far as possible from this unfolding drama involving one of their own.

If all the drama of the story was like thick icing covering a cake, the cake itself was the spy story. In substance, my father was just no good. The traitor rumour had not been entirely quashed by Wilson's denial in the House of Commons on 17th December, because many considered it a cover-up. Once the dramatic icing came into full view people reconsidered the spy allegation and thought it was probably true. If he could collude with his mistress and fake his own death, he could also be a spy. The problem with it, from our point of view, was that being called a spy holds emotional content: everyone loves their country, and love holds emotion. Being accused of being a spy releases that emotion in other people – except it's not the emotion of love for their country, it's the hate for someone who would harm their country. On the 10th January, *Private Eye* carried this by Auberon Waugh (who routinely called Wilson 'Wislon' to avoid legal action): 'In the House of Commons we hear Wislon announce that there is not a shred of evidence for believing John Stonehouse was a Czech spy apart from the first-hand testimony of his Czech spymaster. No wonder Wislon decided to let him stay in the Government ... I have never attempted to hide my belief that Wislon is a Russian agent.'[8]

In a debate on 'Subversive and Extremist Elements' in the House of Lords on the 26th February, Lord Clifford of Chudleigh said this: 'Once again, will our leaders take note that in a book by the Czech defector, the ex-intelligence agent, Josef Frolik, which I think is coming out in May, there will be mentioned three fairly well-known people as having supplied information to the Czechs. It would be comforting to know for certain that these reports are false, and that if they are not that they will be dealt with without fear or favour.' He didn't need to mention my father's name because Frolik had revealed that in the *Daily Mirror* in December and everyone knew he was included in the 'three'. For us, it was like having a bully living in the backyard, with the additional problem that people believed the bully was in the right.

As a family, over the years, we were to discover that people love a spy story because it's much more exciting than a non-spy story. And they also loved the salacious mistress angle, especially if it involved 'running away'. What they weren't interested in was the mental health angle. To us, it was patently obvious that a sane John Stonehouse wouldn't adopt alternative personas and fake his death. To others, these bizarre actions seemed normal behaviour for the greedy, adulterous spy. There was also a lot of amateur psychology going on, even among diplomats.

On the 28th January 1975, J.M. Hay of the British High Commission in Canberra wrote to P.G. de Courcy-Ireland at the

Foreign Office, saying that my father had sent a report from his psychiatrist to the minister at the Australian Department of Labour and Immigration, Mr Cameron, and a first assistant secretary there, Andy Watson, had read some of the contents to Mr Hay over the phone. 'Mr Stonehouse, of course, should not find out that we know the contents of the report,' wrote Mr Hay. Paraphrasing what Andy Watson said, Mr Hay reports that the psychiatrist, Dr Gibney, said, 'Mr Stonehouse suffered significant but "atypical" depression. He thought of suicide, but, deciding that this was not the answer, devised a "suicide equivalent" – his disappearance from a beach in Miami … The psychiatrist concluded that Mr Stonehouse is suffering from "significant depression" which requires "on-going" psychiatric care and perhaps treatment in hospital in the future.' Then Mr Hay turns amateur psychiatrist, writing 'Nowhere in the report were there suggestions of the schizophrenia and paranoia of which we have heard so much from other sources. As Andy Watson pointed out, there may well be another report which might either be more confidential between psychiatrist and patient or be held in reserve should Mr Stonehouse require a special defence – such as unfitness to plead – should any legal action be contemplated. Such is Mr Stonehouse's desire to remain in Australia, however, that I would have expected him to use any device to try to soften Mr Cameron's heart – even to the extent of producing evidence of severe mental disturbance rather than the sort of depression which is an everyday part of all too many people's lives.'[9] We were to hear this notion – that what my father suffered was 'everyday' depression – many times over the years. Yet, not 'all too many people' are falsely accused of being a spy. Anyone who thinks that doesn't cause extreme stress has never been accused of something as contemptible as treason and not been in a position to defend himself, in my father's case because the relevant file was behind 'the Iron Curtain' and unavailable to exonerate him at the time.

The same day this letter was written, a motion to set up a select committee to 'Consider the position of Mr John Stonehouse' was passed in the House of Commons. The diplomats, however, decided the committee should not be shown the letter. On the 4th February, Mr A.R. Clark of the Foreign Office South West Pacific Department sent a memo to a select number of colleagues saying, 'I do not think that it would be appropriate to give the letter a wider distribution. If the select committee want a psychiatric report, they will no doubt formally go about getting one.'[10] Sir Thomas Brimelow, the permanent under-secretary at the Foreign Office, concurred, adding a handwritten note to Clark's memo on the 6th: 'The Secretary of State may think it better that letters such as this should be kept in the Private Office under Ministerial Control.'[11]

One aspect of this story that became much misunderstood is that, at the beginning of his time in Australia, my father did want to resign his seat in the House of Commons. He phoned the British High Commission in the capital, Canberra, on the 9th January and asked the director of information services, (H.H.) 'Tommy' Tucker, to pass a classified message to London. First my parents had to get to Canberra. They arranged to meet Tucker in circumstances the US embassy reported to the State Department in Washington as 'best cloak and dagger style at request of Stonehouse'. My father had phoned Tucker and asked him to meet them in a specific hotel car park in Canberra, and to bring his official briefcase as evidence of identity. The reason for the 'cloak and dagger' was that my parents were simply trying to avoid the letter handover being reported or photographed by the press. What Tucker didn't appreciate was that my parents had been forced to move between seven locations in the past five days and were exhausted from trying to avoid the press. My father decided to resign after a particularly gruelling weekend during which my mother and he were followed for hundreds of miles by teams of British reporters in cars who all wanted to know 'when are you going to resign?' A helicopter with press photographers had

even followed them to a beach where it came down so low it sent
sand flying in all directions, annoying the Australians trying to picnic there, who also told my parents to 'go back to the UK'. It must
be said, though, that in general, Australians were very kind to my
parents, casually throwing comments like 'good luck, John', when
recognising them on the street.

Tucker reported the car-park letter handover to his American
diplomatic colleague, Mr Green, who reported to the secretary of
state in Washington that Tucker thought my parents' criticism of
the British press harassment 'a bit hard to understand, as British
High Commission understands that Mrs Stonehouse had accepted
30,000 pounds sterling from London *Daily Express* for her exclusive
story'.[12] In fact, my mother received £4,000 in cash, not £30,000,
and she needed every penny of that to pay for the family's food and
accommodation, and other expenses. Yet this error on the part of
Tucker, or the High Commission, is now part of official diplomatic
history and may well go down forever as 'truth'. If my experience of
being the daughter of John Stonehouse has taught me anything, it is
this: there's nothing new about 'fake news'. In addition, I've learned
from this and other official diplomatic communiques, they're not
always to be trusted either. If Tucker told Green this misinformation,
the chances are it was also communicated to London, where it could
have caused damage to my father's reputation.

The letter my father handed to Tucker was addressed to Edward
('Ted') Short MP, the Leader of the House of Commons, and was
dated 13th January. It said: 'As you know I have expressed a wish to
remain in Australia and my application to do so is being considered.'
He explained the reasons for his breakdown, and said: 'I have already
advised Mr Cameron [the immigration minister] of my intention to
resign from the House of Commons but delayed this action when
it was reported that two Scotland Yard detectives were coming here
to interview me. In fact they made no request to see me and I have
received no official communication whatsoever requesting me to

return to the United Kingdom.' He refers to the pre-judgement he has received from the press, and then says, 'I thank my constituents in Walsall North, and in Wednesbury for their loyal support over the past eighteen years and ask them to accept my profound regret that external circumstances and pressures have forced me into breaking ties I have learnt to value.' The letter ends, 'Will you please, therefore, set in motion the formalities required for my resignation as the Member for Walsall North.'[13]

Ted Short replied on the 14th, attaching a draft of the formal MP's resignation letter, which reads, simply, 'I hereby apply to be appointed Steward of the Manor of Northstead.' Confusing though this text is, there's no appointment being made, simply a resignation under the archaic rules of the House. The Americans were keeping a close eye on the situation because the razor-thin Labour majority put the government in a precarious situation that could lead to an election, and change of ruling party and policies. On the 14th, Mr Spiers at the US embassy in London wrote to the Department of State: 'We anticipate resignation will be accepted expeditiously, opening way for first by-election in current parliament. Press has recently pointed out that absence of Stonehouse and hospitalization of two other Labor MPs theoretically erased Labor majority in parliamentary session which opened January 13. Practical effect of these absences, however, is minimal, as Labor can count on support of single SDLP member and opposition is neither cohesive nor without its own absent MPs.' The communique shows that the Americans were very aware of the mathematics of a by-election: 'As Stonehouse was re-elected by very safe margin (nearly 16,000 votes) in October 1974, there appears to be little chance that Labor will lose his Walsall North seat in by-election, even if many Labor voters fail to go to polls, as is often the case in by-elections. (In percentage terms a conservative win would require a 16.7 percent shift in voter preference.)' Then follows a sentence that helps explain Ted Short's subsequent fury when my father did not, in fact, resign: he wanted the safe constituency for one of his boys – 'Labor party sources report that Terry Pitt, former director of Labor Party Research Department and advisor to Edward Short, is leading contender for constituency party nomination.'[14]

The only people who weren't happy with the proposed resignation were my father's psychiatrist, and his lawyer. Dr Gibney felt that resigning his seat held a great deal of emotional content for him, so much so that it was one of the reasons he feared he would carry out suicide, and that's why he booked my father into a hospital around this time. His lawyer, Jim Patterson, was much focused on the fact that if my father did resign as an MP he'd have to leave Australia within three days. Given that returning to the UK would be so detrimental to his health, Patterson strongly advised against it.

The complication in the situation arose because of the constitutional relationship between Britain and Australia, specifically the fact that under Section 8(1)(*e*)(ii) of the Migration Act my father, as a sitting British MP, had automatic right of entry into Australia and the right to remain. This meant that he had not, in fact, entered the country illegally. However, the law required that he should have sought entry under Section 8(1)(*e*)(ii) before travelling. This was a technical point but, essentially, he wasn't an illegal immigrant although, on the technicality, the Australians could have deported him at any time.

When my father arrived at the immigration desk at Melbourne Airport on 27th November 1974, and got the Markham passport stamped, gaining him entry to Australia, Gough Whitlam was prime minister and Clyde Cameron was labour and immigration minister, and they had what might be termed an independent approach to the British government. During the first few weeks following my father's arrest, that was to show. While the British authorities were falling over themselves to respond to the press hounds baying for blood, the Australians casually pointed out that, under Section 8(1)(*e*)(ii), Stonehouse was exempt from the need to hold an entry permit to enter or remain in Australia and, as the British had no charges against him, as far as they were concerned, he could stay.*

On the 14th January, a front-page headline in the *Daily Express* said: 'Stonehouse quits as MP'. Apparently, Ted Short had made a statement saying, 'I very much welcome this development.' But Short had been too quick to make this announcement as the official resignation letter had not yet been signed, yet alone received in the UK. So, the next day the headline was, 'Stonehouse: I haven't quit'. Obviously this led to the next theme, expressed on the front page of the Aberdeen *Evening Express* on the 16th January: 'Stonehouse told: Make up your mind'. My father wrote to Ted Short on the 16th saying: 'Some newspapers are apparently reporting that I have announced that I will not resign. That is incorrect. The position is as follows. My solicitor has advised me very strongly not to resign because of the curious position with regard to the immigration laws in Australia. My solicitor has said that he would not take responsibility if I signed the document and that he would require an indemnity from me if I did so. My solicitor is examining the legal position more closely ... I will let you know how this legal consideration proceeds and what my final decision is.'[15]

* The head of state in Australia is Queen Elizabeth of the United Kingdom, and her representative in Australia is the governor-general. People tend to think the Queen does nothing to interfere in Australian politics, but in 1975 the democratically elected prime minister, Gough Whitlam, was sacked by the Queen's representative for daring to question the CIA's use of the secret listening post at Pine Gap, near Alice Springs. Whitlam discovered later that MI6 had been spying on the Australian foreign affairs office and Clyde Cameron told him that MI6 had been bugging cabinet meetings and passing the information on to the CIA. Whitlam had wanted to get rid of the post-colonial relationship with Britain, end nuclear testing, and generally have the country's resources and foreign policy in the hands of Australians. The CIA and Britain were having none of that. On the 11th November 1975, Whitlam was called into the office of the governor-general, Sir John Kerr, a man with close ties to both UK and US intelligence services, and summarily dismissed using what's known as 'reserve powers'.

On the 17th January, my father made the mistake of meeting members of the press 'off the record' at the Hilton Hotel, hoping he could explain the series of events that led to his breakdown. It was like sticking his hand in a hornet's nest and hoping not to get stung. He was angry with Ted Short for not releasing the whole text of his letter of the 13th January, which included the lines: 'I now appreciate that the long traumas I suffered were caused by a deep disillusionment with the state of English society and the complete frustration of the ideals I have pursued in my political and business life. The most traumatic frustrations I suffered relate particularly to Africa, Bangladesh, and the British Cooperative Movement.'[16] In his letter to Short on the 16th, he referred to a statement by the government chief whip, Robert 'Bob' Mellish, saying, 'I hope he has been misquoted.' This may refer to the front-page headline on the London *Evening News* that day: 'Angry Mellish accuses Labour's runaway MP, STONEHOUSE "LIKE MANIAC"'. As chief whip of a government with a razor-thin majority, Mellish was much inconvenienced by his runaway MP. He didn't intend to be understanding of my father's mental health issues, but nevertheless arrived at the same point: 'His behaviour does not seem to be that of a normal man.' The opinions of three other Labour MPs were quoted. Marcus Lipton said: 'A simple straightforward motion on Monday to expel him is all we need – cut the cackle and let's get on with it.' John Lee said: 'What we are concerned about is the whole skulduggery of absconding and entering Australia under false names which is conduct unbecoming of a Member of Parliament.' Even my father's friend, William Molloy, was cutting ties with a vengeance: 'Stonehouse has now by his recent action destroyed all vestiges of honourable behaviour. To err is human, to revel in it is repugnant.'[17]

Bob Mellish and Ted Short got lambasted by my father during the 'off the record' dinner with the reporters on the 17th and, the next day, very much 'on the record', the *Daily Mail's* front-page headline ran: 'STONEHOUSE BLOWS HIS TOP. SHORT: "The man is a pusillanimous twit ..." MELLISH: "He's nothing but a crude bore"'. In fact, he'd called Mellish an 'uncouth bully'. Either way, it was not the way to make friends and influence people. The word 'pusillanimous' means lacking courage or resolution, but Ted Short wasn't going to be cowardly now. He wrote to my father on the 21st: 'I very much regret to have to tell you that, as you have not yet signed the application for your appointment as Steward of the Manor of Northstead, I am now compelled to set in hand Parliamentary consideration of your case,'[18] and he set about making arrangements for a select committee to be appointed, essentially to see how they could get rid of him.

During that dinner with the reporters, my father had also banged his hand on the table and said: 'I tell you I am going to stay here. I am going to stay.' This also appeared in the *Daily Mail* article by their chief crime reporter, Harry Longmuir, and it was no doubt relayed to Chief Superintendent Etheridge of Scotland Yard when the two of them met for a prearranged tête-à-tête later that night. This is how it works: the press tell the police what they know, and the police tell the press what they know. Longmuir and Etheridge had such a relationship, possibly forged on their flight out to Melbourne together.

The only journalist who had a good word to say about my father was Bernard Levin, columnist on *The Times*. On 21st January he wrote a piece that began: 'The only surprising thing about the Labour Party's attitude to the case of Mr John Stonehouse, MP, is that there has not so far been a proposal that he should be immediately executed, by hanging, without the formality of a trial.' Bernard had been a friend of my father for 25 years and wrote, 'Perhaps one never knows anybody; but to me, as to others who know him, he has always seemed the most rational, the least wild of men. Yet his behaviour has been that of a man who is seriously disturbed in his mind. (It is true that his descriptions of Mr Short as 'a pusillanimous twit' and Mr Mellish as 'a crude bore' have the stamp of a man who is in full possession of his faculties. But nobody is so crazy that he has no lucid intervals.) Is it not reasonable, then, to assume that mentally disturbed is precisely what he is?' Bernard clearly picked up on the collective negativity of the political party my father had dedicated his life to: 'the sheer indecency of the Labour Party's behaviour, in assuming the worst of a colleague, in presuming him guilty of crimes with which he has not even been charged, in ignoring the obvious and tragic fact that, on all the evidence, he is clearly suffering from a severe breakdown, and in making such unseemly haste to rid themselves of possible embarrassment and to restore their tiny majority in the House of Commons, should not pass without censure'.[19] Bernard's voice was like a short sweet whistle in a loud howling gale that would go on and on.

Also in contrast to the cacophony of press and parliamentary hate was the warm sympathy we experienced from constituency officials. My father had been MP for the constituency of Wednesbury for seventeen years until it was abolished in the boundary changes set for the February 1974 election, when he was elected to Walsall North, which included part of the old constituency. We'd built up close relationships in the old constituency – particularly with the chairman, Sam Stevenson, and agent Vic Steed, and their families, and in the new constituency there was Harry Richards. They were all, throughout the whole long nightmare, steadfast and understanding and our family will always be grateful to them for that.

The motion to agree to the setting up of a select committee took place on the 28th January. The issue was vexing for the members. They knew that if a precedent was established, it could affect them all. The parliamentary columnist Andrew Alexander summed up the problem in the *Daily Mail* the following day, asking 'what is the select committee going to say … After all, if it is going to say that strange behaviour, telling lies, ignoring one's parliamentary duties, making utterly contradictory statements on television and so on – that all these are grounds for disqualification, then we must be prepared for the biggest rash of by-elections in British History.'[20]

Alexander noted that the Labour MPs were pulsating with 'righteous indignation'. One of these was Dennis Skinner, who said: 'When BBC television has to announce that it is broadcasting photographs from Australia by kind courtesy of the *Daily Express*, that is enough for me to suggest that the right hon. Gentleman, or someone very closely attached to him, was of a sound enough state of mind to get involved in that.' He was implying that my father's mind was sound enough to make a financial arrangement with the *Daily Express* for their taking of photographs. Skinner didn't know that it was my mother who had made a deal with the newspaper, simply so she could get herself to Australia on Christmas Day.

Members were concerned that my father's behaviour would call their own integrity into question, an idea voiced by Mr Fernyhough: 'But the one thing that we must try to understand and appreciate is the feeling of the general public. I am certain that they will come to the conclusion that this place is the best club in the world and that once again we are trying to cover up, to shove matters under the carpet and to conceal something which does none of us any good and which, unless it is dealt with, is bound to leave some further mark upon what I would call the general integrity of this House. It is the integrity of the House which is suffering in these circumstances. It affects every Member; some of it rubs off on him.'

The mental health issue was raised by Emlyn Hooson: 'That is a matter which it will be extremely difficult for a select committee to decide. For example, I know, from my experience at the Bar, of a medical certificate or a medical report relating to an accused man which on the face of it disclosed a certain state of affairs. However, when the medical expert was questioned and cross-examined thereafter, a totally different state of affairs was disclosed. How would a select committee, for example, be able to judge and assess a medical report from an Australian psychiatrist who was not present to be cross-examined by the committee? That medical issue might be the very issue which the House would eventually be asked to decide. I can think of many difficulties that would face a select committee now.'

Members were conflicted about whether they should discuss the matter at all. Sir John Langford-Holt noted: 'My right hon. Friend the Leader of the Opposition said that we could act only on the fullest information. We have not had that information. We have had speculation in newspapers. I know what the right hon. Member for Walsall, North is supposed to have said in one newspaper but when I read another newspaper I find that he has said something different. We read what his wife has said, what his secretary has said and what his secretary's husband has said. But there is nothing of authority.' (Sheila had no husband; they'd been divorced for years.) Mr Fernyhough thought differently: 'I do not think it is fair to say that we are not entitled to discuss the matter. The whole of the press has discussed it. It has been discussed on television. It is not fair to say that the House somehow must not say one word on this issue.' After three hours, the motion was passed by 237 for, and 30 against.

The first thing the select committee did, on the 30th January, was to write to my father asking him to answer two questions, either in person or in writing: 1) Do you intend to remain a member of parliament and 2) Is it your wish to remain in Australia? At their next meeting, a few days later, on the 4th February, the select committee took evidence from Sir David Lidderdale KCB, clerk of the House of Commons. Their first question related to absence: 'In the past there have been many occasions when members have been absent for a long time?' – 'Yes.' It was established that if the select committee asked an absent MP to come, and they didn't, they could get a resolution from the House ordering him to come. If he did not then come, it would be 'contempt of the House'. They discussed precedents for 'expelling' or 'discharging' members, or for 'disgraceful conduct' and 'constructive contempt'. They discussed cases of errant MPs going back to the 17th century. It was ascertained that there has never been a case where prolonged absence in itself was taken as a reason for expulsion. And they reminded themselves that there are republican MPs from Northern Ireland who, with the backing of their constituents, never set foot in the House of Commons because of ideological objections. There was an option of dismissing my father on the basis that he was obstructing the House in the performance of its functions, but there was no precedent that, simply for being absent, an MP had been dismissed on those grounds. At the end of the discussion, they seemed to have settled on one point. Michael Stewart asked the question: 'It is clear, is it, that actions which one considers tend to lower the esteem in which the House is held by the country, are contempts?' Sir David replied: 'They have been so treated and could be again.'[21]

My father replied to the select committee on the 18th February: 'The advice of my psychiatrist is that a return to England would be extremely dangerous to my psychiatric health. The reason I wish to remain in Australia is because the conditions here are more conducive to my recovery. It may be that after a period of convalescence I would be fully recovered and able to return to the UK in which case I might make a personal statement to the House and resume my Parliamentary duties. But at this time I must be guided by my psychiatrist who has said that the circumstances would be better for me away from the conditions which brought on the traumas to which I have been subject.'[22]

That same day, the Australian minister for immigration made a statement saying: 'While Mr Stonehouse remains a Member of the House of Commons and there is no formal charge or request for extradition, it seems inappropriate to require his departure.'[23] On the 26th February, the Australian House of Representatives in Canberra considered an urgency motion on the subject and, in this, the minister revealed that on the 15th January he'd instructed his department that if my father resigned he was to be given three days to leave Australia, or be deported. During the debate the minister also said: 'The Commonwealth Health Department had recommended to me that Mr Stonehouse not be granted permanent residence on January 29, after he was given a psychiatric examination. The department's report to me said: It is considered this man has had a mental breakdown which has resulted in a depressed, paranoic state of mind.' It went into some detail: 'This breakdown was due to him overloading himself with responsibilities beyond his capabilities to handle himself in political and business life. To this has been added the extra strain of things beyond his control going wrong. One result of this illness has been irresponsible acts without proper heed to the consequences in order to try and escape from his trouble.' This was relayed to the select committee in London, along with the note that, 'His mental illness is such that he fails to satisfy the criteria for permanent entry. Mr Stonehouse was not previously aware that he would have to leave Australia but he now knows he has to make plans. He could have fled from Australia and he will probably try to do so now.'[24]

So here was the catch-22: if my father resigned as an MP he'd have to leave Australia immediately and return to the UK, where they were universally antagonistic towards him and didn't seem to recognise he'd had a mental breakdown – the same mental breakdown that made his stay in Australia impossible due to their immigration laws. What was my father supposed to do? He didn't know. So he didn't resign, and just stayed put. He continued to see his psychiatrist and started work on a book, *Death of an Idealist*, the writing of which became a form of therapy.

On the 28th February, the Australian High Commission wrote to the select committee, clarifying that Mr Stonehouse would only be allowed to stay in Australia if he remained an MP. They pointed out that there was a provision in the Migration Act to disallow an MP to stay – a 'declaration' under Section 8(2) that could be instigated by the minister or an authorised officer – but that 'In the existing situation the Minister does not have any present intention to make a declaration under Section 8(2) of the Migration Act.' So there they had it: the Australians weren't going to throw him out, so if they wanted Stonehouse back, or expelled, they'd have to do something themselves. The British parliamentarians remained unsympathetic and indignant. The Leader of the Commons, Ted Short, said if he didn't resign or return to the UK he could be expelled from the House, and party officials continued to explore the procedural options. Some of the less aggressive MPs pointed out that the only known alleged charge was obtaining a passport in an assumed name and, as that appeared to be a remarkably easy thing to do, nobody was sure it was actually illegal. Plus, they knew that many other MPs had been absent from the House of Commons for various reasons for much longer periods of time. The press were baying for blood and whipping the nation into a frenzy of hate and the poor parliamentarians felt impotent, and didn't like it.

Then my father slapped them right across the face with an exclusive excerpt from the book he was writing, published in the *News of the World* on 16th March. The part that hurt was this: 'The Commons became even more oppressive and the childish banter even more irrelevant and irritating. In the Division Lobbies as I shuffled through to have my name ticked and my nod counted, I realised that most MPs around me were robots, too, voting on issues which they did not bother to understand after debates to which they had not bothered to listen.'[25] Five days later he was arrested on the instructions of London's Scotland Yard.

12

Three's a Crowd

My father was in love with two women at the same time: his wife, Barbara; and his secretary, Sheila. He once said to me that 'men are different', meaning men, euphemistically, 'sow their oats'. Sheila said my father told her he felt relaxed with her, and I don't doubt that, but at some point the cheat has to get up and leave his mistress, go home, and lie to his wife about where he's been. He'd been doing that for about five years. At what point does the strain of lying become a crack in the persona, because lying to anyone, about anything, is always a strain, and the more lying there is, the more of a strain it becomes. In May 1976 my parents, unusually, had a row, during which my mother called him a cheat and a liar, and he replied, 'That's why I had to get away from Stonehouse. Don't you realise how I hated him?' My father had become disassociated from his emotional self.

One might wonder, with two women devoted to him, how he managed to get into such a mess with the BBT. My mother blamed herself for not recognising what was going on. She later said, 'If only John had taken me into his confidence and let me have a go at his business interests I might have done well for him. I actually asked him on several occasions if I could help, but he always shunted me sideways. I think he felt I was the little wife in the background being supportive.'[1] But my mother had always supported him in an active way in his political career, and she had always worked to support the family while he was engaged in his various unpaid idealistic ventures.

What made the BBT different was that my mother disapproved of the whole project from the outset and generally stayed away from it, and my father was too proud to admit it had defeated him. Also, my father didn't encourage my mother to come to his office, because Sheila was there nine to five, five days a week. Until August 1974 Sheila was a director of several of his companies, and was a signatory on the accounts – that's what caused her to stand trial with my father at the Old Bailey.

My mother didn't know my father and Sheila were having an affair. Her suspicions had only been raised once. She'd gone to Dover Street with a business associate and they were asked to wait outside my father's office while Sheila went to see if he was free. My mother and the associate heard a squeak – the kind of sound that comes from a woman when she's having her bottom pinched. It seemed that flirting was going on. Sheila came out and said to my mother, 'You look so smart today,' but my mother's appearance was always stylish and immaculate and she chided Sheila with, 'Try not to sound so surprised, that could have sounded like an insult not a compliment, which I'm sure you meant.' As she left the office that day, my mother noticed the book on Sheila's desk – a romantic novel, and thought to herself that Sheila was not my father's type. He always chose very intellectual women, and Sheila said many times that she was not that.

My father's philandering started early on in my parent's marriage. The first affair was with Birgitta, a beautiful Swedish woman my father met when my parents were travelling, with my one-year-old sister Jane, by overnight sleeper train to an International Union of Socialist Youth conference in Sweden. Six months later, when my mother was giving birth to me in hospital at Isleworth, my father was supposed to be at an international socialist event in France but, when he returned, the date stamps in his passport told a different story. When my mother questioned him about inconsistencies in his stories, he couldn't lie very well – it always showed in his eyes. Although he told her the usual 'she doesn't mean anything' story, with him, it was always love. He fell in love with beautiful, intelligent women, and they with him, and the affairs could last a couple of years. As well as Birgitta, another long-term relationship was with an English *Financial Times* reporter. My mother stayed with my father because her own parents had divorced, and her childhood had been difficult as a result. She didn't want that for us and, above all, tried to keep the family together. One day my mother was at home with their three children and there was a phone call from number 10 Downing Street. Usually my mother wouldn't bother him but this was possibly urgent, so she phoned the hotel where she knew he was staying in Birmingham, and the receptionist said 'Oh, Mr and Mrs Stonehouse have just gone in to dinner. Shall I give him a message?' My mother replied 'Yes, tell him his secretary phoned.' He was always sorry, always begging her forgiveness. In 1974 he knew, because my mother had previously told him, if she found out he'd had another affair, she'd divorce him.

It came as a complete shock to me to find out that my father had been having an affair with Sheila and, moreover, had phoned her from Hawaii two days after disappearing in Miami, and met her in Copenhagen two weeks later. We'd all known Sheila for years. She'd once given me a lift in her Mini to the constituency, and on that long journey I talked about my boyfriend and asked about hers. She said she'd only ever loved one man, and he was married. It didn't occur to me that she was talking about my father. During the 'missing month' between 20th November and 24th December, my mother, sister and I went to my father's office in Dover Street to see what needed to be done. Sheila said to me, 'Oh, your eyebrows are so nice.' At the time, I thought it was an inappropriate comment in the circumstances, but as the truth of her relationship with my father emerged, it seemed cold. I didn't want to hear about eyebrows; I wanted to hear that my father was alive.

Betty Boothroyd recalled in her autobiography that following the disappearance, and as a former secretary herself, she was worried about Sheila being out of work and invited her to tea on the terrace of the House of Commons. Betty asked Sheila if she'd be interested in taking a job with another Midlands MP, Bruce George, who was looking for a parliamentary secretary: "'Shall I speak to him? You know the area and the local authority. Your knowledge could be quite valuable to him.' 'I am only valuable to John,' she replied, looking me straight in the eye ... She fooled me completely ... She was the best liar I ever met.'[2] Coming from a former Speaker of the House of Commons, that's quite something. To be fair, Sheila had her reasons for not letting anyone know my father was alive. She was terrified he'd kill himself and, after he was discovered in Australia, that became the family's number one concern as well.

My mother left Melbourne on the 16th January, and would be in London for three weeks, making various urgent arrangements before returning to Melbourne. On the 17th or 18th my father returned to Yellingbo, where the trunk he'd sent out to Melbourne before faking his death had been delivered. On the 19th, my fourteen-year-old brother, Mathew, arrived in Melbourne. He was expecting to meet my father at the home of the British consul general in Melbourne, Ivor Vincent, where my father had stayed overnight, but the location of the reunion had to be changed when the British high commissioner in Canberra, Sir Morris James, found out my father was staying with Vincent and gave instructions that my father was to leave immediately. It wouldn't look good if the British authorities were seen to be fraternising with the enemy.

While my mother was in the UK, my father became obsessed with the idea of bringing Sheila out to Australia. She was being hounded by the press, it was true, but as my mother was due to return on the 6th February and had told my father she wouldn't tolerate Sheila being around, my father's lawyer, Jim Patterson, was very much against the idea. My father made the mistake of turning to

Ian Ward, a *Daily Telegraph* correspondent who was lurking around looking for an 'in', and asked for his help. My father was looking for an ally, but had instead found a snake who was going to cause him and Sheila irreparable harm. To begin with, Ward appeared helpful. He arranged for his friend, Lionel Blake, to fly with Sheila to Amsterdam on the 6th February, the very day my mother was due back in Melbourne, to get inoculations before flying on to Singapore. There, Ward had arranged for Sheila to stay a few days with his friend, Miss Yeo. Sheila thought they were just being friendly and supportive but, of course, she was being set up, and in girly chats Sheila told Miss Yeo she'd met my father in Copenhagen. Miss Yeo duly relayed that information to Mr Ward.

On the 5th February, my father and brother moved into a small 'unit' at 840 Toorak Road, fronting a drive-in cinema, where Ian Ward found my father unpacking the trunk he'd earlier had delivered from customs to Yellingbo. Mr Ward took mental notes that, a week later, he'd turn into an elaborate distortion of the truth that would utterly destroy my father and help to get Sheila a two-year conviction. My mother arrived the next day.

A couple of evenings after arriving, my mother picked up the phone and found Sheila on the line. 'Where are you?' my mother asked. 'Singapore,' replied Sheila, 'John asked me to come.' My mother handed the phone to my father and heard them making arrangements to meet in Perth. My mother was terribly upset, and felt she was being used. She told my father, 'If she comes to Australia, she can take on the role of nursemaid, secretary, chief cook and bottle washer. I'm going home.' There was a silence, and then my father lost control. He grabbed my mother and threw her to the floor, yelling, 'Why can't you understand?' My mother was face-down on the floor and my father leant down, grabbed her hair, and used it to bang her head up and down on the floor. Mathew was in the sitting room and came running in shouting, 'Stop it, Dad, stop it!' and pulled him off, telling my mother to get in the kitchen and shut the door.

My mother stood with her back to the door, panting and amazed because nothing like that had ever happened to her in her life before. He'd turned into a monster. Usually, my father was so gentle. He could be emotionally cruel, but never violent. In the bedroom, he was banging his head against the wall and crying his heart out. My mother reached for the phone to try and contact his psychiatrist, but my father burst in, snatched the phone from her hand, and shouted, 'Who are you calling? I suppose you're calling the police.' 'I'm trying to get the doctor, you need help,' my mother replied. He shouted, 'Yes, I do need help, your help! And what do you do? You call the police. You bitch!' He then pulled the phone cord from its socket and started beating my mother about the head with the handset. It broke, shattering on the floor. Then he put his hands around her throat and started banging her head against the wall. My mother thought he'd choke her to death, but Mathew managed to drag him off, and into the hall. My father broke loose, and rushed out the front door, shouting, 'I'm going. Do you hear? This is the last you'll see of me! I'm going to kill myself. That's what everybody wants and then you'll all be happy.'

Mathew ran after him, but he was in the car and away. Despite her injuries, my mother and Mathew set off into the street looking for help – a policeman, a phone box, a taxi, anything. They were terrified he'd do something to himself or drive so carelessly he'd hurt someone else. The first phone box was broken. Eventually they found a cab and took it to Jim Patterson's house. His wife, Peggy, opened the door. Jim was out but she got on the phone to him immediately. After finding out what happened, Jim spoke to his son, Kevin, who ran out to his car and drove away. My mother tried to track down the psychiatrist on the phone, but his wife would only suggest they take my father to a hospital. Jim and Kevin tracked my father down and took him back to the apartment. After several hours, Kevin returned to my mother and said, 'It's OK, Pa says you can go home now. I'll take you back.' 'What sort of state is he in?' she asked, and

Kevin replied 'Oh, he's as good as gold. Very subdued. Probably in a bit of shock.'

Jim was at the front door when they got back. 'He's terribly upset about tonight. I've been talking to him for two hours flat and it's like walking on eggshells. I don't think he really knows even now what he did. I'll take you in.' As they stood there talking, my father suddenly bounced out of the sitting room, smiles all over his face, wrapping my mother in a big embrace and kissing her, but with tears streaming down his face. 'I'm so sorry, darling, I'm so sorry I hurt you.' These quick mood changes weren't unusual in Australia, but in these new circumstances of violence and abuse, my mother suddenly felt very frightened again. 'I'm not staying,' she told Jim, 'I'm going back to England and taking Mathew with me. Sheila Buckley will be here tomorrow and can cope with him.' My father looked surprised and upset. Jim told him, 'You could have killed her tonight, you can hardly expect her to feel differently. Perhaps we can sort things out tomorrow. Sleep on it.'

The next day my father went to Perth to meet Sheila. At the airport, out of nowhere, Ian Ward and a photographer appeared. My father and Sheila were desperate not to be photographed together and went in different directions, without even having said 'hallo'. My father had a taxi waiting, and Sheila grabbed another, and they both took off, eventually losing Ward but staying in communication through the taxis' radios. They pulled over in a side street, and Sheila got into my father's taxi. They flew to Adelaide but by this time all the press knew they were together and although they got off the plane separately, both were besieged. Again, using the two-taxi ruse, they avoided having their picture taken together. They hired a car and set off for Sydney. My father told Sheila that although my mother wasn't happy about her coming to Australia she was 'slightly mollified' by the fact that Sheila would be staying with friends in Sydney.[3] In fact, my mother and brother were already packing.

My father's manic behaviour in Australia in 1975 was so out of character it was frightening. It could well have been a symptom of him withdrawing off Mandrax, a procedure so dangerous it often necessitated hospital supervision. He no longer had his regular suppliers at hand – the doctors in the House of Commons who were unaware he had suppliers additional to them. He only had one bottle of pills in his washbag and what they were, I do not know. Perhaps he had taken some Mandrax or Mogadon to Miami when he faked his death and these were the last of his supply. Perhaps they were another drug altogether, prescribed by his psychiatrist. In the 1970s people were so trusting of doctors, and talked in generic terms about 'sleeping tablets', without being too fussed about what they were or their possible side-effects, whereas today we have the internet and can all be pharmacology experts. Eventually the medical profession became wise to the dangers of the highly addictive Mandrax and it was banned in the UK and USA in 1984 – ten years too late for my father.

Sheila later explained to the readers of *Woman* magazine why she'd gone to Australia: 'Yes, of course, I was upset when I realised that we were now having the same set-up in Australia as we had had in London – John back with his wife, and just seeing me when he could. But – and I think only a woman who has ever been in love with a married man will understand this – I understood. And I was prepared to put up with the situation just to be with him. I felt then that this was what he wanted and my main concern was that he should *have* what he wanted. I know it might sound extraordinary and as if I had absolutely no pride but that's how it was. I loved him, you see, loved him more than myself. And, if this was how he wanted it, this was how he should have it.'[4] With this level of blind devotion, my father loving both Sheila and my mother, and my mother not prepared to put up with it, there was bound to be a showdown.

It happened at Albury. Somewhere on his road trip east with Sheila, my father had phoned my mother and, getting no reply, phoned his lawyer, Jim Patterson. My mother had been to his office to give him the apartment key and told him she was going to Sydney.

Jim calculated that they'd stop at Albury and phoned all the hotels and motels until he located my mother and Mathew late in the evening at the Boomerang Hotel. Jim persuaded my mother it would be good for them all to talk and, against her better judgement, she agreed to wait there until my father and Sheila caught up with them. The next day, my mother and brother drove around the town and discovered a nice seating area near the dam. Back at the hotel, as it began to get dark, my brother went downstairs and saw a policeman and a cameraman eating in the restaurant, near the door. They'd probably found them because, as we discovered later, Jim's phone was being tapped by the police (who, of course, passed information to the press). My mother and Mathew sneaked out while the policeman and cameraman were still eating, and my mother stayed in the parked car while my brother went around the back, in case my father and Sheila arrived that way. Clearly, any meeting would have to be far away from the hotel. They only needed to wait half an hour before my father drove into the car park. He walked towards the hotel but my mother leapt out of her car and told him they needed to get away. She picked Mathew up from the back of the hotel and, in two cars, they drove towards the dam which, at this time of the evening, was likely to be deserted. On the way, my mother saw in her rear-view mirror that my father was flashing his headlights. They were low on petrol, so my father and Sheila got into the rear of my mother's hired car and the strange party drove in silence to the dam, and parked up. Mathew stayed in the car while the love triangle sat at a picnic table.

My father told my mother he wanted them both in Melbourne: my mother so she could transcribe his book; Sheila so she could help him with impending questions from the DTI inspectors, who would be arriving in Melbourne shortly. The insensitivity of his request didn't seem apparent to him even if, as he suggested, they live in different places. My mother told him, 'No. I won't have that girl there. If she goes to Melbourne, I go back to England with Mathew.' Now they got to the nub of the problem: he shouted 'I want you

both. You are both important to me.' My father completely failed
to appreciate the situation he was asking my mother to put herself
in, plus they were already being hounded by the press and he didn't
consider that his proposed living arrangement would fuel the media
circus. But his needs were more important to him at this moment
than any other emotional or logical reality. 'Look,' my mother said,
'our suitcases are packed and in the boot of the car. I'm ready to fly
to England tomorrow with Mathew and I will do so if you bring
that girl back to Melbourne.' My mother meant it. At that moment
she could quite cheerfully have got on the first plane and never seen
him again. Suddenly, he jumped to his feet and yelled, 'If you leave
me, Barbara, I'll kill myself,' and started running towards the dam.
Sheila and my mother stood up, and Sheila screamed at my mother,
'Barbara, *you must do something*.' Something inside my mother
snapped and she turned to Sheila and said, '*You* do something.' Sheila
ran after him. My brother had seen all this and had started the car
and turned the headlights onto the scene of my father climbing up
onto the dam. He drove up to my mother and she slipped into the
driving seat and they sped towards my father and Sheila. By now, he
was off the dam and he and Sheila were sobbing in each other's arms.

My mother drove them back to their car. She told my father
that she was going to Sydney in the morning and if he wanted to
contact her, he could call her old friends from Potters Bar, Mike
and Billie Kirlew, who were now living in Sydney and would give
him her phone number, but not her address. She followed them to
a petrol station, then returned to the hotel with Mathew. Sheila and
my father stayed in a motel. Sheila wrote: 'John seemed to go all to
pieces. For once he didn't seem able to talk to me. It was as though
he was going backwards again, back to the awful highly strung state
he'd been in when he first had his breakdown. I was desperately
depressed. I'd got him almost back to normal again during those
first two days in Australia but now here he was, a wreck once more.
I felt utterly exhausted and, worse than that, for the first time I felt

I'd really taken enough. That night, I lay awake for hours. I said a prayer of thanks that he was still alive. Then I started worrying. I was terrified that he was going to think it was really all my fault, that terrible scene. I thought, maybe he wants Barbara really and I'm in the way. Next morning, he was still very quiet but as we drove towards Sydney he seemed to become more and more like his old self.' My father told Sheila he was going to try and get my mother to go back to Melbourne. Sheila wrote: 'I said that if that was what he wanted then that was what we'd try to achieve. I said I would stay in Sydney but that I'd miss him a lot and that I loved him very much. And, if that sounds saintly, it wasn't. I'm really terribly selfish about him. I love him, you see, and he comes first. Before me, before everyone. I'd do absolutely anything for him.'[5]

My father took Sheila to her friend's house, then started looking for my mother. She and Mathew had decided to rest in Sydney for a couple of days and the Kirlews had found a hotel where she could drive the car into an underground car park and take a lift directly to the floor where she'd booked a room, thus avoiding any press who might be in the foyer. It seemed a perfect hideaway and, as an extra protective measure, the Kirlews booked themselves into a room next to my mother and Mathew's. The next evening, the phone rang in my mother's room. It was my father, wanting to have dinner with her. She told him she was still too upset to see him and, anyway, didn't want to leave her hotel. 'There's no need to,' he said, 'I'm in the room next door to you.' My mother nearly fainted. She phoned the Kirlews in the adjacent room on the other side and they said they'd come so the four of them could have dinner together in the sitting room of my mother's suite. My father arrived holding a Valentine's card. He'd already given Sheila hers. Over dinner, the Kirlews tried to explain to my father that my mother's nerves couldn't take any more, that it would be better for her to return to London and make a new life while he could stay with Sheila. My father put his head in his hands and said, 'I can't cope without Barbara. I'm desperate. I need her and she knows I love her.' My mother succumbed to my father's appeal, and they returned to Melbourne with Mathew, leaving Sheila in Sydney.

While all this drama was going on, Ian Ward was stirring a big pot of trouble. On the 12th February he had two exclusives in the *Daily Telegraph*. The front-page story was innocuous enough, 'Secretary flies in to greet Stonehouse', but on page three he delivered a devastating work of fiction: 'Stonehouse Had Secretary's Clothes Sent On'. (In later editions that day it would be headlined 'Stonehouse shipped secretary's clothes three months ago'.) It began: 'A trunk-load of clothes belonging to Mr John Stonehouse's secretary, Mrs Sheila Buckley, 28, who was reunited with him in Perth this morning, was sent to Australia last November at about the time the Labour MP disappeared … it would suggest that the MP for Walsall North had intended all along to meet Mrs Buckley in Australia. The metal trunk containing Mrs Buckley's day and evening dresses, slips, shoes and handbags as well as some of Mr Stonehouse's personal effects lay, unbeknown to Australian police, in a Melbourne customs warehouse for some weeks.'[6] In fact, the trunk arrived at Melbourne docks with no female clothing in it whatsoever, was examined by a customs officer named Robert Rowland Hill who saw no female clothing in it, only a man's clothing. It was delivered to Yellingbo, where my mother had stayed with my father, and where my father put into the trunk the clothing my mother had left behind while she was in London for three weeks. They couldn't have been Sheila's clothes, because she'd not yet arrived in Australia.

Ian Ward's story continued: 'On Wednesday Mr Stonehouse transferred all Mrs Buckley's clothing from the trunk to a red suitcase and arranged for this to be stored in a Melbourne suburban home. Yesterday, although no one was in at the time, he entered the house and retrieved the case, leaving a bunch of flowers and a note for the occupier.'[7] Anyone reading this in the *Daily Telegraph* would be convinced that my father was a dastardly cad who wanted nothing more than to run away with his much younger secretary. And this story couldn't be dismissed as the made-up fantasy of a cheap tabloid because it was in the most 'serious' establishment newspaper in the country – read by politicians, lawyers, judges and DTI inspectors. This was *their* newspaper, and they believed every word. The Ward trunk story led, inevitably, to Sheila being implicated in the plan to run away. The story was so damaging because, if Sheila was planning to be in Australia before my father left England for Miami, that indicated my father had a plot, not a nervous breakdown. It also pointed to a conspiracy between my father and Sheila.

Ward's trunk article was copied by other newspapers. On the 13th February 1975, under the *Daily Mail*'s headline 'The love trap triangle', the country read: 'Some of Mrs Buckley's clothes, Mrs Stonehouse also learned, were sent by trunk to Australia last November, before the Member for Walsall North was found by police and his plot to fake his death was uncovered.'[8] And just to confirm the conspiracy angle, they said that in one of her letters she'd said she was pregnant, which was 'a reminder to him that they had a pact for a life of love on the other side of the world'.

The Ward trunk story had legs that would run all the way to the very last day of the trial at the Old Bailey, and beyond. The truth of the matter – there were no woman's clothes in the trunk when it left London – got lost along the way. Ian Ward spent over two days, between the 7th and 9th June 1976, defending his article in the witness box. Although the police interviewed the customs officer Robert Hill in 1975, in a classic case of non-disclosure his testimony wasn't included in the court documentation. At the Old Bailey in August 1976, Judge Eveleigh told the court his 'name did not appear on the back of the indictment. He was not a witness that the prosecution were under an obligation to bring to this court.'[9] The prosecution only decided to tell the defence about Robert Hill

on 10th June after Ward had given evidence. The defence then had
a mad scramble to locate him on the other side of the world, and
get his statement into court. Michael O'Dell, my father's solicitor,
described the difficulties to the court, which the Judge summarised
for the jury: 'His mother would not disclose his address and he was
not at home. Then he was found, and at first there was difficulty
because of bureaucratic obstacles in getting a statement from him,
and you can understand that because he was a Customs Officer.
In the end a statement was obtained.' But he couldn't get to court
because he 'had broken his legs, and it might be necessary for him to
be accompanied by his wife'.[10] With all this delay, Mr Hill's statement
could only finally be read to the court on the very last day of the
defence, 20th July. Mr Hill said: 'I saw this item of baggage opened
in my presence and under my supervision. I did not see a blouse, a
black slip or any ladies shoes or any article of ladies clothing.'[11] By
that time it was too late – everyone had already been convinced that
Sheila was in it from the beginning.

My sister Jane arrived in Melbourne and the family settled into a
routine. Their 'unit' was a tiny two-bedroom flat but at least the
majority of the press didn't know where it was, and that became its
greatest redeeming feature. Jane and Mathew took turns sleeping
on the living room floor. My father started writing his book out in
longhand in the bathroom, and my mother would type it out in the
sitting room. They didn't talk about Sheila. My father and Mathew
played endless games of backgammon and Scrabble. Dramas came
and went.

   Ian Ward delivered another bombshell on the 25th February. In
a *Daily Telegraph* article, 'Secretary's secret Copenhagen days with
Stonehouse', he said that: 'She flew to the Danish capital after receiving an urgent telephone call from Mr Stonehouse *a few hours after
his arrival there*' (my italics).[12] That once again made it look as if he

was in cahoots with Sheila. But it wasn't like that at all. The facts are that my father arrived in Copenhagen on the 29th November 1974, but didn't phone Sheila that day, or on the 30th, or the 1st, or 2nd, or 3rd. He phoned and asked her to come to Copenhagen on the 4th, she arrived on the evening of the 6th, and they both left on the 8th – she back to London, and he to Australia.

Sheila described herself as 'a bit puritanical, a bit prim',[13] and while I might not admire her capacity to have an affair for years on end with my father, she was never the wild sort of character who'd go along with the mad escape from reality 'Plan B' growing inside my father's head over the course of 1974. But what all the misreporters did over 1975 was create a distorted picture of collusion and conspiracy where there was, in reality, just love and loyalty. The reason for that is simple – as a narrative, Bonnie and Clyde was a money-spinner.

The 25th February also saw the start of six days of grilling by DTI inspectors, carried out by Michael Sherrard QC and Ian Hay Davison. Backed up with an array of recording equipment, they tried to find out what had been going on with his businesses. Reliving the whole experience was emotionally exhausting and left my father utterly depleted. The air conditioning in the offices they were using was on full blast and the place was freezing, making the experience even worse. They gave my father an undertaking he'd be given an opportunity to make comments on the DTI's report, but that never happened.

Jane soon learned that our father was still at breaking point. She was 26 at the time and had never seen my father in such a horrendous state. He would cry, scream, bang his head on the floor repeatedly, rush around the flat shouting, and even lose complete control of his body. She was terrified. They all were. The real concern was that he'd go into one of these episodes never to return, for his mind to literally explode into unrecoverable madness, or for him to simply kill himself. Some days he would be found curled up in a ball on the sofa. Or he'd just cut out when my mother was talking to him about something that needed to be dealt with, by simply falling asleep in the chair. He really should have been in a psychiatric institution, but simply refused to go. Instead, the family were on constant guard, trying to calm the outbursts and keep him on an even keel. It wasn't easy. The bad press reports kept coming, and issuing denials seemed pointless as they were rarely printed, or became one-liners at the very end of otherwise damning articles. This is such a feature of British journalism that, even today, I go straight to the last lines in damaging newspaper reports about other people to find the denial they issued if, indeed, it was printed.

My father was talking to Sheila on the phone regularly. My sister overheard him one day saying, 'Remember, I love you madly and passionately.' Jane asked him straight out why he stayed with our mother if he loved Sheila and he said he loved and wanted them both. This is something we all had to get used to. On the 5th March, Jane and my father went on a trip to Canberra to visit the Bangladesh and Brazilian High Commissions, hoping for permission to travel there. On the journey, he announced they'd be meeting up with Sheila and collecting her from the bus garage that evening. There was a convention in town and all the hotels were full but, with luck, they managed to find a two-bedroomed apartment they could rent for a few days. Jane wrote in her diary that Sheila was 'definitely in command' and 'seems to boss him a little'. Rather awkwardly, my father and Sheila shared a bedroom, and Jane slept in the other. She wrote: 'I've retired quickly to my nasty room – she and pa are preparing themselves for their lovemaking – I hope to God they're quiet – *that* I could not bear.' For the next few days, this odd threesome went swimming from deserted beaches, and sightseeing. Jane also accompanied our father when he made a short visit to the immigration minister, Clyde Cameron, to thank him for his treatment and apologise for the embarrassment.

❖

On the 21st March, my father was at the 'unit' in Toorak Road working on his book when there was a knock at the door. It was Detective Inspector Robert Gillespie of the Australian Commonwealth Police, with DI Craig and DSS Coffey. 'Hallo, Bob, come on in,' said my father. After the introductions, Gillespie said, 'Sorry, John, I've got some bad news for you. I have here a warrant for your arrest.' This came as a complete shock to my father, because he'd not heard anything at all from Scotland Yard, and the DTI enquiries had been over for weeks. My mother and Mathew had gone shopping for a school uniform in expectation that the family could be in Australia for some time, and they now arrived back. My parents were allowed to have a word together in the bedroom, watched by Gillespie, and as my father got something out of a bedside drawer, Gillespie spotted documents in the name of Markham. He said, 'I deem those documents would be relevant to the subject matter of the charges mentioned in this warrant. Would you like to examine them with me?' My father said, no, he wouldn't examine anything unless his solicitor was present, and Gillespie said, 'By virtue of this warrant I intend to seize these documents.' The three policemen then gathered up every single piece of paper they could find. Mathew watched as DI Craig searched behind the pictures on the wall.

Gillespie had received a phone call from Chief Superintendent Etheridge of Scotland Yard at 5.20am that morning, and a telex message followed two hours later. The telex had instructed Gillespie to gather all paperwork, and refuse bail. All the pages of the book my father was working on were seized and copied for Scotland Yard, which included a chapter about the Scotland Yard investigation into the BBT in January 1973. The magistrate at the Melbourne Court granted my father bail on the low surety of A$1,000, despite the instructions from London.

The next day, the front page of the *Daily Mail* blared out: 'Yard Want MP's Girl Friend to Return'. The smaller front-page story had two headlines in two editions, one being, 'He needs me now says

Mrs Stonehouse'. Although it may have looked like a contemporary interview, the journalist Rupert Massey was calling on notes he'd made in late January at Faulkners Down, when my mother was clearing out the house: 'Of course I am sad that my husband should love two women. He says it is quite possible for a man to do this and I know that a man's physical needs are different from those of a woman. I have forgiven him. I love him … divorce has raised its head in the past and I suppose it's on the cards in the future. Sometimes I feel like a lemming going to my fate, but I am a beaver about my marriage.'[14] She also said: 'Besides him, other men are pygmies,' and that was the problem: as a man, he was impressive. That's precisely why other women found him attractive.

On the 24th March, the *Daily Mirror* banner headline read: 'MP IN NEW SPY PROBE'. It seemed the police had sold them pages copied from my father's book, taken during the police search of the family's 'unit', in which my father denied the allegation and explained the meetings he'd had with Czechs in the course of his ministerial duties. This was exactly why my father was angry about the police taking the papers in the first place: he suspected the police couldn't keep their mouths or their pockets shut. The *Daily Mirror* completely misrepresented what he'd written in the book, saying 'Stonehouse – after flatly denying any involvement with the Czechs – is now hinting that there was more to it than that.'[15] He was doing no such thing. There was no 'hinting'; there was a flat denial, with all contacts fully explained, but the *Daily Mirror* had spun it 180 degrees into a completely different story.

The family heard a warrant had been issued for Sheila's arrest from a reporter who phoned from Adelaide. Sheila was still staying with friends in Sydney and, because the phone at the 'unit' was bugged, Jane called her from a public phone and broke the news that she too would be facing extradition charges. Her warrant contained six charges, relating to my father's case. It seemed best that Sheila make her way from the State of New South Wales to the State of

Victoria, where all charges could be faced together, and my father's solicitor, Jim Patterson, agreed. Sheila's friend, Denis Streeter, immediately left work to drive her the 600 miles in his Volkswagen, so Patterson could accompany Sheila into a police station and place her in the jurisdiction of the State of Victoria. Flying would attract the attention of the press. By dusk the little Volkswagen had made it to a small town near the state border, where Sheila and Denis stayed overnight. Meanwhile, two Scotland Yard officers had flown from Melbourne to Sydney to arrest Sheila, using a hired light aircraft because the airline stewards were on strike. This delay caused them to miss her. They had searched the two friends' houses where she'd been staying, even raking over the barbecue ashes – presumably looking for burnt evidence. Apparently, this was the crime of the century. The front-page headline in the Aberdeen *Evening Express* announced, 'Police hunt runaway MP's secretary'.

The next morning, Sheila and Denis crossed into Victoria and continued driving towards Melbourne. The plan was that Sheila would phone Jim Patterson when she got close to Melbourne and Jim would guide them in. We all knew the phone at the 'unit' where my family was staying was bugged, but nobody realised the solicitor's was being bugged too. That evening my father, mother, Jane and Mathew had planned to go to the cinema with the family of Peter Game. On the journey, just for fun, my father tried to lose the police tail. He did, but it was a waste of effort because the police already knew where they were headed, and were waiting in the cinema foyer. During *Murder on the Orient Express*, my father phoned Jim several times to see how the plan was progressing. He'd heard nothing. He also phoned a sympathetic policeman who told him they should avoid the Princes Highway – the main road into town. All this subterfuge was so that Sheila could walk willingly into a police station, with her solicitor, and not have the indignity of being arrested on the street. Jim had already told the police that he'd be bringing Sheila in the following day, and they were monitoring his calls. But the police felt the need to appear pro-active, so they stopped Denis's car, and arrested Sheila. They also invited the press to take photos of the fugitive, suitably under guard, just in time for the morning papers. The state police then put out a press release congratulating themselves on her arrest. They also said that they had information Sheila was planning on meeting my father on the outskirts of Melbourne, which was nonsense. They had all the phones tapped and knew that wasn't true. Still, it added to their drama. Sheila spent the night in a filthy cell at the old, ramshackle Melbourne Watchtower. Next morning, the magistrate was waiting for her.

On the 26th, my mother phoned her secretary, Margaret Picco, to ask her to call Sheila's parents to let them know Sheila was all right, that my father had spoken to her, and that she had a very good lawyer. Margaret was an exceptional secretary and made verbatim notes of the entire conversation. She had formerly been in the police force and did everything by the book, in triplicate, as well as assertively keeping reporters away from the door whenever possible. She also had her own boundaries. On the 27th March, she wrote to my mother saying precisely and only this: 'Following your phone call yesterday I rang Mr and Mrs Black, as you requested. But may I say one thing: Although in all my working years I have never refused a request by my employer or superior – *please*, I hope you won't ask me to do anything else which is connected with Sheila Buckley!' That was fair enough: Margaret was not prepared to act as a go-between for my mother and the mistress or her parents. When the letter arrived in Australia, my father showed it to Sheila who, on the 7th April, wrote to Margaret accusing her of being prissy and superficial, of having devoured what she read in the newspapers and not spared a thought for the suffering Sheila had endured over the past months. She went on to say that there's so much pain for people to bear because there are so many people like Margaret in the world, adding that she hoped Margaret wouldn't pass her unchristian ways on to her children so their first instinct in life would be to dance on the grave of someone else. She closed by saying she hoped Margaret had spoken to her parents in a civil manner and, if not, she'd be looking for an apology when she returned to London. Given that Margaret was always the epitome of civility, which Sheila knew very well as they'd often had reason to speak on the phone, and coming from the woman who'd been having an affair with her boss's husband for five years, Margaret thought Sheila's letter was a bit much. On the 11th April she sent Sheila the perfect response: a postcard of Annigoni's painting of the Queen on which she wrote 'Many thanks for your letter – it's given us some laughs! I had no idea you'd such a sense of humour. It's a very revealing memento and I *shall* enjoy showing it to people! Thanks again.'

Sheila replied to Margaret on the 18th April with a letter that curiously adopted a 'we' stand, by which she aligned herself with the Stonehouse family, with Margaret as our common enemy. It began by saying that 'we' are concerned that Margaret was apparently showing Sheila's letter to others, and laughing over the deep traumas faced by the Stonehouse family, adding that she and the Stonehouse family were not on a stage to amuse Margaret and her type, accusing her of being callous and brutal. The letter went on and on, saying 'we' would, 'we' thought, 'we' are disenchanted and 'we' can do without correspondence like Margaret's, saying it stabs at them all. Unimpressed, on the 22nd April, Margaret sent copies of the correspondence to her solicitor with the note that 'it is possible they may – in future – be referred to'.

My father and Sheila had to report to the same police station every day and, as she had no car, they'd go together. Although Jane invariably accompanied them, she'd be removed from the press photos. The photographers loved this 'Bonnie and Clyde' photo opportunity and it created a more interesting news story to imply they were living together. But the longer the 'Bonnie and Clyde' narrative continued, the harder it was for people to understand that my father had planned his disappearance on his own and as a result of a nervous breakdown. Day by day, the 'conspiracy' narrative took over until there was little hope of overcoming it.

Sheila was living on her own in a bedsit with no friends around, and no longer thinking she was pregnant. She'd realised that after sending her fourth and last letter to my father on 20th December, and later wrote, 'Worry had probably been the cause of it all.'[16] My mother and father, Jane and Mathew, were in another place a couple of miles away and Sheila was back to being 'the other woman' while the married man lived with his wife. But this time it was different because the law compelled them both to attend the police station, and then they could go and have lunch or spend time together in her sparsely furnished room. It had a gas fire and they'd sit either side of it, talking about what had happened that day. Sometimes they made love in the single bed. They played chess and read. Meanwhile, my mother had to endure the knowledge that her husband was with his mistress, and Sheila had to endure her lover going back to his wife. The only person who didn't think three was a crowd was my father.

My mother returned to London, leaving my father in the care of my sister and brother. He and Sheila were facing extradition, and sleeping together. Nevertheless, my father was sending my mother love letters. He usually began his letters to her 'My darling love', and in the month of May 1975 alone, his letters say: on the 1st, 'You are most beautiful and I love you'; 2nd, 'I am missing you, much love'; 3rd, 'It has been a marvellous and beautiful relationship which will – whatever happens – live forever. Much love'; 9th, 'It was marvellous talking to you this morning. You sounded so strong despite everything. I am so proud of you'; 11th, 'I love you darling'; 12th, 'I am missing you very much sweetheart. I hope you are getting some rest now. Please don't worry about me. I am getting stronger every day. Do love you – take care'; 13th, 'I dreamt about you last night'; 15th, 'It was wonderful talking to you. I miss you so much'; 23rd, 'I love you rather desperately. And I long for your company and kisses. You are the most beautiful woman in the world. Much love.'

My mother still loved him too. On the 8th June 1975 she was interviewed by *The Observer*. At this point in time, my parents had been married for 26 years. She said: 'I knew John when he started out, progressed, achieved something and during all that time he has acted honourably. What has happened lately are aberrations of his personality: I just don't think they are basically John Stonehouse, apart from the Mrs Buckley thing, which is a completely separate subject and is something that many men might do. It is all very well for people to take the holier-than-thou position because he's a public figure. But in public life men are more exposed and vulnerable to this kind of thing. To me, he isn't just my husband, he is somebody who embodies certain ideals. If he had been making money all his life by doing people down I wouldn't have respected him and perhaps wouldn't have given a damn what happened to him. But I don't intend to join in the national sport of kicking a man when he's down and I won't apologise for backing him, because he's been a damn good man, a very good husband. I've had a very good marriage all these years and it may well be over. I don't know, but I can't forget it. I don't intend to bash him about like everybody else is. He doesn't need me to do that: he's got plenty of other people doing it.'[17]

After the trial at the Old Bailey, Sheila wrote a series of articles for *Woman* magazine in which it became clear that my father had been giving her the adulterer's usual, 'You couldn't break up our marriage. It broke up years ago' story. Sheila said, 'I believe in marriage. Yes, even though I've had an "affair" (a word I hate just as I hate the word "mistress") with a married man. But, you see, I think marriage is sacred only when there is love there. When love dies then the marriage is not a marriage at all. It's phoney.' Like so many mistresses before her, Sheila had been strung a line and if she thought my parents' relationship was without love during any of that time, she was being fooled. In *Woman* magazine, Sheila said, 'Divorce was not at all acceptable in politics in those days and it could have harmed his career.'[18] Labour lost the June 1970 election and my father was not offered a position in the shadow cabinet, nor a position in the February 1974 Government when Labour scraped in with a hung parliament. He was still an MP, but there was no 'career' to worry about. My father could have got divorced from my mother in 1970, had he wanted to.

In the article Sheila says, 'Only once did we ever quarrel. That was over his silver wedding party. Barbara was very anxious to throw a big celebration. John was against it. So was I. It was the only time I made a stand. I told him I thought that it was almost obscene and totally hypocritical. The wrangling went on for days. And then one evening John came to the flat looking very distraught and said: "It's no good. I've just had to give in to that woman. It's the only way to keep her quiet." I was beside myself.' Sheila told him: 'If you're going to carry on with this ridiculous charade I don't know if I should have any more to do with you. I'm beginning to lose my self-respect.' She then picked up a sherry glass and threw it at him. Good for her. She recalled, 'It shattered into pieces all over the place. John didn't say anything. Just bent and slowly started to pick up the pieces. As he did so he cut his finger.'[19] I was 22 at the time and involved in the preparations for that party. My father was all for it, highly enthusiastic one might say. I still have the paperwork, including the table plan laid out in his own handwriting. It was held at the Chanticleer restaurant on Palace Street, SW1, on the 13th November 1973, and was attended by 56 guests. The most important of these was Sir Charles Hardie, an old business contact who was now head of the firm which had audited BBT's accounts in June 1973, and would be called upon to do so again in 1974. No doubt my father wanted to impress him because he also invited Sir Frank Woods, Sir Arnold Hall, Sir Charles Forte, Sir Alexander Glen, Sir Ray Brown, Lord Jim Peddie, Sir Leckraz Teelock (the High Commissioner for Mauritius), and their wives. They were my father's business associates and friends and they were joined by my mother's business associates and friends, and family. This was as much my father's party, as my mother's. After a four-course meal accompanied by Pouilly-Fuissé and Château Pichon Longueville Baron, there was dancing. We all had a great time, as proven by the thank you letters. One said: 'We had a lovely time and you both looked so much more like a young couple about to go off on their honeymoon than celebrating their 25th wedding anniversary … Hope you enjoyed it as much as all your guests did. Barbara you looked beautiful.'

Whatever he told Sheila, my father loved my mother. And my mother loved my father. And my father loved Sheila. And Sheila loved my father. Perhaps if there hadn't been so much love, our lives would have been simpler.

13

Where to Next?

My father disappeared because he had a nervous breakdown brought about by, or exacerbated by, overdosing on a cocktail of Mandrax and Mogadon. With that breakdown, he now had to deal with a daily tsunami of negative press. Plus, he physically had to try and escape the pack of reporters and photographers that were constantly on the hunt for him. If he tried to talk to them, they twisted what he said. John Stonehouse couldn't win. Nobody was interested. Nobody believed him. They all thought he was lying about having a breakdown because they'd read in the newspapers that he'd phoned Sheila, met her in Copenhagen, she'd sent him letters, and her clothes had been sent out in a trunk. Clearly, it was a conspiracy, and he was a spy. His old comrades in the House of Commons were yelling indignantly that he should be brought back to the UK, and the diplomats were trying to achieve that goal, as shown by voluminous diplomatic extradition files in the National Archives at Kew. My father left England a broken and disillusioned man in November 1974, but three months later he was more tired and angrier than before. At the beginning of January, he'd been willing to go back to the UK, but the more hounded he was, and the more vitriolic the commentary became in the UK, the less he wanted to return. By the end of February, he didn't care if he never saw the place again.

The hatred of my father was palpable, and a complete and utter horror show. I was in London 'holding the fort' while trying to earn a living and be as anonymous as possible. One day I was at my desk at work when a temp sitting nearby having her lunch and reading a newspaper spat out the words, 'He should be hung!' I knew who she was talking about without looking. She didn't realise who I was. 'Who's that?' I asked, knowing full well the answer. 'Stonehouse!' she spluttered. 'Why?' I asked. 'Because he left his wife and children to run away with his secretary.' If I saw someone reading a story about him in a paper, standing at a bus stop, next to me on the tube, or at the bar in a pub, I'd ask, 'what's that Stonehouse been up to today?' and they'd repeat as fact what had been reported. I'd overhear people behind me on the bus saying vile things about him and knew, without looking, what newspaper they were reading because I read them all every day. And I knew the 'facts' in them were invariably wrong or had glaring omissions. The whole country was flooded with rivers of negative 'fake news', and there was no escape from it. Nor was there escape from the reporters themselves. They followed me up the stairs on the bus, and down the escalator on the tube. They knocked on neighbours' doors, phoned friends or harassed them on the street. They were everywhere, like an endless swarm of biting midges.

Before police charges were laid, the press were free to say whatever they wanted. We had no time to challenge them before the next assault arrived. It was like the daily 'Two Minutes Hate', or more like 'Hate Week', in George Orwell's novel *1984*, when people vented their hatred at the image of the 'Enemy of the People', Emmanuel Goldstein, the renegade who'd mysteriously escaped and disappeared. Goldstein was a traitor, and many still believed my father was a traitor too, never mind that the prime minister had denied it. They thought, 'He would say that wouldn't he? They all cover for each other.' The general distrust of politicians within the country became pinpointed on the figure of my father. Politicians hated him because they thought he reflected badly on them and defiled their integrity. The Tories hated him because he was a socialist. Labour politicians were venomous in their contempt, seeing him as a backslider who'd abandoned the great cause. Fascists hated him because he was anti-fascist. Communists hated him because he was anti-communist. Men hated him because he was tall and handsome, had a beautiful blonde *and* a beautiful brunette by his side, and was too clever by half. Women hated him because he'd abandoned his wife and children. They were all glad to see he got his comeuppance. You could hear the hissing, booing and snorts of disgust.

Only the *Guardian* and *Observer* managed to dispatch their role as reporters with honesty. They'd get facts wrong too, of course, but not deliberately, and only when they copied another paper. On the 26th January, my father wrote to the Leader of the House, Ted Short: 'Press freedom is a false god to worship: it has become a weapon in the hands of callow, cynical and completely irresponsible men who delight in undermining and destroying the active people in politics and business who are the constructive and positive elements in society. The negativism of much contemporary journalism is a cancer in the body politic and is gradually eating away at the vitals of British democracy.'[1] Having lived an entire lifetime through the press tornado, I would go further. The intensity of negativity was a form of brainwashing, so much so that even today – 40 years later – there's hardly a true word written about my father. Recent reports just plagiarise the old, then twist them and spin them to get more juice out of them. In researching this book I've not seen a single book, article, web page or post that's not riddled with inaccuracies to do with time, place, people, events and all other facts.

After Sheila arrived in Australia, the press were frantic to know if my father and she were going to try and run away together, possibly to New Zealand. No charges had been made against him in the UK and the Australians had lost interest – so long as he didn't resign as an MP, he had the legal right to remain. On the 13th February, British diplomats were discussing the issue: 'the Australian authorities are no longer keeping Mr Stonehouse under surveillance and … they would not arrest him on charges of contravening the Australian Immigration Act should he attempt to leave the country, as they had said they would on 1 January.'[2] On the 15th February, an article in a New Zealand paper said he and Sheila, or my mother, could go to New Zealand and get a six month temporary visitors' visa, 'so long as they had the normal travel documents'. British diplomats contacted the NZ immigration minister's office to find out if this was correct, and were perturbed to discover that 'a passport would not in fact be required if they travel from Australia (so far as we are aware, the latter point is not yet publicly known)'.[3] The diplomats confirmed that his UK passport had been confiscated and taken back to the UK by Scotland Yard, and the Australian police had the Markham passport. Nevertheless, they began to get nervous: maybe he'd run away again.

On the 28th February, Jack Dixon of the Nationality and Treaty Department at the Foreign and Commonwealth Office (FCO) in London, wrote to a colleague: 'We have told Canberra and Wellington that the only passport facilities that may be given to Mr Stonehouse if he applies are to be a passport restricted to a single journey to this country.' They wanted him back. It continued: 'There have been suggestions, repeated by Reuters yesterday, that Mr Stonehouse may be able to obtain a passport of Bangladesh of which he claims to be an honorary citizen. It is not known whether this claim is correct but the High Commissioner in Dacca suspects that if Mr Stonehouse decided to go to Bangladesh the authorities there would not stop him.'[4]

On 4th March, my father wrote to his old friend, the prime minister of Sweden, Olof Palme, but didn't realise that in the open society of Sweden, mail sent to the PM can be examined by journalists before he or she even sees it. His letter began, 'In view of the persecution I have received from the English authorities and the British press, I have decided to resign from the House of Commons in due course and renounce my United Kingdom citizenship. At that time I shall have to leave Australia and I am therefore writing to earnestly request that you grant me a Swedish passport.' He outlined four reasons for this request, briefly: 'I am advised that my enforced return to England could cause irreparable psychiatric damage to me'; 'I have not been charged with any criminal offence'; 'I have suffered the most vicious campaign of persecution by the British press'; and 'I have adequate means.'[5] This appeal was published in the Swedish press, and the news soon reached Westminster. Olof Palme's office wrote back saying my father couldn't have a Swedish passport unless he resided in the country, but he could apply for resident status. On the 5th March, my father went to Canberra with Sheila and Jane and visited the Bangladesh High Commission to ask for a passport, and also to the Brazilian High Commission, to see what travel options they could offer.

On the 11th March, the select committee that was established to tackle the issue of their errant MP stated in their first report that they 'cannot advise the House to take any action for the present'. Their opinion changed, however, when they saw the letter to the Swedish prime minister, and were told a warrant for my father's arrest had been issued by a Bow Street magistrate on 20th March. In their second report, published on the 6th May, the members refer to the Swedish letter, and say, 'Mr Stonehouse has abandoned his Parliamentary duties.' Moreover, as there was now a warrant, they considered 'it irreconcilable with membership of this House for a Member of Parliament, when charged with serious criminal offences, not to submit himself to the processes of justice established by Parliament. For these reasons Your Committee consider that a Motion to expel Mr Stonehouse would now be justified. They recommend that such a Motion should not be moved earlier than one month after the publication of this Report, in order to give Mr Stonehouse the opportunity to attend the House or resign.'[6]

On the 1st April, someone at the Australian Consulate General in San Francisco decided to play an April Fool's Day joke on the

British. On the 2nd April, Mr Scullard of the British embassy in Washington DC reported the events to a Mr Blair at the Foreign Office in London: 'Upon my arrival home last evening I was given a message to ring the duty officer at once. I did so and learned that the Australian embassy had alerted him to the fact that Mr John Stonehouse had just arrived in Los Angeles and was being held there by the immigration authorities pending instructions. We telephoned Los Angeles and told the unfortunate duty officer there to get in touch with US immigration and find out at once what document Mr Stonehouse had travelled on. At the same time my Australian cousins were telephoning Canberra for instructions. I was about to send you a Flash telegram (at midnight your time) when we learned from Los Angeles that the whole thing was an April 1st occasion … I have received abject apologies from my Australian colleague but personally I think this was one of the best jokes I have heard for many years.'[7] He got an irate reply back from Jack Dixon at the FCO, dated 8th April: 'Robin Blair passed me your letter of 2 April as I am the extradition man. Remember? As one who, for three months, spent about half his official time and a fair part of his private time on the Stonehouse affair and who went home at Easter believing that the case was wrapped up as far as was humanly possible I would not have been best pleased if the Resident Clerk had awakened me in the early hours of 2 April and I had in turn to awaken the others in Whitehall who would have needed to be told. And we would all have been furious if we had then learned it was all a hoax. As it was, a fair amount of official time and money was spent as a result of the hoax, including a telegram from Canberra repeated to Los Angeles and Wellington, and I cannot bring myself to regard it as a joke. I hope the Australian was suitably disciplined.'[8]

The humourless Jack Dixon had already been busy trying to head my father off at the pass. On the 19th March, he'd drafted a telegram to the British High Commission in Port Louis, Mauritius, about how they could dissuade the Mauritians from taking Stonehouse

With HM Queen Elizabeth II at the opening of The Postal Museum, 19th February 1969.

Postmaster General,
15th May 1969.

Barbara and John being greeted by the chairman of the Greater London Council, Leslie Freeman, and his wife, County Hall, 24th July 1969.

Playing cowboys with Mathew outside Faulkners Down House, 1971.
© Julia Stonehouse

With the extended family at Faulkners Down House, Christmas 1972. John bottom left with Julia behind, next to Beatrice, behind whom John's sister Betty, Barbara to left, Rosina to far left.
© Julia Stonehouse

John and Barbara in 1973.
© Julia Stonehouse

Designer of the first set of stamps for Bangladesh, Biman Mullick, left, with Justice Abu Sayeed Chowdhury and John Stonehouse, 27th July 1971.

© Unknown

Viewing graves of victims of the 1971 war in Bangladesh, 1972.

© Julia Stonehouse

Barbara with Syed Abdus Sultan, the first Bangladesh high commissioner to Britain, between photos of Justice Abu Sayeed Chowdhury on left and Sheikh Mujibur Rahman on right.

Photo by Brian Worth.
© Julia Stonehouse

The bomb that destroyed my father's car at a Heathrow Airport car park, 19th May 1974.

Bomb explosion at the House of Commons, 17th June 1974.

Michael Cummings, *Daily Express*, 18th December 1974.

Leaving Commonwealth
Police Headquarters, Melbourne,
26th December 1974.

First meeting of John
and Barbara at detention
centre, Melbourne,
with Jim Patterson
to the left of John,
27th December 1974.

John in Melbourne pub
opposite court, 1975.

John, Mathew, Jane and Barbara in Australia, 1975.
© Julia Stonehouse

John and Sheila in Australia, 1975.
© Julia Stonehouse

(Left to right) Sheila, Jane and Mathew at a press conference in Melbourne, 26th May 1975.

Photo by the AGE. © Getty images

With Jane, heading for the boarding gate and a London-bound plane, just prior to arrest, at Tullamarine Airport, Melbourne, Australia, 10th June 1975.

© Keystone Press / Alamy Stock Photo

Barbara meeting Jane at Heathrow Airport, London, 11th June 1975, following John's arrest at Melbourne Airport.

© ANL/Shutterstock

Heathrow Airport, arriving back from Australia under police escort, 18th July 1975.

© ANL/Shutterstock

Heathrow Airport, Sheila being led from the plane by police woman, 18th July 1975.

Photo by Jimmy Jarrett. © ANL/Shutterstock

John leaving Bow Street Magistrates' Court in a prison van after being remanded into custody, 19th July 1975.

© ANL/Shutterstock

in, including pointing out 'the embarrassment to them which you foresee his presence in Mauritius might cause'.[9] The prime minister, Sir Seewoosagur Ramgoolam, was an old friend of my father, and had initially replied warmly to his request for a passport, but the situation became a lot more complicated after the 21st March, when the warrant for his arrest was carried out. On the 11th April, Jane went to Mauritius, after being strip-searched at Melbourne Airport as well as having her luggage searched. They said they were looking for a large amount of money, but were probably looking for the letter from my father that Jane carried to the PM, saying he'd now have to deal with the criminal charges, but would thereafter still be interested in getting a passport from them. Jane stayed part of her time there with Sir Harold Walter and his wife, Yvette; Harold had been friends with my father for fourteen years and was now the minister for population control. The press in Mauritius, Australia and the UK wanted to know what she was doing there. British diplomats reported on the 12th that Stonehouse had told the press: 'It is well known that I have applied for passports from a number of countries. Mauritius is one of them. I pointed out that if I secured the defeat of the attempts to extradite me I would still have to leave Australia within 72 hours, once I ceased to be an MP, and for that I would need a passport. It is persecution and twisting of the facts to suggest that I am trying to get away.' They noted that 'Mr Stonehouse is further reported as saying that he planned to renounce his British citizenship "at an appropriate time".'[10] On the same day, the high commissioner of Mauritius in London was at 10 Downing Street being advised of the British position. He said he'd 'been instructed by Mr Ramgoolam to elicit directly from the Prime Minister whether he would be embarrassed if Mr Stonehouse were to be granted a Mauritian passport', adding that 'Mr Stonehouse had many friends in Mauritius, including his Prime Minister, who had been touched by the personal tragedy of the present situation'. The high commissioner was given details of the legal charges and told of the British concern that 'if he is given a Mauritian passport, Mr Stonehouse might attempt to get to a country from which there would be no hope of obtaining his extradition. The Mauritian Government might well pause before agreeing to facilitate such an evasion of justice.' He was reminded that the assistant high commissioner had already spoken to the Foreign Office, 'and had been left in no doubt as to the displeasure that would colour any British Government reaction to a decision to grant Mr Stonehouse a Mauritian passport'.[11] The high commissioner reported back about Britain's 'displeasure' to Mr Ramgoolam that night. By the time Jane left Mauritius, everyone knew the decision was 'no', but privately Jane had been told that if the extradition proceedings failed, he would be given travel documents. When she arrived back in Melbourne, she was again strip-searched, and her luggage gone through.

My father had written to other old friends who were now leaders of their countries but, being Commonwealth countries, they too feared the 'displeasure' of the British government and were bound by the same extradition treaties. None relished a diplomatic incident. Only silence came back from the president of Bangladesh, Sheikh Mujibur Rahman, who'd given my father honorary citizenship of that country in thanks for all he'd done for them. A secretary in the office of Seretse Khama of Botswana sent a formal and negative reply. Not a word was forthcoming from Presidents Nyerere of Tanzania, Kenyatta of Kenya or Kaunda of Zambia. The prime minister of Canada, Pierre Trudeau, eventually replied in a friendly tone, saying he'd discussed the matter with Harold Wilson and Gough Whitlam at the Commonwealth Heads of State Meeting in Jamaica, held between the 29th April and the 6th May, and it was a 'No'. My father had to face the fact that political expediency now drove the men he'd been so close to over many years, usually in the capacity of helping them forge independence for their countries. This hurt him very deeply. If the African leaders had at least sent a letter saying they couldn't help because it would jeopardise their relationship with

Britain, my father would have understood that, but their deafening silence echoed in his heart.

❖

The extradition proceedings were due to begin in Melbourne on 5th May, but the prosecution asked for a three-week adjournment. The select committee's second report on the 6th May complicated things because they were asking my father to either resign or attend the House, or a motion could be put before the House to have him expelled. That would be the last straw, and a sense of urgency gripped us all, including Dr Gibney, who thought such an action would have serious emotional content for my father. With the three-week adjournment, the court would resume on 26th May. With the time frame implied by the wording of the select committee report, my father thought he would have to be in London by 6th June. Even if he pleaded guilty to all charges – which he wasn't about to do – he could never make it back to London in time because anyone being extradited must spend a mandatory fifteen days in an Australian jail before leaving the country. He began to panic. As well as the extradition proceedings to worry about, he had this catch-22 to get around as well.

My father was desperate to avoid being returned to London in handcuffs because of successful extradition proceedings, and his lawyers were convinced they could win his case and he could then do as he wished. During the preliminary discussions at the magistrates' court, my father instructed his lawyer to propose to the prosecution that the extradition case be withdrawn, allowing him to fly to London immediately. The prosecution agreed, but only on the condition that Sheila also agreed. Her counsel, George Hampel, however, did not: he thought the case against Sheila was flimsy and they could win. So the opportunity to return without extradition proceedings was lost. My father had been caught in another catch-22: pressure to return to the House of Commons before they expelled him, set against pressure from Sheila's lawyers to remain in Australia and fight the charges. Their cases had to be dealt with together because, by this time, the prosecution had added the charge of conspiracy.

Back in London, it was announced that the House of Commons would hold a debate on the motion to expel my father as an MP on Thursday 12th June. The pressure was rising. At the resumed court hearing in Melbourne on the 26th May, the magistrate proposed another two-week adjournment, and the prosecution agreed, but my father was desperate for proceedings to progress so he could attend the debate in London and, at the request of the defence, it was reduced to four days. By this time my father had become convinced that people back in London were deliberately trying to prevent him getting back in time. The select committee said in their fourth report that 'between 5th May, when extradition proceedings were commenced, and the resumed hearing on the 26th May, it was open to Mr Stonehouse to announce his willingness to submit to an order of the Australian Court which could still have resulted in his return by now'. The select committee never seemed to be aware of the legal catch-22 in Melbourne, and my father sent a cable to the prime minister, saying 'The select committee have made this observation without in any way consulting me or my lawyers, or obtaining advice on the legal position here in the State of Victoria.'[12]

Completely exasperated, my father made the decision to get on a plane and fly back to London. He made no secret about his plans. On the 30th May, he wrote to the chairman of the select committee, George Strauss, saying: 'I have a booking on British Airways flight 419 from Melbourne at 12 noon on Sunday 1 June arriving Monday 7a.m. on 2 June in London. However, the magistrate has said that if I attempt to catch this plane I shall be in breach of bail and I will be arrested by the police here. The failure of the UK Government to agree to my leaving on this plane is tantamount to impeding my attendance in the House of Commons.'[13] In fact, he never caught that particular flight, because he wanted to try one last time to see if he could leave legally. He went to the magistrates' court to request a hearing on his extradition so he could be allowed to leave Victoria, but was refused. Then he made a personal plea, exempting his solicitor from blame for what was to come, and told the magistrate he was going to remove himself from the jurisdiction of the court, and catch a plane to London.

On the 9th June, Jane delivered to the consul general in Melbourne a petition from my father to the Queen, written in his capacity as a privy counsellor. It was a desperate move, that expected no response, but my father was becoming a very desperate man. In London, my mother described it as his 'last weapon' in the effort to get the debate to expel him postponed.[14] Jane then headed for Melbourne's Tullamarine International Airport with my father and Mathew, where around 60 reporters, photographers and television crews were waiting for them. Some reporters had bought tickets to London. My father, Jane and Mathew struggled past the crowd. Checking in was too easy, and porters were waiting to whisk their bags away. My father kept his with him. They went through customs and immigration. With each step closer to the plane they wondered whether, miracle of miracles, the authorities were allowing him to return to the UK – which is what extradition was designed to achieve. It had all been so easy, but Jane began to get suspicious because there was a half-hour delay in opening the doors to board the plane. She thought the police would be behind the doors, but my father was daring to be hopeful. The doors opened and they went through, but they were locked behind them. Now they were trapped, and Inspector Bob Gillespie appeared. Jane wrote in her diary, 'the energy of misery was overpowering'. My father leant against the wall in a daze as Gillespie read the charge of attempting to obstruct the course of justice. My father turned his back on him and Gillespie threatened to charge him with resisting arrest. To drown out his words my father kept repeating, 'I want to talk to John Sullivan.' Jane held my father's hand. They went upstairs to the security check,

Jane in tears. Gillespie wanted to leave immediately but Jane said, 'For God's sake, let us say goodbye.' They sat and gripped each other in an embrace, both sobbing their hearts out, with my brother looking sadly on. Jane wrote, 'Pa saying that he was so terribly in love with us all and me telling him to be strong and keep himself together … The heart-wrenching sobs were terrifying and he wiped his tears saying "give my love to mummy", and hugged Mathew.' Then he was taken away.

Shaking and sobbing, Jane and Mathew boarded the plane to London. They ordered two brandies. Jane wrote in her diary, 'I just cried and cried. Am still crying. Mathew is thoroughly unhappy. It was just so lonely him not being there. Poor, poor daddy – it's all so very unfair. He knew he'd be arrested but it is still a ghastly shock. At Perth I rang Peter [Game] and he said pa appeared in court and was mute – he looked very miserable and haggard – I hope he isn't going to snap but it sounds as if he is.' At Heathrow, Jane and Mathew were met by our mother and held a press conference at which they said they fully supported my father, and would do what they could to stop the proposed debate on his expulsion from the House of Commons. Back in Melbourne, my father refused to say a word in court and didn't request bail, so was sent to Pentridge Prison. He remained mute and refused to eat.

Nine hours behind Melbourne, the Cabinet met at 10 Downing Street in London that same day, the 9th June, at 11.30am. They had three items on the agenda: 1) The leaking of speeches to the press; 2) Deciding whether to go ahead with the debate on the 12th to expel Stonehouse; and, the rather more important item, 3) The statement the prime minister was to make that afternoon regarding the outcome of the referendum on continuing membership of the European Community (in which 67 per cent had voted 'yes'). On item two, Edward Short outlined the issues: 'It would be unsafe to agree to his return to this country except in custody and as a result of extradition proceedings, since otherwise there would be no power to prevent him absconding. These difficulties were, however, largely of Mr Stonehouse's own making and would not have arisen if he had not opposed extradition in the first place.' Short wanted him returned in custody, but the last thing my father wanted was the stigma of being brought back in handcuffs and, according to my father's lawyer, the extradition warrants were incorrectly drawn, and thus invalid, plus they thought they had good grounds to challenge the charges. The attorney general was concerned that a debate would prejudice the possibility of my father 'receiving a fair trial in later criminal proceedings', even though the Speaker had indicated that he could prevent Members breaking *sub judice* rules. He thought the issue should focus on non-attendance and being unable to perform parliamentary duties, and was worried that any delay meant there could be no by-election before October. As my father had a safe Labour seat, and the government had a wafer-thin majority, this was important to consider. In the discussion, it was noted that 'it appeared that Mr Stonehouse was now making genuine efforts to return to this country; and that being so the public might well consider it unjust that he should be expelled from the House of Commons in his absence'.[15] Cabinet deferred the decision for 48 hours, when it was decided to cancel the debate on the proposal to expel him.

When he heard that, my father started talking and eating again. He'd been in prison in Melbourne where, on the 10th and 11th, he was seen by the consultant psychiatrist in charge, Dr Bartholomew, who had a hard time conducting his consultations with a man who wouldn't talk and would only write his answers down on a piece of paper. His report stated that he 'considered the man to be grossly mentally disturbed – hysterical – but wonder about the possibility of an underlying schizophrenic illness'.[16] Court resumed on 13th June. The prosecutor, Mr James, had made it clear right from the outset of the extradition proceedings that his instructions were to oppose bail, but despite my father's flight or, rather, missed flight, the magistrate granted him bail with a low surety of A$500.

The purpose of extradition is not to decide whether a person is guilty or innocent, but to establish whether there's a charge to be answered. The prosecution can't extradite on charge 'A' and then add charges 'B', 'C' and 'D' at home. In Australian law, all the charges came under one 'information', which meant that if any charge was deemed answerable, the whole package transferred to London. My father's lawyer, Jim Patterson, and Sheila's, George Hampel, tried to disentangle the 'information', but the rather confused magistrate went along with the prosecution. In the State of Victoria, stipendiary magistrates were not legally qualified and attained their position by a rise through the ranks of the court clerks. This means that they often take direction on points of law from the prosecution lawyers, as in this case. There are differences between UK and Australian law plus, on the 29th May, the Supreme Court of the State of Victoria had indicated that my father's case raised issues regarding the constitutional relations between the UK and the States of Australia, and advised that only the High Court of Australia may be competent to adjudicate. But my father and Sheila wanted to avoid a long legal delay, so that option was not followed.

The financial charges against my father amounted to around £29,000, mostly in the form of cheques alleged to have been stolen from one of my father's companies, Export Promotion and Consultancy Services (EPACS). Patterson made the case that my father had a right to that money, and there was no evidence to the contrary. Sheila was charged with signing some of those cheques, but her lawyer made the point that 'if every secretary or clerk or person in an office who signed cheques were to be committed for trial if it were found that the cheques were illegally dealt with subsequently, there would be a great many people in jail or awaiting trial'.[17] Nevertheless, this connection made their legal fates inextricably linked and would introduce the charge of 'conspiracy'. The defence was not allowed to question the depositions, large bundles of which had been brought from London. None of the witnesses had been brought to Melbourne, and my father's solicitor's request to be able to question them in London was refused. Australian witnesses couldn't later be compelled to go to London.

Dr Gerard Gibney, my father's psychiatrist, appeared as a witness for the defence and explained to the court that people with depression can withdraw within their own shell, carry out their own suicide or, as my father had done, perform a kind of suicide equivalent by adopting a new personality to escape into. Dr Gibney thought that after coming to Australia, there was a part of him that hoped for detection, largely because of the feelings he had towards his wife and children, and that when he was detected he felt something like relief to know the whole experience was coming to an end. The prosecution lawyer, Mr James, also questioned Dr Gibney extensively. He did this not in a challenging or sceptical manner, but as a man who wanted to be clear about the psychiatric reasons behind my father's actions. This same professional approach was not going to be found in England.

The magistrate decided that there was a case for extradition, and my father and Sheila had to spend a mandatory fifteen days in jail. The magistrate, trying to be kind, committed my father to the Maribyrnong Detention Centre without knowing, apparently, that it was more cold and inhospitable than Pentridge Prison – where my father elected to go. He wrote to Jane on the 7th July, 'it is extremely bitter here. There is something curious about the Australian cold it has an intensity about it which I do not remember from Europe.' Sheila was equally cold when her friend from Sydney, Denis, visited her at the Fairlea Women's Prison – which was nowhere near as nice as the name suggests. On the 16th July, the *Daily Mail* published extracts from the letters Sheila had sent to 'Mr Mildoon' in Melbourne. As official evidence, those documents should have been secure in the hands of Scotland Yard, yet here they were, for all the world to see. The symbiotic, not to say financial, relationship between the police and the press appeared to my father to be once again on view.

The question 'where to next?' was answered on the 17th July: my father and Sheila were escorted back to London by Chief Superintendent Ken Etheridge and other officers from Scotland Yard on flight BA 979, which left Melbourne at 17:00 hrs.

14

Bonnie and Clyde are Back

The arrival of the notorious runaways at Heathrow Airport on Friday 18th July provided a fantastic opportunity for press photographers, who'd been corralled behind metal railings on either side of the steps leading from the door of the British Airways jumbo jet. My father came down the stairs first, and was funnelled through the tunnel of flashing lights by detectives on either side of him, quickly put in the back of a waiting car, and driven off. Sheila appeared next, looking as if she'd lost weight, and was guided into another car by one of the two plain-clothed policewomen who'd been sent to Australia to collect her. They were taken to Bow Street Magistrates' Court, where another crowd of photographers waited, along with my sister Jane. The plane had been delayed and it was too late for a bail hearing before a judge, so they both spent the night in the court's grubby cells. The next morning, in a courtroom full of reporters, Sheila was given bail, but my father was not.

The following Monday, a bail appeal was refused by a judge in chambers, Mr Justice Kerr. My father was represented by Sheila's barrister from Melbourne, George Hampel, who'd been quickly admitted to the English Bar. He and Jim Patterson had flown to London at their own expense to help with the cases. Michael O'Dell became my father's solicitor in London, and was to prove an absolute gem and true family friend. The press emphasised that the charges against my father came to £154,000 but I don't think the public realised that £125,000 of that related to life insurance policies which had never been claimed. However, emphasising big numbers made a good story and sold newspapers. Meanwhile my father was remanded to Brixton Prison, where he would spend the next six weeks, during which Josef Frolik was doing the publicity rounds and generating reviews for his book *The Frolik Defection*, which was published on the 25th July. For him, the timing couldn't have been more perfect.

The first chance I had to see my father was that same day, Wednesday 25th July, five days after he'd been escorted back from Australia, when my mother and I visited him in Brixton. After eight months of trauma, it was a phenomenal relief just to hug him, and have the opportunity to say we loved each other. He felt thinner, and his hair had gone slightly grey, but I was relieved to find him in good spirits. He had no idea, then, that he'd be incarcerated on remand for weeks to come. The guards did what they would always do, whether in prison or at court – stand a few feet away trying to overhear his conversations. There was no privacy.

The next bail hearing was on Monday 28th July, my father's 50th birthday. He made the appeal himself, and failed. There had been reports in the newspapers that he'd been on hunger strike. This wasn't true, and he told the judge that he occasionally goes on a starvation diet for health reasons. Indeed, he said, Brixton is 'like a health farm and extremely good for me' because, outside, he'd be harassed by the press. Each Monday he applied for bail. Michael O'Dell tried. His newly appointed barrister, Geoffrey Robertson, tried. And John Mortimer, QC and playwright, tried. They all failed. My sister and I were in court during the fourth attempt, on the 11th August, and heard our father complain to the judge that while the prosecution had access to all the documents, and had had eight months to prepare their case, he'd had no access to documents and barely eight minutes to consult with his solicitor because there were 1,000 unconvicted prisoners in Brixton Prison and only ten rooms in which they could consult their legal representatives. He was also desperate to get out so he could explain to the House of Commons, by way of a personal statement, what had happened to him, and felt his continued incarceration was the result of political, rather than legal, considerations.

My mother made the journey to Brixton Prison practically every day, collecting laundry and delivering books, food and other extra things to try and keep up my father's morale. The warders some-times escorted her to a small back door exit so she could avoid the press photographers out front, but that ruse was soon discovered and she'd find them there too. If my mother couldn't go, Jane or I would. The longer he was there, the more depressed my father became. There were eighteen bars on his cell window, through which he could see four houses with sixteen chimney pots and four TV aeri-als. Apart from visits, he spent 23 hours a day in his cell. The prison was old, overcrowded, noisy, unsanitary and claustrophobic. On the 15th August, he heard on his radio that Sheikh Mujibur Rahman, the first president of Bangladesh, had been assassinated. This tragi-cally disappointing news from Bangladesh was accompanied that day by another news item: the Labour Party in Walsall North had disowned their MP.

On the 27th August, my father was finally given bail, with the condition he reported to the local police station once a day, exclud-ing Sundays. By this time, the House of Commons was in summer recess. It would resume on 13th October, but the courts decided that 13th October would also be the day committal proceeding would begin, and couldn't be persuaded a slightly later date would do. This meant there was no time in which my father was free to make his statement of explanation to the House of Commons, and he became even more convinced that the government was trying to silence him.

If the Department of Public Prosecutions (DPP) thought that locking my father up in the appalling conditions of Brixton for six weeks was going to break him, they were wrong. As he collected his belongings from the remand prison, he told reporters, 'Five hundred inside there should be out here with me.' The justice system and prison reform were to become his new causes. He also said, 'Wake up England – be aware of what's happening in this country.' From this point on, he went public with the hypocrisy and inadequacy of British politics that had, when internalised, driven him to despair. He had nothing to lose, his reputation was in tatters, and he intended to speak his truth. My father emerged from his unsympathetic treatment as the system's most vocal critic.

The press, as far as I know, never reported on the fact that while my father was fighting extradition in Australia and, later, in Brixton Prison, he'd been submitting written questions to various ministers, for answering in the House of Commons record. Before the Freedom of Information Act of 2000, the only way facts could be prised out of government departments was if a member of parliament asked the appropriate minister. This could be done through normal correspondence, during a debate in the House of Commons, in the form of an oral question, or by requesting a written answer for recording in Hansard. Often, parliamentary questions are rhetorical, in that the questioner knows more about the subject than the replier and the question is just a way of drawing attention to a particular subject, or getting information into the public record. Between 22nd May and 31st July my father asked 21 questions.

Regarding problems in his constituency, questions included those about unemployment, the depressed state of the automobile industry, and the cash-flow problems of car-component manufacturers. His concern about British exports was expressed in questions about submarines, Nimrod aircraft, and diplomatic staff doing more to promote trade. On British politics, he asked the secretary of state for employment to introduce legislation to enforce trade unions to conduct elections by secret and postal ballot. He asked the minister of the civil service what the annual saving on national expenditure would be if the number of civil servants was cut by 20 per cent. One question asking for 'details of the overseas loans to United Kingdom authorities' revealed that the entire country was deeply in debt. Fired by his experience in Brixton Prison, he asked the home secretary 'if he will take steps to strengthen the resources of the Probation Service to assist in dealing with the problems of juvenile homelessness'. Always with an eye on post-colonial exploitation, he asked about the accountability of UK-based multinational corporations and whether a strategy could be developed so countries around the Indian Ocean such as Mauritius, the Maldives, India and Bangladesh would benefit from the extraction of ocean bed mineral resources. And he asked what consultations had been had 'with the Governments of Mauritius, Seychelles, Kenya, Tanzania, India, Sri Lanka, Bangladesh, Malaysia, Singapore and Australia regarding the intentions of the United States Government to build a military establishment on Diego Garcia in the British Indian Ocean Territory; and whether they have indicated their approval'.

When my father returned to 21 Sancroft Street in Kennington on the 27th August, he'd been gone nine months. In that long time, he'd not had a moment's peace, and he desperately needed to rest. But first, we celebrated with a glass of wine over a dinner of quiche Lorraine, French beans and new potatoes, followed by fresh greengages. It was the first time in many weeks that my father had not eaten alone in a cell. My mother, Jane, Mathew and I took a deep collective breath. He was alive.

From now on, my father would have to prepare for the committal proceedings with Michael O'Dell, and without the advantage of access to all the necessary papers. Apparently, the DPP thought only they had the right to see them. This non-disclosure is an issue that's always plagued defence teams, then as now, and has led to many injustices far greater than in my father's case. There's 'the law' and there's 'how the law is applied' and, shockingly, they are not the same thing.

On the 7th September, I accompanied my father by train to his constituency. It was a Sunday, so we didn't have to worry about being back in time to sign in at the police station as part of the bail conditions. Everyone was very nice. We met none of the hostility or outrage the press had led the country to believe was occurring there. The *Daily Express* report was headlined: 'In the streets of indifference, the Rt Hon Member for Walsall North returns after nearly 11 months …'[1] My father's constituency work had been carried out by neighbouring MPs Bruce George, Geoffrey Edge and Betty Boothroyd, and they were the people most agitated by his absence. When my father explained that he'd had a breakdown, the constituents were sympathetic and understanding. It gave my father faith that regular folk were a better kind of person than those with vested interests in the House of Commons, or financial interests in selling newspapers. Although he'd been deselected by the local party, which was understandable in the circumstances, he would remain as their MP until the next election, or until he resigned.

On the 30th September my father went to the Labour Party Conference in Blackpool and during the breaks, while the delegates went to drink in the bar, he sat defiant and alone in chair number G30. Nobody spoke to him, except the prime minister's wife, Mary Wilson. At that conference, the chancellor of the exchequer, Denis Healey, announced that he would be seeking a loan from the International Monetary Fund (IMF) to bail out bankrupt Britain. On Sunday 5th October, we were all devastated to hear that Jim Patterson, my father's lawyer in Melbourne, had died of heart troubles. He was only 53. My mother told the *Daily Mail*: 'Mr Patterson became very personally involved in the case, and helped my husband come through a breakdown, and once or twice almost saved his life.'[2] Jim had been a godsend to us in so many ways, and his sad passing served to remind us that, whatever our troubles, they were nothing compared to what other people were going through.

I sat in the public gallery of the House of Commons with Jane when my father finally made his personal statement on the 20th October. Sheila sat a few rows behind us. The statement had been severely cut over the preceding few days by the Speaker, Selwyn Lloyd, who told the members: 'The convention of this House is that a personal statement should be listened to in silence.' Everyone was very surprised to see him speaking not from the Labour benches, but from the Opposition side, which he explained, 'has no party political significance whatsoever. I am standing here because this is the place that I occupied for most of my time in the House in the last nearly nineteen years, and indeed it was from this bench that I made a personal statement when I returned from Rhodesia some sixteen years ago on 13th March 1959.' The Speaker was irritated: 'The right hon. Gentleman must say only what has been passed by me.' After some back and forth, my father began:

'I deny the allegation that I was an agent for the CIA. I deny the allegations that I was a spy for the Czechs. I can only regret that the original stories were printed. The purpose of this statement is to explain, as best I can within the traditions of the House, why I was absent from the House for such a lengthy period.

'The explanation for the extraordinary and bizarre conduct in the second half of last year is found in the progressions towards the complete mental breakdown which I suffered. This breakdown was analysed by an eminent psychiatrist in Australia and was described by him as psychiatric suicide. It took the form of the repudiation of the life of Stonehouse because that life had become absolutely intolerable to him. A new parallel personality took over – separate and apart from the original man, who was resented and despised by the parallel personality for the ugly humbug and sham of the recent years of his public life. The parallel personality was uncluttered by the awesome tensions and stresses suffered by the original man, and he felt, as an ordinary person, a tremendous relief in not carrying the load of anguish which had burdened the public figure.

'The collapse and destruction of the original man came about because his idealism in his political life had been utterly frustrated and finally destroyed by the pattern of events, beyond his control,

which had finally overwhelmed him. Those events which caused the
death of an idealist are too complex to describe in detail here, but in
the interests of clarity as well as brevity I refer to them as follows.'

He started by talking about his anti-colonial work in Africa, and
the disappointment of 'military dictatorship and despair' in Uganda
now, for example, and then moved on to co-operatives. 'The co-
operative movement in Britain had been a great ideal for me from
an early age. Co-operation was almost a religion for me. It was not
only a way to run a business; it was a way of life from which selfish-
ness, greed and exploitation were completely excluded. I became a
director and later president of the London Co-operative Society, the
largest retail co-operative society in the world, in active pursuit of
those ideals. I did not do it for money. The honorarium was £20 per
year. But I was pursued by the Communists in that position during
that period. I was bitterly attacked, and at that time ...' The Speaker
interrupted. 'Order. The right hon. Gentleman must say only what
I have passed.' And my father continued: 'That time was a most
traumatic one for me and wounded my soul deeply. It had become
cruelly clear that my co-operative ideals were too ambitious, for, in
truth, they could not be achieved, given human motivations. I felt as
though my religion had been exposed as a pagan rite.' This probably
didn't go down too well with the other Labour and Co-operative
Party MPs, of which there were fifteen at the time.

He talked about his part in fighting for an independent
Bangladesh, saying, 'I was enthused at that time with hope, but the
hopes turned to tears as the conditions in that country deteriorated.
Another of my ideals had collapsed.' This led on to the setting up of
the BBT: 'This involved me in very great problems, which could have
ruined my career and public standing, and I was left a broken man
as a result of the nervous tension I suffered throughout that period.
That experience contributed heavily to my breakdown. In 1974,
with the collapse of many secondary banks and the problems of the
British economy, the strains became even worse. There seemed no

escape from the awesome pressures which were squeezing the will to live from the original man. Everything he had lived for and worked for seemed to be damned.'

He tried to explain his breakdown: 'In this House itself, I felt a big weight bearing down on me. It was physically painful for me to be in the Chamber because it was such a reminder of my lost ideals. I was suffocated with the anguish of it all. The original man had become a burden to himself, to his family and to his friends. He could no longer take the strain and had to go. Hence, the emergence of the parallel personality, the disappearance and the long absence during the period of recovery.' He explained why he had been absent from the House: 'That recovery took time, and in the early stages the psychiatrist in Australia advised that I should not return to England until I had recovered, as a premature return would inevitably do further harm to my health. At the time of the disappearance, no criminal charges were laid or anticipated; they did not come till four months later. In view of the facts, I hope that the House will agree that the right hon. Member for Walsall, North had no intention of removing himself from the processes of justice as established by Parliament.' He extended thanks to some MPs who had been supportive, and within fifteen minutes, it was over.

In November, *Death of an Idealist* was published. MPs had already been made aware of some of his criticisms of parliament when extracts of the book had been printed in the *News of the World* in March and April. Now they were to read more: 'What I saw and felt increasingly alarmed me and, most seriously, what we were doing in Parliament was, at best, irrelevant and, at worst, extremely damaging to Britain and her standing in the world. Parliament had become a raucous rabble concerned only to shout the ephemeral slogans of the day. The few intelligent leaders cynically pandered to the appetites of their supporters so they could ride along on their unthinking support. Principle, except on rare and isolated occasions, was thrown out of the window. What leaders wanted was power; their political aims as politicians were subverted to this end, rather than power being seen as the means to achieve those aims. Power and office became the cruel masters of men as ends in themselves.'[3]

What he said about his own political party was damning: 'The 1964–1970 Labour Governments had been conspicuous failures in the fields of National planning, but this did not deter Labour leaders from further adventures in state manipulation. In this they acted like alcoholics who had felt the effects of earlier drinking, but were not to be deterred by that experience, as the intoxication was already in their blood.' And 'I was sick to death with the way most Labour Members were afraid to say what they really thought about the Trade Unions because they feared the repercussions from the militant members of their constituency party organisation. I recalled with a shudder of disgust that Dick Taverne, the talented Member for Lincoln, had been forced out of his seat by such militants.'[4]

Individuals within the Labour Party came in for criticism. He wasn't too hard on James Callaghan, who became prime minister on 5th April 1976, three weeks before my father's trial at the Old Bailey began, saying he'd been 'one of the best Foreign Secretaries since the war, although disastrous, at some stages, as Chancellor', noting that 'Jim Callaghan is a skilful politico, always with his eye on the main chance; a man without the impediment of strong convictions.'[5] He had little good to say about Tony Wedgwood Benn, who he'd followed into two ministries, feeling he'd been left to clear up Tony's mess – for example, the two-tier postage system, GIRO banking system, and the expensive postal HQ in Birmingham. He felt that he'd become the scapegoat for Tony's flamboyant but expensive and time-wasting decisions. Meanwhile, Tony would gladly take credit where he could, such as over Concorde: 'Tony Benn was never involved in the detailed talks but always turned up, as he was entitled to do as Minister of Technology, when there were important public occasions.'[6]

In 1978, I had the opportunity to ask Tony Benn to help my father when I happened to be at Khan's Restaurant in Westbourne

Grove with my friend, Steve Abrams, while Tony was there with his family. My father was in prison recovering from open heart surgery and needed all the help he could get. As usual I was sitting with my back to the other tables, when the waiter came up, very excited, and said to Steve 'It's only because I know you're Lord Snowdon that I'm telling you Tony Benn is over there.' This was bizarre enough as Steve was a tall, long-haired American who'd started SOMA, the campaign to legalise marijuana, while Lord Snowdon was short, immaculately groomed and dressed, and the very English ex-husband of Princess Margaret. How the waiter could confuse the two, I do not know. Anyhow, I went over to Tony's table and gave him the details of what was going on. His eyes went dead. Not glazed, not distracted, just so dead they ceased to look alive. I've never seen anything like it. And Tony wasn't going to do anything to help. None of them did.

In the period between my father's arrest in December 1974 and his imprisonment in August 1976, he was something of a loose cannon on the deck of the big ship H.M.S. Establishment. He criticised parliament and parliamentarians, the press, the police, the legal system and the security services. On the 9th February 1976, the *Daily Mirror* reported on the November 1975 US Senate Committee hearings on communist bloc intelligence activities, at which Josef Frolik had been the CIA's star witness, and where he had named my father as an StB agent. The same day, the House of Commons held a debate on 'Foreign Policy and Morality', and this coincidental conflu-ence of events gave my father the opportunity to both deny the spy claim, and challenge the UK security services to be more account-able. He began, 'It is true that when I was a minister and, indeed, before, I associated with Communist agents. I did not know at the time that they were spies. Also, I am convinced that most ministers of both administrations have in past years associated with agents. There is no escaping from it, if one is going to engage in any sort of discussion with the Czechs or with anyone else. Indeed, the man I had known from the Czech embassy turned up when I was a minister negotiating with the Czech minister responsible for the Czech aircraft industry and I was trying to sell him the VC10. Associated with that sale was a negotiation to provide the Czech airline with landing rights at Heathrow, so that the Czechs could fly their VC10 through the United Kingdom into the United States, and the very man who at that time, apparently, was a Communist spy turned up as the interpreter. He has since been named as one of the Czechs' leading agents in this country at that time. I therefore suggest that it is impossible for anyone, if he is a minister responsible for negotiating with the Czechs or with anyone else, to escape from having some association with Communist agents. When I was in Czechoslovakia I apparently met some others who were involved in this business.'

He then turned to the subject of the debate by quoting from a report by US senator Frank Church into the CIA's plots to assassinate foreign leaders, and their 'Mongoose' plan to sabotage Cuba by any means, including 'incapacitating sugar workers during harvest season by the use of chemicals; blowing up bridges and production plants; sabotaging merchandise in third countries – even those allied with the United States – prior to its delivery to Cuba …'.* In particular, he wondered whether the *Daily Mail* was correct in February 1975 to question 'Did the CIA organise a collision on the Thames to stop British Leyland sending 400 buses to Castro's Cuba?' The story concerned an East German freighter called the *Magdeburg* that sunk in the Thames at Kent, in October 1964. He then suggested that the UK government should establish a select committee to investigate the *Magdeburg* and attempts by the CIA to prevent the export of UK

* From page 274 of 'Alleged Assassination Plots Involving Foreign Leaders, An Interim Report of the Select Committee to Study Governmental Operations with Respect to Intelligence Activities', Chairman: Frank Church, Senate Report No. 94–465, Washington: US Government Printing Office, 20th November 1975.

civilian goods to Cuba, adding, 'We should investigate other areas involving activities of our own secret service and foreign affairs officials.' He then talked about the USA and Soviet Union subsidising foreign political parties, and added that he believed 'a select committee should investigate the secret donations that have been made by British Governments to foreign political parties to enable them to win certain elections, to the advantage of the United Kingdom. As a former minister, I know of examples, which I should like to give to a select committee … If the Americans have thought it right to establish the Church Committee and the Pryke Committee to carry out full investigations into the secret operations of the CIA – I am not suggesting that our activities have been so serious – I believe that we should investigate our operations in other countries.' Although any such investigations would be done behind closed doors, I doubt the British security services were happy about this suggestion, and it told them and everyone else that my father had had enough of keeping his mouth shut about what really went on in the geo-political world.

On the 5th April 1976, three weeks before his trial at the Old Bailey was due to begin, my father asked this of the attorney general in the House of Commons: 'Is he not aware that the Directorate of Public Prosecutions is headed by a geriatric who is well beyond the retirement age and is given to making ridiculous decisions about prosecutions – given that 25 per cent of the prosecutions at the Old Bailey result in acquittals?' The *Financial Times* reported that 'a Labour MP shouted "Give him another passport"'.[7] It probably wasn't wise to attack the director of public prosecutions, Norman Skelhorn, who would undoubtedly have an influence on his own case. Indeed, Skelhorn was an influential man all round, having been Master of the Freemasons' Western Circuit Lodge 3154, based in Duke Street, St James's, and favoured by judges. Judge Edward Eveleigh, who would preside over my father's trial at the Old Bailey, was also a Freemason.

❖

On the 7th April my father resigned from the Labour Party. The American embassy in London sent a message to the Department of State, laying out the consequences: 'Renegade Labor MP John Stonehouse – scheduled to stand trial later this month on thirteen counts of fraud arising from his questionable business dealings and "disappearance" – tossed a spanner in the government's parliamentary works April 7, adding to Prime Minister Callaghan's political problems. Stonehouse publicly announced that he had resigned the Labor Party Whip and in future would vote as independent. ... This is one problem Prime Minister Callaghan really didn't need at this time, following loss of Labor MP by death. Stonehouse resignation, if it becomes official, will diminish government's working majority (roughly eight to ten seats) and place its control of committees in jeopardy ... this situation will increase uncertainties, enhance bargaining power of minority parties, and make government whip's already trying task even more difficult.'[8]

Now that he was free of the miserable, unfriendly Labour Party, my father started representing a group that his barrister, Geoffrey Robertson, called 'a collection of fairly harmless oddballs, who dressed up in Robin Hood costumes and held tea parties'.[9] The 'English National Party' my father represented for four months were along the lines of 'Merrie England', and their main objective was a devolved English parliament. They were a fun bunch who enjoyed themselves without being too serious, and their whole eccentric outlook was a relief from the usual dogma of British politics. (They disbanded in 1981 and shouldn't be confused with the racist organisations that adopted that name during the 1990s.)

In my father's defence 'dock statement' to the jury at his trial at the Old Bailey, on 27th July 1976, he accused the prosecution of lying, deceit, cheating and trickery: 'The lying and cheating is as bad as anything I have seen in the House of Commons. But the humbug is even worse, because it is dressed up in this decorum and in that way you are not supposed to notice it.'[10] Judge Eveleigh threw his comments right back in my father's face on the last day of the trial, saying: 'You falsely accused other people of cant, hypocrisy and humbug when you must have known all the time your defence was an embodiment of all those three.'[11] That was right before he sentenced my father to 95-and-a-half years.

15

Off with Their Heads!

M y father's trial at the Old Bailey was like the scene in *Alice in Wonderland* where the Queen of Hearts shouts 'Off with their heads!' except in our real-life version, the Queen was replaced by Mr Justice Eveleigh. I suppose we were lucky that Eveleigh allowed the 95-and-a-half years of prison sentences he handed down to run concurrently, so my father 'only' got seven years. Eveleigh was the last stop on a long journey that began with arrest on the immigration charge on 24th December 1974, arrest on extradition charges on 21st March 1975, arrest at Melbourne Airport when he was trying to return to the UK on 10th June, arrest when he was brought back to London on the 18th July and denied bail for six weeks, and the committal proceedings in October 1975 in front of a magistrate. My father had already spent months in four jails.

Proceedings began on 28th April 1976 in Court 1 of the Central Criminal Court, known as the Old Bailey. The lead prosecutor was Michael Corkery QC, who appeared to have a further four QCs by his side. He started with a three-day outline of the prosecution case, followed by 40 days of prosecution witnesses. Then came my father's six-day statement from the dock, followed by eight days of defence witnesses. The prosecution took 43 days, and the defence fourteen, yet it would be my father who'd be accused of dragging the trial out.

Sheila and my father sat together in the dock, not speaking a word to each other. The prosecution were determined to paint a picture of a pair of devious, selfish conspirators and Sheila and my

father didn't want to feed that narrative by whispering conspiratori-
ally to each other. They shared six charges: conspiracy; the theft of
four cheques that belonged to his company EPACS, worth £7,500,
£6,981, £2,112, £3,029; plus an EPACS US dollar banker's draft
that converted into £5,343. My father faced an additional fifteen
charges. These included theft of another EPACS cheque for £3,118;
taking out two bank overdrafts for £7,500 and £10,000; and not
paying his most recent credit cards bills in the sums of £385, £355
and £422. He was also charged for applying for a credit card in the
name of Joseph Markham, as well as falsely obtaining a passport
in that name, and birth certificates in the names of Markham and
Mildoon. Finally, he was charged with taking out five life insurance
policies that were never claimed, totalling £125,000.

The committal proceedings had been held in October 1975
at the Horseferry Road Magistrates' Court, presided over by
Mr Kenneth Harrington, and my father had been represented by
barrister Geoffrey Robertson, supported by the solicitor, Michael
O'Dell. At the trial, they'd both be involved again, along with a
senior QC, Richard 'Dick' du Cann. Geoffrey Robertson was 29 at
the time, and at the beginning of what would become a very illus-
trious career; he's now a famous barrister and Master of the Bench.
In his book *The Justice Game*, he outlined a fundamental problem:
'What nobody heeded was the fact that John had no crime to run
away from: on the contrary, his only crimes were committed in
order to run away. The passport forgeries, the £29,000 taken from
his one-man company for his expenses, the insurance policies taken
out to console his unwitting wife – these were crimes committed in
the course of fleeing from his middle-class English existence. But
why? There would have been no great difficulty about leaving his
wife for Sheila, his bankers would never have forced an MP into
bankruptcy and his creditors would have compromised.' I find
these remarks quite interesting. First, there was only one passport
charge, not plural. And could not Geoffrey see that the insurance

policies would never have consoled his wife because, as short-term policies and without a body, they could never have been claimed? He wrote 'At lunchtime we would retire to our room to feast on the contents of a picnic basket provided each day by the much-forgiving Barbara, replete with silver cutlery and silk napkins.' They weren't silk, they were linen, and the cutlery was stainless steel Maya, still used by my mother today. We were not the kind of family that possessed silver cutlery, yet alone 'silk napkins' – if such absurd items even exist. My father wasn't happy with his legal representation and sacked them half-way through the trial. He wasn't satisfied with the amount of time he was being given by Dick du Cann to discuss the case, and also felt that he had no understanding of the mental breakdown that had led to his disappearance and, consequently, the charges. Even Geoffrey Robertson wrote later: 'If it were madness, there was too much method in it ever to convince the jury.'[1] With that kind of support, no wonder my father decided to defend himself.

My father considered himself innocent of all charges and would fight them all the way. That stubbornness, and his pride, infuriated a court that demanded contrition. His decision to defend himself further infuriated Judge Eveleigh, who revoked his bail as soon as the defence began. (Bail conditions since 29th May had entailed reporting to the police station twice a day.) So my father then had to struggle with briefcases full of papers while handcuffed to another prisoner until he got to the unsanitary, overcrowded Brixton remand prison where he had to prepare for the next day at the Old Bailey. This is where he would reside for the rest of the trial. After a sleepless night, he decided against testifying in the witness box, questioned and under oath, and to instead make an unsworn statement from the dock, an old legal right that allowed him to speak without interruption or cross-examination from Crown counsel or questioning from the judge. This decision made Eveleigh even more irate, and my father then went on to make the longest dock statement in British history, six days long, by which time the Judge was apoplectic. On the last day of his summing up, Judge Eveleigh turned to the prosecutor, Mr Corkery, and expressed his displeasure about dock statements: 'Its history is not entirely clear, but I believe a great deal of time and money would be saved and far less deception entered into if we considered, if not abolishing it, at least modifying it.'[2] Eveleigh was later appointed to the Royal Commission on Criminal Procedure and successfully lobbied for the abolition of 'the dock statement' – and an ancient legal right was brought to an end.

By the time the jury took their seats at the Old Bailey in April 1976, they'd been through the Miami disappearance in November 1974, the Melbourne arrest in December 1974, the extradition proceedings in June 1975, and the committal proceedings in London in October 1975. They'd seen so many front-page headlines about my father, it must have been hard for them to think he was anything other than a lying cad and traitor. The front-page headlines included, in brief: 'Riddle of Girl in Lost MP's Flat'; 'Lost MP Insured His Life for £119,000'; 'Stonehouse Security Sensation'; 'Concrete Coffin Probe'; 'MP was Named as Spy Contact'; 'Was Stonehouse working for CIA?'; 'Missing MP was quizzed by MI5, says Wilson'; 'Secretary knew secrets of missing MP'; 'Missing MP ran his empire on borrowed cash'; 'Did Mafia cut in on Stonehouse's £6½ million deal'; 'Why I Came To Hate England'; 'Captured In A Dead Man's Shoes'; 'Yard Ready To Fly Stonehouse Home'; 'Riddle Of Calls By Stonehouse'; 'Stonehouse Insurance Cash Probe'; 'He *Did* Talk to Sheila'; 'What "S" Wrote to Stonehouse'; 'Stonehouse quits as MP'; 'Stonehouse: I haven't quit'; 'Stonehouse told: Make up your mind'; 'Police hunt runaway MP's secretary'; 'Stonehouse Stole My Wife by Mr Buckley'; 'Police Will Extradite Stonehouse'; 'Body in concrete link'; 'Astounding! Outrageous! Bloody unbelievable!'; 'Sheila Buckley faces ultimatum – help or risk legal action'; 'MP in New Spy Probe'; 'Get him back, MP and secretary face extradition'; and 'Mistress "was in plot with Stonehouse"'.

Not once did anyone suggest that the bad publicity might have prejudiced the defendants' right to a fair trial. We were way beyond that. By this time, everyone thought they were guilty of something. The spy allegation was the worst because that was a smear that couldn't be wiped off, and it stuck to my father not only through the trial but right up to the present day. He referred to it in court, and the judge had this to say to the jury on the matter: 'You may have noticed during this trial that I tried once or twice to stop him bringing in the contents of newspaper articles. Nobody asked to be told about the Chezk [*sic*] Spy story, for example, but there it was, you heard it was reported in the papers. Matters that appear reported in the papers are not facts proved in this court, and must not be regarded as such.' Later, the judge said: 'The Chezk [*sic*] spy. I told you when I began this summing-up, this was raised by Mr Stonehouse. You otherwise would not have heard about it, and the prosecution attach no importance to it.' The idea that the jury 'would not have heard about it' was disingenuous because the entire country was well aware of it. So too were the prosecutors and judge, and all the establishment figures that stood, invisibly, behind them. Prejudice is something that those who have not experienced it can dismiss as just a word because it has no experiential or emotional content for them. But to the person who experiences prejudice of any kind it's palpable, like a wall before them that can be touched. The judge continued, 'It is relevant to this extent. Mr Stonehouse tells you that is an indication of the kind of attitude there was towards him, and the kind of pressure he had to endure.'[3] What Eveleigh clearly didn't acknowledge was that the jury may have had an 'attitude' and, equally importantly, so might he himself.

The prosecution rode the wave of press misinformation to promote their narrative that Sheila was involved from the beginning and it was a two-person conspiracy, not a one-person mental breakdown. In the summer of 1975, the customs officer who'd opened my father's trunk of clothes when it arrived in Melbourne had been interviewed by the police, so the prosecution knew that Robert Rowland Hill had seen no woman's clothing in the trunk. But they didn't disclose that to the defence, instead allowing everyone to believe what they'd read in the newspapers, that 'Stonehouse Had Secretary's Clothes Sent On'. Ian Ward's February 1975 story had said that, 'A trunk load of clothes belonging to Mr Stonehouse's secretary, Mrs Sheila Buckley, 28 … was sent to Australia last November at about the time the Labour MP disappeared.'[4] At the committal proceedings in October 1975, the prosecution presented a statement from Ward to the court saying my father had told Ward the clothes were Sheila's, adding, 'Having said this he took the black slip, held it to his waist and took a couple of dance steps as if he was dancing with its owner.' The prosecution had told the press reporters when the salacious trunk story was likely to be addressed in court, but some had missed it, so, on the 30th, a member of the Department of Public Prosecution team held an impromptu press conference after the court adjourned, reading the Ward statement at dictation speed, using court documents. The judge censured them later, by which time it was too late. The next day the headlines included the *Mirror*'s, 'The Night Stonehouse Danced with Sheila's Undies'. The *Daily Express* headline was 'Runaway MP's "petticoat polka"', and began: 'In his bedroom John Stonehouse dances alone – holding Sheila Buckley's black slip to his waist.'[5]

There'd been so much in the press about Sheila being phoned from Hawaii, met in Copenhagen, and sending letters to Melbourne – all of which was true – it was hard for anyone to accept the argument that Ian Ward's article about the trunk containing Sheila's clothes was untrue. But, while the phone calls, meeting and letters all happened *after* the disappearance, the trunk was sent from London *before*, and apparently 'proved' that Sheila was in the runaway plan from the beginning and the Stonehouse story was about a conspiracy, not a breakdown. This made the trunk a crucial issue.

On day 27 of the trial at the Old Bailey, the prosecution called Ian Ward to give evidence. Over the two days of the 7th and 8th June, and the morning of the 9th, my father cross-examined him about the trunk article, but Ward resolutely stuck to his story. Shortly after proceedings resumed on the morning of the 8th, the judge interrupted my father and basically told him to get a move on, or they'd be there until Christmas, at which point my father shouted back, 'it is not my wish to be here until Christmas', and the judge ordered him down to the cells to calm down. After fifteen minutes he was allowed to come back, and he apologised.

Ian Ward and my father were the only two people who knew what had been said in the 'unit' when the trunk was unpacked. Now they stood facing each other in the Old Bailey. Ian Ward's police statement, already aired at the committal proceedings, now became part of his testimony. It said: 'I noticed at the time that he was unpacking a considerable number of items of women's clothing which included a black slip, several dresses, what appeared to be a woman's evening bag, a daytime handbag, some shoes – possibly two pairs of women's shoes – and what appeared to be blouses. The latter were carefully folded up. I asked him who they belonged to. He said they were Mrs Buckley's and having said this he took the black slip, held it to his waist and took a couple of dance steps around the bedroom as though he was dancing with the owner.'[6] My father told the court his version of events: 'My wife went back to England leaving her things behind. When Ward came and saw the trunk I made a joke, saying "Wouldn't it be fun if they thought this was Sheila Buckley's clothing".'[7]

It could be said that Ward simply misheard, but his version of events went on to paint a graphic picture of a man hiding his mistress's clothes from his wife – aided by Ian Ward himself: 'I immediately considered the fact that his wife was arriving the next day and remarked that he would be ill-advised to retain these clothes in his apartment. He agreed and then began packing them in a red Samsonite suitcase. He suggested that we leave the suitcase at my home in Melbourne. Subsequently we drove to my home and the

red suitcase along with the contents were placed under the bed in my
room. There it stayed until the day before the arrival of Mrs Buckley
in Perth from Singapore. Early that morning I left with a photographer for Perth. Some time after my departure Mr Stonehouse called
at my mother's home. My mother was out at the time but the door
was open. Mr Stonehouse left a note to my mother together with a
bunch of flowers. When I returned from Perth the following day I
noted that the red suitcase was missing from under my bed.'[8] Ward
didn't know that the customs officer who examined the trunk when
it arrived in Melbourne would later confirm my father's version
of events – no women's clothing had been sent in the trunk from
London. Sheila had not yet arrived in Melbourne, so they could
not have been hers. The clothes belonged to my mother, who'd left
them in Yellingbo, where the trunk first arrived from the customs
warehouse. Her first trip to Melbourne was between 25th December
and 16th January, when she'd returned to London, and she'd need the
clothes again when she returned to Melbourne on the 6th February.
So why would my father transfer her clothes to a red suitcase and hide
it under Ian Ward's bed at his mother's house on the 5th February?
That made no sense at all. But the court was so reluctant to accept
this simple truth, witnesses had to be called to verify my mother had
been in Australia before Ian Ward saw the clothes in the trunk and,
given that her arrival had been on the front page of every British
newspaper, this seemed to us somewhat unnecessary.

The trunk story was causing a lot of fuss and taking up time.
On the 10th June, the day after Ward had finished testifying, the
prosecution decided they'd better admit to the defence that they'd
taken a statement from the customs officer in Melbourne, Robert
Rowland Hill, the previous year. They knew that what Ward was
saying in court was directly contradicted by Hill's statement, which
confirmed there was no women's clothing in the trunk when it
arrived in Melbourne, but embarrassing though this late disclosure might be, non-disclosure could be worse because it might give

grounds for an appeal. So it was that my father's solicitor had to set about getting a statement from Robert Hill, in Melbourne. It took some time for a variety of reasons, but eventually the statement was received and read out at the Old Bailey on the 20th July. It was the last piece of evidence to be submitted at the trial: 'I am employed by the Federal Bureau of Customs at Melbourne, Australia. On the 30th December, 1974 at Brambles Bond, Melbourne, Australia I examined trunks and cases. One of these items was shipped in the name of Joseph Arthur Markham and marked J.A. Markham. I saw this item of baggage opened in my presence and under my supervision. I did not see a blouse, a black slip or any ladies shoes or any article of ladies clothing. The item was passed for collection as being non-dutyable.'[9] Although these were some of the most important words heard at the trial they were completely ignored by the press at the time, and over the subsequent 45 years, and nobody can see the Robert Hill statement because the files pertaining to the trial at the National Archives at Kew, five in total, have nothing whatever in them from the defence side. Files one to four consist entirely of prosecution documents. File five is top secret – it's been redacted for 56 years. Following a Freedom of Information request, I've been told it's a psychiatric report – but I won't be able to read it until 2033.

The Robert Hill statement conflicted with the narrative the press had been exploiting for seventeen months – Sheila was in it from the beginning – and they weren't about to admit that. Plus, it was immediately followed by Sheila's Statement of Mitigation and the press were agog because this was the first time Sheila had spoken throughout the trial. For 45 minutes her voice could hardly be heard above thunder, the sky went black and a desk lamp had to be found for the judge so he could read his papers. Hers was the story that would be reported the next day. *The Sun's* front-page headline was 'I Thought I Was Having His Baby', the *Daily Mirror* had 'Our love-child scare, by Sheila', and the *Daily Express* 'I thought I was pregnant – Sheila'.

Judge Eveleigh made it clear to the jury that it was not their business to consider mental health issues. In his summing up, he told them: 'His condition, the pressure under which he was is a matter relevant to you to take into consideration when deciding whether you can infer he intended this, or he intended that, or was acting dishonestly and so-on, but if you come to the conclusion that he did intend to steal, if you are satisfied of that, your verdict is guilty, whatever you may conclude drove him to it. The mother who steals from the gas meter is nonetheless responsible for stealing even though she did it because she was driven to distraction by her young children and the poor state of their clothing. Those are matters which can be taken into consideration in mitigation by the court, if appropriate, but they are not matters which affect guilt itself.'[10]

At the end of the trial, Corkery spent four days summing up the prosecution case. He told the jury 'there was no question of insanity in the case, or even diminished responsibility. Mr Stonehouse's conduct was based entirely on survival, not psychiatric suicide as one doctor for the defence had suggested.'[11] Four psychiatrists gave evidence, but the judge said: 'Every person is presumed to be sane and accountable for his actions until the contrary is proved. There has been no attempt in this case to prove the contrary.'[12] The difficulty faced by the defence was that my father only saw the psychiatrists after he'd been arrested. Dr Gibney, who my father first consulted on the 1st January, said this: 'I diagnosed a depressive illness. There was severe reactive depression, which means a reaction to the circumstances in life.'[13] But, said the judge in his summing up, 'The prosecution say it is not surprising as he had just been discovered and was, in effect, in the custody of the police.'[14] They were trying to say the only reason he was crazy in January 1975 was because he got caught by the police on 24th December 1974. *That's* what made him crazy. Dr Gibney said my father had carried out a form of psychiatric suicide and that 'he had begun to cast around in a furtive inappropriate way for ways out, and for these reasons he evolved a bizarre scheme, that of establishing a new identity. He described it as a relief.'[15] The judge's response to this was: 'Doctor Gibney said there was evidence that Mr Stonehouse had been suffering from depression which had disturbed his judgement to some extent and led him to a degree of irresponsibility. However, in Doctor Gibney's view he was aware of what he was doing although he seemed able to justify his actions to himself. That means to say he told himself, well, what I have done is all right for me.'[16] If Eveleigh had been the judge at an inquest after, hypothetically, my father had thrown himself off a cliff, he would have said he was just being selfish.

The psychologist Dr Heywood said: 'It does happen with hysterical personalities that a change of identity is used as a form of escape.'[17] The judge reminded the jury that under cross-examination from the prosecution, '[Dr Heywood] agreed that the state in which he found Mr Stonehouse was possibly as a result of the failure of his plan, and the fact that the press were hounding him.'[18] Once again, the court was trying to press the idea that he wasn't crazy *before*, he was crazy *because he'd been arrested.* Professor Watson told the court: 'It seems to me quite understandable that he should feel less depressed and less anxious in moments when he could function as Markham. In that sense it seems reasonable to say it served a psychological purpose. It is possible to disappear in order to get relief and not for any other reason.'[19] Doctor R.D. Laing said: 'There was anxiety and a sense of guilt, which, on the story given to me, there was no reason to feel, and there was no way for Mr Stonehouse to escape from the pressures.' In terms of the Markham personality, Laing said: 'We have here a parallel personality running alongside Mr Stonehouse.'[20] Another witness was Maurice Miller MP, a GP my father casually consulted at the House of Commons, along with Dr John Cronin MP, and any other doctor MP he could find wandering down the corridors of power who'd give him a prescription for the Mandrax or Mogadon I saw lined up in rows of tablet bottles in his bathroom cabinet. If this trial was happening today, experts would be brought in to describe the mental effects of these two drugs, taken individually and in combination, over a two-year period. But this was 1976, when those drugs were handed out like candy, and they didn't even come into the conversation.

To us, the family, the prosecution's drive to say my father didn't have a breakdown was offensive. In Australia, during the first six months of 1975, my mother, brother and sister witnessed crazy incidents with my father behaving like another person altogether. But by the time he got to the Old Bailey in April 1976, those who came into contact with him were a step removed in time from his dual personality madness and it was easy for them to blank the breakdown out of the equation. On top of this, my father was proud and wouldn't let his weaknesses show if he could help it. He worked hard, looking as competent and mentally in control as anyone else. The essential problem – the breakdown – thus became several steps removed from current reality and people forgot about it, or ignored it, or chose not to believe it.

Sheila spoke only once during the trial, when she made her Statement of Mitigation on the last day. In this, she said that in 1974, she'd 'noticed that without any doubt Mr Stonehouse was suffering from considerable strain which had become more intense and his health, in my opinion, had greatly deteriorated. I saw him resting frequently which I had never seen him do before. Much of his zest and enthusiasm had left him – he gave the impression of being a very, very tired man. I felt he was suffering greatly as a result of the considerable pressures he was under at that time.' She talked about his state of distress when he phoned her from Hawaii and when she met him in Copenhagen – speaking in the third person, and suicidal. She had no regrets about keeping quiet about him being alive when the family thought he was dead. She said: 'Even though I find myself in this dock as a result of those actions, I cannot change my mind even now. If I had the same decisions to make all over again tomorrow, I feel certain that those decisions would remain the same. My long ordeal has been, to say the very least painful – but the safety of a man or a woman is of far greater importance than pain and humiliation. I have no regrets.'[21]

It was entirely because of my father that Sheila was in the dock at the Old Bailey. She said: 'I had no real interest in business and had, I am afraid, never really understood it.'[22] She did what so many admin people do within business organisations: sign cheques and forms without really knowing their significance. Sheila shared with my father five charges of theft, and conspiracy to defraud the creditors of EPACS – the company my father 98 per cent owned, and whose income relied totally on his efforts. Four of the charges related to cheques prepared by the accountant, Mr Le Fort, on the instruction of my father and signed by Sheila, in the amounts of £7,500, £6,981.25, £2,112.10, and £3,029.87 (totalling £19,623.22). In addition, there was a banker's draft dated 15th August payable to EPACS for US$12,500 (£5,343.97) from the Garrett Corporation, in payment for a report my father wrote for them, which had been endorsed over to my father by Sheila's signature on the reverse, as company secretary, three months before he disappeared. For the prosecution, Michael Corkery QC told the jury: 'She knew perfectly well what she was doing, removing funds from the company to use jointly when she went to Stonehouse in Australia.'[23] However, the DTI inspectors, after spending two years going through my father's business affairs with a fine-tooth comb, had a different opinion of Sheila. They asked her why she resigned in August: 'You were not, as it were, beginning to clear the decks with a view to eventual emigration?' Sheila replied, 'No, I certainly was not ... I was not a very good secretary, in that I had no knowledge of what is really required of a company secretary and/or director.' The inspectors asked again, 'Are you sure that you were not laying the ground for a departure?' Sheila said, 'I am absolutely positive, but I don't expect anybody to believe it.' Significantly, a year after the trial ended, the inspectors declared 'We do.'[24] Although the jury found my father and Sheila not guilty of the conspiracy charge of 'enabling Stonehouse unlawfully to receive payments from EPACS in the knowledge that the company would thereby become insolvent and unable to pay its lawful debts to its creditors', they found them guilty on five charges of stealing the cheques themselves.

Judge Eveleigh thought Sheila was just my father's puppet. He told her: 'You will be sentenced to two years' imprisonment on each count concurrent suspended for a period of two years. That means if you commit no further offence punishable by imprisonment in this country during that period you will hear no more of it, and I have every reason to think you will not.' With this conditional discharge, she'd walk out of the Old Bailey a relatively free person. Eveleigh told Sheila, 'I have no doubt that you were fully aware of what was going on … I have no reason to believe that deviousness is in your nature. I think you were extremely unfortunate to meet this persuasive, deceitful man, and an ambitious man. I know you will not recognise it, women in your position so rarely do.'[25] (About that statement, Sheila later wrote 'He was so wrong.'[26]) Eveleigh continued, 'Fortunately for you I recognise it, because were it not for that you would be sentenced to a term of imprisonment … but I do recognise that John Stonehouse's influence must have been tremendous. One had only to see the manner in which he sought to mesmerise the jury in this court to know that he could have told you anything, and while it is clear, as I say, that you knew the situation, I have no doubt he persuaded you your duty was to go along with him, and while you regretted having to do it, you did it.'[27] For the same charges Eveleigh sentenced my father to six years apiece, for which he'd serve prison time. In addition, he got six years for another EPACS cheque, for £3,118, which didn't involve Sheila. The way my father saw it, he was sentenced to 36 years in prison for taking £28,085.19 out of his own company.

The law relating to the taking of money from a company that is, essentially, one's own, was explained by the judge using this analogy:

'A company in law is regarded as an individual in itself, and its property belongs to it, just as the council dustcart belongs to the council and not a particular rate payer, however big his rates may be.' He elaborated: 'People may feel morally right in doing a number of things. It is said that Robin Hood felt that way, but, members of the jury, a moral right is not the same as a legal right.'[28]

The lead prosecutor, Michael Corkery QC, accused Sheila of being 'a shrewd and tough operator' and the police and DDP spent a lot of time trying to nail her into 'Plan B' before my father carried it out. But, having read all the trial witness statements I see nothing to indicate Sheila had any idea what was going on inside my father's head before he faked his death on the 20th November 1974. He phoned her two days later from Honolulu, that's after the event, and she met him in Copenhagen, after the event. They might, at that point, have discussed Sheila joining him in Australia or New Zealand in the future but, if so, it's still after the event. There's actually no evidence to indicate Sheila knew of 'Plan B' before the event; all the evidence against her was circumstantial.

But the police and prosecution were determined to paint a picture of my father and his mistress engaged in criminal conspiracy, and this can be seen in the language they used and the facts they omitted, not only during the trial but in the paperwork they submitted to the appeal judges as well. On the 24th October 1974 my father accompanied Sheila to look at a hotel at 62 Fitzjohns Avenue, Hampstead, and this is recorded in the trial appeal notes as 'Stonehouse (name?) found a room for Mrs Buckley at Highfield House Hotel, NW3'.[29] There's nothing in the receptionist's statement to suggest he 'found' it for her, and as her sister lived a ten or fifteen-minute walk away in Howitt Road, it's likely she 'found' it herself. Sheila paid £20 in advance for the room, starting on the 30th. The receptionist said the man with her said, 'I would like my wife to stay somewhere while I am away,' and the police found that very deep and telling, indicating Sheila knew he was going away. It doesn't actually mean anything other than he wanted the receptionist to know there was a man in the picture, as a kind of protective move. Strange men are more likely to stay away from a single woman when they know there's a 'husband' around. That's a fact, although men might not be as aware of it as women are.

In the timeline of events that the prosecution put before the judges, for the 29th November, they say '"Markham" arrives in Copenhagen. In Copenhagen he is visited by Mrs Buckley who travelled under the name of Mrs Morgan.'[30] What it leaves out is that my father arrived on the 29th, but didn't phone Sheila until the 4th December. She then arrived on the evening of the 6th and left on the 8th. The appeal notes give the wrong impression, especially as the next timeline entry is 8th December: 'Markham purchases air ticket to Melbourne.' The prosecution made it all too easy for the appeal judges to assume that Sheila was in Copenhagen from the 29th November to the 8th December.

The prosecution made a big deal out of the fact that my father wanted Sheila to have the financial benefit of his personal stamp collection. He'd started selling them in March 1972, when $14,516 from the sale of some of his personal collection was put directly into the EPACS account to support the company. But by 1974, he clearly wanted Sheila to have the funds from sales because on the 7th October, following a stamp sale, $1,000 had been sent to her via my father's company in Liechtenstein called Victa. On the 23rd October, he wrote to stamp dealers Stanley Gibbons saying the stamps they held for him should be considered the property of Sheila Buckley, and the payments arising from three auction sales should be sent to her. As the auctions occurred over the first two weeks of November, and he disappeared in a blaze of publicity on the 20th, Stanley Gibbons never sent Sheila any payments, preferring to wait. Sheila was also sent $970 from America, again, from a sale of some of his personal collection. To the prosecution, this sounded like collusion; to me, it sounds like a man trying to be nice to his mistress; to

Sheila, it was her lover giving her the proceeds of his own property so she could get some money together to put down as a deposit on a flat.

The police were desperate to link Sheila to 'Plan B' and their best hope related to 'Markham' phoning the Astoria Hotel sometime after the 16th October saying, according to the receptionist, thank you, he was going to Australia, and wasn't expecting mail but if it came could it be forwarded to a hotel. The police hoped to make a link to Highfield House, and Sheila. The receptionist at the Astoria thought he mentioned the hotel was in the UK but she didn't write it down. I wonder if Markham said anything of the sort, otherwise why didn't the receptionist make a note of it? All she'd have to do is write the address on any received envelope and pop it back in the post; in the event the few letters that did arrive just cluttered up the reception area. Aside from this, Sheila's association with Highfield House was well after the 16th October: she and my father first went there to make enquiries about a room on the 24th October, and Sheila first stayed there on the 30th. The police also made a lot of enquiries when trying to track down a mystery woman who phoned the Bank of New South Wales on the 29th October, saying she was Mr Markham's secretary and that he'd gone to Australia on the 25th October. Try as they might, they eventually had to admit Sheila hadn't made the call, and they never found out who did.

There were an additional fifteen charges against my father alone, including two for obtaining birth certificates in other people's names which were dropped during the trial when it was shown that there was nothing illegal in doing that. Two charges related to credit card bills of £355.95 and £422.65, for which he was sentenced to twelve years. Both amounts related to business travel that was, in the normal course of events, routinely reimbursed by the company. £355.95 was a Diners Card payment due to National Airlines for the flights London–Miami–LA–London that my father took for business in early November – when he first tried to disappear, but freaked out and couldn't. The witness for Diners Card told the court my

father had that card 'from July 1959, and it had been satisfactory
until September of 1974'. The payment for £422.65 was on my
father's American Express card and was used to pay for the ticket
Jim Charlton used to fly on that fateful 19th November, London–
Miami–New York–London for £281 plus £1.15 tax, plus £140.50
for my father's one-way ticket London–Miami. No credit card company brought charges against my father. It was only the DPP who
wanted him to go down, and they didn't seem to get the irony of
charging him for paying for his business colleague, Jim Charlton,
to fly. By the time the bills arrived my father was in the middle of a
breakdown, and on the other side of the world. If someone had said
'Look, John, you've got these two unpaid credit card bills that need
paying', he would have paid them, even if it was from his Markham
bank account. Instead, Scotland Yard quietly put the bills in a file,
waited three months, and then charged him for 'falsely pretending'
he 'intended to pay', and watched as British justice slapped him with
six years in prison for each.

He got another six years for buying £385.38 (US$870) worth
of traveller's cheques on his Barclaycard, which was unpaid at the
time of his disappearance. The sentence for applying for an American
Express card in the name of Markham was six months, and for the
forged Markham passport he got one year. He also got five years
apiece for taking out two company overdrafts, one for £7,500 and
another for £10,000, which led to charges of obtaining 'pecuniary
advantage by deception'. He applied for the first one on 29th August,
almost three months before he disappeared, at the Midland Bank,
giving a personal guarantee. I was watching the committal proceedings when the manager of Lloyds Bank, who'd given EPACS the
£10,000 overdraft on the basis of a personal guarantee, was called
as a prosecution witness. He said he still believed that guarantee to
be of value, 'because I think Mr Stonehouse has a good life ahead
of him, and is a potential force for good'. The prosecution took a
double-take: his evidence sounded like it was part of the defence.

So far, the sentences amounted to 65-and-a-half years, but the DPP weren't finished yet. They wanted to bring in charges relating to the five life insurance policies my mother had taken out in 1974, but never claimed. At the committal proceedings the magistrate, Mr Kenneth Harrington, had dismissed the life insurance charges on technicalities. The first was that the 'attempt' to defraud occurred outside the jurisdiction of the court – in Miami. The second reason is explained by my father's lawyer in these proceedings, Geoffrey Robertson QC, in his book *The Justice Game*: 'to be found guilty of "attempt" to commit crime you must have had a real go at pulling it off: the legal test is whether the act charged as an attempt (the disappearing act in Miami) was "sufficiently proximate" to the notional completed crime (the eventual payment of the insurance moneys to Barbara in England). Since Stonehouse, in order to achieve this objective, would have to remain hidden for years, and in Melbourne (then one of the world's dullest cities), my argument was that what he had done by faking his death was not close enough to the anticipated insurance claim to be punished as an "attempt".'[31] Geoffrey won the argument and the charges were dropped, but the DPP reinstated them for the trial at the Old Bailey. My father put down a question in the House of Commons asking if this was usual practice. On the 20th July he got his answer, the last written answer of his political career. The question had referred to 33 other cases, and the reply was: 'No charges were reinstated after being dismissed by the magistrates in any of the cases mentioned in the Questions for written answer on 10th May.' My father had suspected that such reinstatement of charges was unprecedented and that his treatment by the judicial system was exceptional – exceptionally harsh – and this parliamentary answer appeared to prove that true.

The DPP probably felt they had to include the life insurance charges to justify all the hoo-ha the extradition had caused, plus the press hounds wanted blood – and not much of that could be squeezed out of £29,000. There were five insurance policies that, together, totalled £125,000 – a nice big, fat, number that made his crimes look dramatic and the police heroic for nabbing him. He would be sentenced to six years for each policy, 30 years, bringing his total sentence to 95-and-a-half years. We could never understand how my father could be charged on the insurances, yet alone convicted, because they were never claimed and were, in any case, short-term, which meant they would have run out of term before any claim could be made, because, obviously, there was no dead body.

In UK law, a person can't be declared dead, or a claim made on any life insurance, until either a body has turned up, or a minimum of seven years has passed. These were the policies: Canada Life: five years – £25,000; Norwich Union: five years – £25,000; Phoenix Assurance: five years – £25,000; Royal 'Temporary Assurance': seven years – £30,000; and Yorkshire General: ten years – £20,000. The first four policies could never have been claimed; they would simply have run out of term before a court could be applied to, and a claim made. The ten-year Yorkshire General policy was taken out on the 17th July, two months after my father's car was blown to smithereens in a Heathrow Airport car park by an IRA bomb, and four months before he faked his death. This is the only policy that could have been claimed if, after seven years, a court accepted he was actually dead and there was no doubt in the form of 'sightings'. Lord Lucan's son had to wait 41 years before he was allowed to have a death certificate. There had been 'sightings' of his father, so that kept the missing file open. Given that everyone thought my father was a spy and there'd been speculation that a submarine had taken him from Miami to Cuba, they'd be looking for him in Moscow and keeping the file open. But, crucially, no claims were ever made by my mother.

The Old Bailey judge was fully aware of the short-term nature of the insurances because questions had been asked in court on that very point. In his summing up, the judge referred to what had been said: 'Cases without a body are relatively rare, because usually in this world when someone dies there is a body. Absence of seven years can lead to a presumption of death, and that is the kind of evidence that would satisfy directors ... A body is not absolutely essential. You may ask how would one proceed in the case of someone who is missing at sea. How would one proceed in the case of an air crash where perhaps bodies cannot be identified. The answer would be that same proof satisfactory to the directors should be given, and the nature of that proof you may think will vary depending on the circumstances of the death. So much for the insurance counts.'[32]

But my father didn't fall overboard from a ship, and he hadn't been in a plane crash. He didn't leave a trail of blood; he left his clothes at a beach cabana. He was missing. Each year around 200,000 people go missing in the UK and although 99 per cent are eventually found or return home, around 2,000 are lost forever. All this uncertainty explains why life insurance companies wait seven years before allowing a claim on a missing person. Before he was an MP my father sold insurance for Canada Life, including a policy to the governor of the Bank of England. At the trial he said, 'I knew quite a lot about insurance because I had worked for an insurance company ... I knew that no claim could be made without a body, or without a court decision.'[33] The judge told the jury, 'when he says he knew, of course that would presuppose it is taken for granted by everybody concerned in this case that is so. What he is meaning there is that it was his belief.'[34] Either way, what my father believed conflicted with the charge, namely that he 'dishonestly attempted to enable' my mother to claim on the insurances. If it was an 'attempt', it was risky in the extreme to expect British law to change its usual procedure in the case of no body and making the beneficiary of an insurance wait seven years before they can apply to a court for a death certificate. My father continued: 'My wife in fact approached all of them except the Royal, which I approached, because they had offices in Dover Street. Why there were so many policies was to achieve flexibility and we could let one or two lapse if required. All the premiums were paid by my wife.'[35] There was plenty of speculation, both inside and outside the family, that my father might have committed suicide but, if he had or had been suspected of having done so, the life insurances would have been invalid because life insurance does not pay out in the case of suicide.

When people are convinced someone is guilty, guilt seems the only explanation for otherwise perfectly logical events. On the 19th May 1974 my father's car was destroyed by an IRA bomb at Heathrow Airport and later that night another bomb went off at the Navy, Army and Air Force Institutes HQ, around the corner from where my parents lived in Kennington, London. My mother started thinking it would be a good idea if there was life insurance on my father, especially as he was travelling so much, and to some quite dangerous places. On the 17th June, the IRA bombed the Houses of Parliament, injuring eleven people. My mother requested a Canada Life agent to come to the house in Kennington, where they met at teatime on the 4th July. He left her with a five-year proposal form for my father to sign. On the 17th July, a bomb went off at the Tower of London, killing one person and seriously injuring 41, many of them children. On the 22nd July, Norwich Union received a proposal form from my mother, along with a letter which, according to the agent's witness statement, 'intimated that the proposal form was for temporary insurance cover on her husband's life'. This was another five-year term policy, as was the Phoenix Assurance policy my mother arranged shortly after.

London was a very dangerous place at the time. IRA bombs were going off left, right and centre. In 1973, 100 people had been injured in London by bombs at King's Cross and Euston stations, and the five car bombs that exploded outside key locations including the Home Office and the Old Bailey. 1974 was much worse, and in February twelve people were killed on a bus. A further 28 would lose their lives in pubs in Guildford, Woolwich and Birmingham, with 226 injured. In London, five bombs were placed in letter boxes, injuring 40, and other targets included Harrods, Selfridges, and various restaurants. Nowhere was safe in 1974, and we were not the only family taking out life insurance that year. On the very day we were told about my father's disappearance, 21st November, an IRA bomb in Birmingham killed at least seventeen, with innumerable life-changing injuries.

The judge was very keen to emphasise the fact that my mother's solicitor had written to the insurance companies three weeks after he disappeared, even though those letters made it clear my mother was not making a claim and just noted she was aware of the insurance policies, and the judge overlooked the fact that my mother was replying to mail she'd received. For example, on the 28th November 1974 – eight days after my father disappeared – Martyn Jones of Canada Life wrote saying, 'no doubt you will keep us informed of the position as appropriate'. My mother replied to him on the 3rd December, saying, 'As you can imagine we are going through a form of nightmare here, hoping against hope that it has all been some ghastly mistake. We are still making all kinds of enquiries and obviously this is going to take some time. I'm about to see the police this afternoon to ask them to look into another area of search as a result of a very similar case we've just heard of. But it's all pretty depressing and nerve-wracking. The press have been unbelievable but at least we have been surrounded by good friends and family. I'll be in touch if I have any news.'

My parents had a big row about Martyn Jones of Canada Life on the 26th May 1976. Arguments between them were so unusual that my mother made a note about it, from which I quote now. She wrote: 'Tonight, the first real words of anger to pass between us since John's return from Australia.' She'd picked him up in the car from Lambeth Bridge, finding him 'lower and more dejected than at any time during the trial. Apparently, a young insurance man named Martyn Jones had been a prosecution witness during the day and had followed a question-and-answer exchange with completely unsolicited remarks of his own to the effect that when he met me to discuss the insurance scheme I had said that my husband had asked me (instructed me, I'm not sure which) to acquire the insurance cover. John felt that the prosecution regarded this as the best and biggest break in the trial hitherto.' When they got home my mother went through the file and found a letter to her from Jones which hadn't been submitted by the prosecution. 'Of course they wouldn't,' said my father, 'they're only interested in anything that would link me with the insurance, so they've omitted yours and produced one sent to me after I'd been to the doctor.' My mother wrote, 'What must have happened was that he had transposed remarks I'd made about discussing the question of insurance with John into an instruction to purchase the insurance. It was an understandable mistake in the circumstances.' But my father said, 'It was no mistake. The police have been drilling him all day. He's been waiting around all day and only came on the stand about 3pm. He's so hostile to me.' This is what my father was dealing with – conniving police and prosecution, all determined to see him do jail time for the insurances.

At committal, the defence lawyers had focused their attention on two technical points relating to the insurance: the 'attempt' to defraud occurred in Miami – outside the jurisdiction of the court; and the 'attempt' was not 'sufficiently proximate' to where the insurance pay-out might occur, namely England. Lawyers would obsess about these two points through several further legal proceedings, but they were red herrings. The essential point was that they were short-term policies and literally couldn't be claimed. Unfortunately though, the Old Bailey judge instructed the jury to convict on the insurances on the basis of the technical red herrings, and the more common-sense point about them being unclaimable short-term policies was lost in the fog of law. Judge Eveleigh took the decision about the insurances out of the jury's hands by telling them that a higher court would rule on it, if his direction was wrong: 'There is an attempt by the accused within the legal meaning of that word attempt if you are satisfied that the matters I have stated to you are proved. I am going to repeat that, that he falsely staged his death by drowning, dishonestly intending that a claim should be made and the money obtained in due course, sooner or later. If I am wrong about that, there is a higher Court that will put me right. That is the definition you have to follow in this case.'[36]

That direction of Judge Eveleigh led to a change in law – 'the law in Stonehouse' – whereby a judge cannot any longer instruct a jury to find the defendant guilty. The proceedings that led to the legal change is found under 'Director of Public Prosecutions v Stonehouse: HL 1977' and in them Lord Salmon said: 'Anyone in the judge's position might easily have made the slip which he did of not leaving the jury to decide whether the facts proved amounted to the attempt charged,' adding, 'I am completely satisfied that no miscarriage of justice could have resulted from what technically was a misdirection.'[37]

Judge Eveleigh's summing up was long. It began on 2nd August and went on until the 4th and, to read it, it covers 130 pages. My father wrote to me from Cell No. 11 at the Old Bailey on the 3rd, saying of the judge: 'He is awful and cunning with it, skilfully giving the impression to the jury of objectivity but all the time weighing the balance decidedly against me.' On Thursday the 5th August, the jury retired at 10.55am and returned at 8.10pm with four unanimous verdicts. The jury were already down to eleven members due to the ill health of one, and the judge told them, 'I am in a position now to accept a verdict from you upon which at least ten of you are agreed,'[38] and sent them off to a hotel for the night.

Early the next morning, before the jury had decided the final seventeen verdicts, and before Judge Eveleigh sentenced my father to 95-and-a-half years, the front page of the *Daily Express* blasted like a bomb into our family with the headline: 'Stonehouse guilty on 4 counts as wife says: I'll cite Sheila WHY I'LL DIVORCE JOHN'.[39] The newspaper had made it look like an exclusive interview with my mother but, in fact, the reporter, Paul Hopkins, had cobbled together a two-page story using information from various sources. In the spring of the previous year my mother had told a friend, who we later discovered had been sleeping with an editor in the Beaverbrook Newspapers group, that she would probably eventually have to divorce my father. At that time in 1975, my mother had recently returned from Melbourne, where it had become clear to her that my father and Sheila had been having an affair for years and that divorce was probable some time in the future. She had told the friend in confidence, but that so-called friend had told her lover and he had told Paul Hopkins to use the information when it would have maximum impact. That day had come, fifteen months later. My mother was warned about the upcoming *Daily Express* story on Thursday 5th by a phone call from a journalist at another newspaper, and she immediately phoned the editor of the *Daily Express*. He wouldn't take her calls, so she phoned her lawyer and they both spent most of the night frantically trying to get an injunction to stop the fabricated story. They failed, and by dawn the presses were running. Jane wrote in her diary on the night of the 5th: 'Ma has a story breaking tomorrow – about divorce. Poor thing. She's under so much strain she doesn't really know how to cope. Paul Hopkins has finally done the dirty.' Isolated as he was in Brixton Prison and at the court, my father didn't know the background to the story, which we all thought influenced the judge to hand down the excessively long sentences. My mother wrote to my father as soon as the final sentences were announced on Friday 6th August. He replied to her the following Wednesday, from his cell at Wormwood Scrubs Prison: 'I appreciate the difficulty you were put in by H**** and of course it is for you to handle the situation in the way you think fit … I shall always be grateful for your love, which I treasure. As you so rightly say we achieved great things and some marvellous happiness.'

Also that morning, Friday 6th August 1974, the *Daily Telegraph*'s front page had twenty passport-sized photographs of my father, that had been in his attaché case when he was arrested. They'd come from their correspondent, Ian Ward, eighteen months earlier. The caption referred to one of the four guilty verdicts delivered the previous day: 'uttering a forged application for a passport in the name of Joseph Arthur Markham'. My father immediately knew the source of these images was Ian Ward, and it reminded him, as if he needed it, of all the trouble Ward had caused. In early February 1975, while my mother was in London and my father vulnerable and looking for an ally, Ian Ward had suggested he could help my father write a book. In his police statement Ward said: 'Mr Stonehouse some days prior to the arrival of his wife, gave to me for safe keeping his black attaché case, this contained according to him all the private papers, concerned with his disappearance in Florida and his subsequent trip to Australia. It was his stated intention that these would be used to illustrate the proposed book. This attaché case was also kept under the bed next to the red suitcase.' Ward arranged for a photographer, Mr Howe, to photograph 'the entire contents of the attaché case'. The negatives and one set of prints were given to my father, apparently, but 'the other set of prints I sent to my office in London'.[40] My father did not give Ward his attaché case 'for safe keeping' only for Ward to send photos of the entire contents to his newspaper. Undoubtedly, Ward did not have my father's permission to do that.

At 4pm, the jury returned their final verdicts, and then Judge Eveleigh passed sentence. My sister Jane recorded in her diary what she saw in court: 'The judge was absolutely obscene – he said Pa was a hypocrite, deceitful, all the things he accused others of being. That's why he broke down dummy. I could shake him by the neck – tightly. I have never witnessed such vitriol – he loathed Pa. Obviously thought he was lying all the way through. The adjectives, dishonest, deceitful, persuasive, ambitious, greedy – on and on. Didn't believe he was an idealist. Didn't mention the breakdown. His venom was shattering. Pa stood impassively. Gave a sincere thank you and mitigation – about the years he's worked for others. About nobody being hurt except his family. Judge not listening *at all*. Callous. He *hated* Pa attacking the establishment.' Judge Eveleigh said about a deterrent sentence: 'Its principal object is to inform others that they cannot profit by this kind of behaviour or any criminal behaviour.'[41] Well, I'm sure the sentence of 95-and-a-half years sent that message out loud and clear.

❖

My father instructed his lawyers to appeal on all charges and sentences, but they had other ideas. For the appeal, he was represented in January 1977 by Louis Blom-Cooper QC and Geoffrey Robertson. The paperwork for Appeal 4265R76 shows that 'counsel having abandoned in court the application for leave to appeal on the remaining counts',[42] they pursued just one tiny legal technical point to do with the insurances: the red herring concerning the 'attempt having occurred outside the jurisdiction of the English Courts'. My father was furious. He wrote to me from Blundeston Prison on 26th January 1977: 'You will have heard the result of the so-called Appeal. Well, if that doesn't confirm the prejudice I have been up against then nothing will. It also confirms the incredible self-orientation of counsel. I gave clear instructions to Blom-Cooper QC through my solicitor that appeals must be lodged against all convictions and grounds for appeal were available in the judge's summing up which was rigged against me. Instead he decided to appeal only on legal points on the insurance charges and dropped the rest in court without advising me, of course … He did ask for the sentence to be reviewed but leave to appeal was refused on that so he couldn't even deploy the arguments and, as you know, his previous legal argument was knocked down flat. And the price he paid for that was to say on my behalf that I accept conviction on all the other charges which I damned well don't.'

On 6th February 1977, he wrote again, saying, 'My disgust is strongest for counsel who regard the whole sordid business as a game with clients merely props to be used for their own grotesque and arcane pleasures. Mine never followed my instructions and actually <u>abandoned</u> the appeal against convictions on all charges except the insurance ones although there were powerful reasons for complaint in the twisted summing-up of the judge on these counts quite apart from the basic illogicality of being convicted of stealing from oneself. I understand only too clearly what went through his mind. He calculated that by abandoning them he could curry favour with the appeal judges and would then be able to argue his favourite insurance points in a favourable climate. But they threw it all back and made him look silly. He came on Friday. Full of bounce and blasé as hell. Appointment was for the morning postponed until 3.30pm then they arrived ¾ hour late so giving us very little time. One feels at the end of everyone's list of priorities. I said "what have you got to say" BC said "I have nothing to say, what have you got to say to me." Which made me speechless for fifteen minutes.'

The appeal judges had had before them a letter from the senior medical officer at Blundeston Prison, Francis Eteng, which read: '[He] went on to say that he "had a nervous breakdown progressively from 1974 and on looking back it must have been coming on since 1971 because a psychiatrist called L. Howard in Sussex, after examining his paintings, thought that he was heading for a nervous illness." Describing this nervous illness he said that following the collapse of his ideals he became tense, sleepless, perspiring at night, behaving in an hysterical manner and disorientated; in fact, he attributes all his anti-social behaviour to this condition but he did not seek medical advice because "reason had gone out of him".' Eteng then goes through the usual physical medical history, and concludes: 'He has "doubtful" insight into his condition and I think he has a tendency to exaggerate the normal stresses and strains of life and to wishfully think that he had a nervous breakdown which gave rise to his irresponsible conduct, and, as such, wants to be pitied.'[43] I don't know what Eteng considered 'the normal stresses and strains of life', but I suggest that being branded a communist spy during the era of threatened nuclear war is not one. And neither were the other major stresses being put upon him from 1972 onwards.

In a confusion of ignorance, a huge whirlpool developed, generated by the suspicion he was a spy, exacerbated by his obvious infidelity, fuelled by his financial difficulties, and driven faster ever downwards by the money-making potential of negative or false press stories. I wish my father had never been caught in Melbourne and had succeeded in his escape from reality, living a calm life playing chess, listening to jazz and classical music, soaking up the sun. He might have lived to the age of 83, when he could have used the newly released StB file to prove to the world that he was, in fact, innocent of that heinous charge of treason. As it was, he very nearly died in prison and, aside from Sheila and the family, nobody cared. They all thought he deserved it.

16

Prisoner 334093 and the Broken Heart

My father was escorted from the dock of the Old Bailey and taken to the 19th-century Wormwood Scrubs Prison, where he would join another 1,200 men. He described it as 'an ancient series of buildings with gross overcrowding'. As a 'long-server' he was allowed the privilege of working, riveting strips of aluminium together to make louvres for windows destined for DIY stores. In a good week he could earn £1 to spend in the canteen. He wrote: 'I had a succession of inmates to share my room (always three of us) and got on very well with all of them, which was important in view of the long hours spent together.' He wrote to Jane two weeks after the end of the trial, saying, 'when I look back I realise just what a terrible job we had to push back that wall of prejudice. I suppose there was no way in which we could have won against the combined pressure of the media and the establishment. It was too much to hope for.' From his prison cell, he resigned as a privy counsellor on the 17th August and, finally, as an MP on the 27th. The Home Office press release announcing that he was being transferred to Blundeston Prison, near Lowestoft, on the 25th November, referred to it as an 'open' prison, and the press would consistently refer to it as such. It wasn't. Blundeston was a high-security prison, with all that entails.

Two days later, he wrote to Jane, saying, 'I have been feeling happier and more relaxed than for at least four years and possibly longer. I feel more like a whole person. As I look back I realise how unhappy I was during the period of Labour Government (particularly when

I was in the Post Office and after). It was such a fraud on the British public and I was part of the squalid sham. Trying to break out of it worked for a time in 1970 and 1971 but Bangladesh was a truly terrible trauma for me. And those vicious attacks on me in connection with the formation of BBT were the last straw. My breakdown began then. I was desperately unhappy carrying that burden and working against such odds. I was always disguising from everyone just how depressed I was because I didn't want to worry or hurt anyone. And nearly everyone around me went blithely on behaving as if everything in the garden was lovely while my world and my life was gradually disintegrating. Of course I was foolish not to confide in you and others but I was anxious to save them the terrible anguish I was suffering hoping, as I did, that I would find the solutions to the impossible problems. But there are no solutions for the simple reason that idealism and politics, and idealism and business do not mix. Anyone trying this impossible mix is bound to be crushed – although circumstances sometimes are not serious enough for them to realise it and they muddle on.'

'I am telling you all this – not because it is new to you as you have understood so well and you have been so good and kind in listening – but simply to emphasise the wonderful joy I feel now. I am free in the real sense of the word for I have both found my identity and I have shed those terrifying burdens. It is truly wonderful to be treated as an ordinary human being. Carrying a public persona (even when things are going relatively well) is a strain and when one is reviled, abused and pilloried as I have been for the past nearly two years it is sheer torture. But now I am treated as an ordinary prisoner it is a marvellous relief for me. There were some idiots who thought I wanted special treatment. From their subjective point of view it is probably what they expected of a man who had apparently earlier enjoyed privilege. That, of course, was a complete reverse of the truth – I wanted nothing but to be treated as badly or as well as the most unprivileged member of the community. And the fact that I have had such treatment has been the real cause of my amazing recovery. I have had no suffering since August 6th, it has been a pleasure to experience, the worst possible conditions at the Scrubs are so much better than the tension and desolation that I had to bear before.' He writes that the conditions at Blundeston are so much better, then says, 'I was happy at the Scrubs but I expect to be even happier here. I will soon be working of course in one of the workshops (as I did at the Scrubs) but even so I find it more relaxing than anything I've done in twenty years (or even 30 years). There is simply no pressure. I am learning at last what a joy it is to have an "ordinary" life.'

Sheila sent my father four letters a week, and was allowed a visit once every two weeks. He was put to work making box files for the government, which seemed ironic, and was paid £1.30 a week to produce 120 boxes while standing on his feet seven hours a day. He spent the money on tea, powdered milk and honey. To exercise, he practised yoga. In December, he heard that the appeal would take place in January and decided not to attend because, 'my presence will make hackles raise and personal resentment return. They do hate me so – and I don't know why – except that I attack all their sacred cows.' The day before the appeal he wrote to Jane: 'I have had no opportunity of discussing the matter with counsel. They were too busy to come all the way out here. The last time I saw Geoffrey was briefly in August at the Scrubs ... I've written out copious notes on the judge's summing-up but of course have no idea how counsel react to them. As you can imagine my blood boiled on re-reading that stuff. It was so cunningly done. I was an innocent crucified in a sacrificial rite. And it is called justice. I still ask myself "how can one steal from himself?" Do you know that of the miserable £27,000 or so £10,000 was salary from EPACS which I was entitled to draw anyway. And to charge me with "pecuniary advantage by deception" for merely giving personal guarantees shows the lengths they were prepared to go to get me. William Stern gave personal guarantees for £110 million and no one suggests he obtained "pecuniary advantage by deception" although it is as plain as a pikestaff that he could not be worth that sort of money in his individual capacity. But that's exactly what they got me on! And the credit cards – just a few weeks overdue. And no complainants. No one saying "we was robbed". As you can see I am still uptight, as you would say, about it and the appeal tomorrow has brought on this surge of resentment on my part. And by golly I am resentful of the system which came down on me on such scanty allegations.'

The next day proved to be a terrible blow because my father learned that his QCs, Louis Blom-Cooper and Geoffrey Robertson, had not appealed all the charges and sentences, as he had instructed them. He was furious. He wrote to Jane on the 7th February, saying, 'The games some people play! I am more than ever convinced that this country has acquired a special tribe of witchdoctors, the sooth-sayers who can never be questioned and who run their own lucrative club – financed by a social security called legal aid – and who play with pawns they call clients.'

In his 23rd January letter to Jane, he'd written about his mother: 'Have just had a most bitter note from my mother. If you can bear it would you ring her and pacify her. If only she could understand. Perhaps if she read *Death of an Idealist* she would get it; trouble is she is part of the early problem but how can one tell her that.' With the stresses of the outside world impinging on the peace of incarceration, it was a blessing that he'd been allocated a share in an allotment. He had to pay for the seeds out of his £1.30 a week earnings but, by 11th March, he wrote to me that he'd planted 50 strawberry plants, a blackcurrant bush, raspberries, gladioli, chrysanthemums and Canterbury bells. He had plans for tomatoes and melons. Some kind stranger called Peters had sent him a book about the agricultural community at Findhorn, and he was contemplating utilising some of their methods.

The following week my father had to meet with the DTI inspectors and, the week after that, attend preliminary bankruptcy hearings.

On the 3rd April, he wrote to Jane about it: 'The examination in bankruptcy was, as you realised from the reports, (although most of those were misleading) a farce. In fact it should not have taken place but deferred, as the Official Receiver intended all the time, to October. They just wanted a bit of circus and expected me to cooperate!' Two weeks later, he had his first heart attack, with symptoms lasting four days. He wrote to me later: 'I think the attack was brought on by the stress and strain of being dragged back to London like a bear on a chain to the circus of the bankruptcy hearings. That experience brought back with a vengeance all the tensions of the three years before; indeed I began to feel similar symptoms to my breakdown in 1974.'

Four days later he had a second heart attack, the symptoms of which were sudden onset of crushing central chest pain which lasted for about twelve hours, accompanied by leg pain, vomiting, sweating and shortness of breath. He was given one aspirin and one valium by a medical 'trustee' and allowed to rest in his cell over that weekend. On the Monday morning a doctor came and told him to get to work. He was put on 'light' duties, which included cleaning the toilets, walking up and down stairs, and moving heavy furniture around. A psychiatrist at Blundeston, Dr Roberto, said his attacks were psychosomatic, which fed into the prison's general theory that he was just malingering. On the 11th May he was taken in the back of a taxi at high speed to Lowestoft Hospital for a mass X-ray, handcuffed and between two warders. This was always how the prison authorities would transport him to his various visits. On the 13th, he was taken to Great Yarmouth Hospital for a 'routine' ECG, but was admitted into intensive care on an emergency basis. It inconvenienced the prison to have two warders at the hospital, so he was only allowed to stay for 36 hours. My father's consultant, Dr Oliver, was horrified to later discover that he'd not been given any medication, specifically glyceryl trinitrate, and out-patient treatment would not be allowed by the prison authorities.

I wrote to the governor of Blundeston on 18th May 1977, concerned that the heart attack hadn't been taken seriously at the time, and that similar casualness might be adopted with any future incident. The Home Office replied saying the current medical management of mild heart attacks 'consists of only a very short initial period of rest and then encouragement to return to a full and active existence as soon as possible in order to prevent the development of what used to be known as cardiac neurosis, which resulted in a person, who had completely recovered from a heart attack, living the life of a complete invalid with the limitations and unhappiness that this entailed under the erroneous impression that this might prevent further attacks'.[1] He was put in the prison hospital wing, where his 'treatment' consisted of valium, from where he wrote to Jane about the view from his window: 'the massive double fence with barbed wire atop (it is put there to keep all my enemies, especially reporters, outside)'.

On the 22nd May he wrote to me that, 'I have resorted to poetry as an outlet for my frustration. Imagine that! And I never had patience for it before!' He'd written a poem to Jane a few days before that included lines he'd penned following the journey to Lowestoft Hospital:

> Today I saw wild bluebells in a wood;
> T'was a glorious revelation which can be understood;
> Only by one who senses the feeling;
> Of the agony that deprivation in my soul was seeking;
> Beautiful innocence of those wild flowers convey;
> Such contrast to the mechanical world of 'obey';
> Their freedom more noble in a sense;
> Than the tulips standing erect, in order, behind a garden fence.

The last verse of the poem gave a clue as to how the initial euphoria of being 'ordinary' had been replaced by the tedium of prison life:

Insignificant little things, maybe to some;
But a whole world of difference to the life, humdrum;
Of keys and locks and tedious sameness;
Day after day, on us inflicted, quite shameless.

At least he was about to get some mental stimulation, because the prison's education department had arranged for him to take a degree in English through the University of London. His focus would now be on Chaucer, Shakespeare, the Gothic writers Hugh Walpole et al, and Keats, Shelley and Byron.

In July my mother's decree nisi came through. It happened to coincide with the death and funeral of my father's uncle – his mother's favourite brother and her best friend. We were concerned that the press would descend on her to ask what she thought about the divorce, and so unfortunately, because the press can't be controlled, we had to break the news about the divorce right after the funeral. A short and innocuous story about the divorce in the *Daily Express* on the 20th was annoying nevertheless, because it contained a 'quote' from my mother that she'd never said. Jane wrote to my father about it: 'I expect Sheila will tell you about the stupid *Express* story. I was sitting next to ma when silly and malicious Don Cooligan rang. I heard all of what she said and she then told us all what he had said. Which was that he'd rung S's pa who said that she was having nothing more to do with you. He was obviously trying to get her going but she was very cool and said she'd heard nothing of that rumour and even if she had she wouldn't make a comment on it as it wasn't her place to. And you must have seen the front page. It makes me so sick … even when you don't talk to the buggers you know they'll print what they feel like anyway and you just pray that maybe that particular reporter will have an ounce of integrity … but that is so rare in Fleet St., if it exists at all. Anyway, you know that better than

I do.' I think it's very hard for people who've never had the misfortune of being 'media fodder' to understand what actually goes on. We felt like 'media fodder' because we were chewed up and spat out, but from the journalists' point of view we were like tubes of paint to squeeze and get whatever material they could to concoct into a picture of their own imagination and liking. The fact that the picture is a fabrication is known only to them, and the tubes of paint, but not to the general reader.

On the 8th September, Jane wrote to the prime minister, Jim Callaghan, asking that our father be moved to an open prison – perhaps to Kirkham, where they had 200 spare beds. He referred the letter to the Home Office, who passed it to the regional director of the prison department, who replied: 'it would not be appropriate for me to discuss the reasons for the decision taken in your father's case.' There were many such letters of appeal over the years, with no success. The government would make a point not to give him the 'special consideration' they would give to anyone else. They didn't want it to look as if they were giving 'favours' to one of their own, so they leant in the other direction. And the length of the sentence was beginning to get to our father. On the 13th September, he wrote, 'out of here in three years four months and twenty-nine days'.

His mother was becoming increasingly ill and on the 28th November he wrote and told me: 'I made a request to speak to her myself which seems reasonable as she is in no fit state to travel here but that cannot be approved here as it is against the regulations. The Home Office has not yet given me a reply but I expect the request will be rejected.' Communication with the outside world was always a problem. He wasn't allowed to receive money, even if it was only to pay for stamps. Everything had to come out of the weekly 'pay' which, in October, was 80p a week for his cleaning job. This had to pay for extra postage as well as shampoo, toothpaste, tea, milk, etc. He wrote: 'It has made me very economical (I practically count the grains of tea).'

Even from his prison cell my father observed politics and wrote: 'The awful thing is that the petty bickering and sheer incompetence is still evident in this Government and is even worse than the 1964–70 vintage. The hypocrisy is rampant. But I must not dwell on such subjects or I shall be getting depressed and that would never do. My health is reasonable in the circumstances; this place is extremely comfortable in the circumstances; the food is very good in the circumstances; I am playing better bridge after hours of practice; the chess is excellent and Jane's old radio, although now split into four pieces, continues to issue forth a wonderful diet of music – so I have no complaints, well almost no complaints, in all the circumstances.'

On 14th December, the Department of Trade published the results of their inquiry into his businesses. The newspapers particularly liked the quote that he was, 'A man for whom truth was a moving target … and who used companies as if they were an additional hip pocket in his trousers.' It was curious how the report managed to both excuse and blame all the other people concerned. The report said 'Justice cannot be done to many of those we have to criticise without an appreciation of the effect of Mr Stonehouse's personality on them. Most held him in awe and great respect. He treated them well, took them for walks along the corridors of power and enabled them to rub shoulders with men and women of considerable eminence.' Is this saying that people who worked with him were so star struck by meeting politicians in the grubby, claustrophobic environment of the House of Commons they became incapable of doing their job? Maybe they just couldn't do their job. Maybe that had a lot to do with why problems developed. The report said of the accountant, John McGrath, that he 'played a direct part in transactions of a most dubious kind'. The young and impressionable accountant, Alan Le Fort, was accused of keeping records 'deliberately fragmented and complicated the entries for the purposes of camouflage'. Sir Charles Hardie of the firm who audited the BBT accounts was accused by the inspectors of 'a serious dereliction of duty' and the audit as 'thoroughly slipshod'.[2]

Despite all the criticism, no charges were brought by the DPP and instead the DTI inspectors recommended changes to the law, specifically the Companies Act 1948. They suggested to the minister concerned that, 'Companies should not be permitted to lend money on the security of their own shares,' and that Section 54 (Sections 190 and 197) relating to loans to directors should be amended because they contain 'exemption for loans made in the ordinary course of business'.[3] The DTI inspectors wrote: 'The DPP has seen the report and no further action is envisaged against Mr Stonehouse neither does the DPP propose to take any action against any of the individuals mentioned in the report.'[4]

A new year began. In January 1978 my father borrowed *The Frolik Defection* from the library, and wrote to Jane on the 12th: 'The country is mad to get excited about such trivia spread about by a renegade who obviously had to ingratiate himself with the CIA. The reason for the ridiculous stories is found in another part of the book where Frolik attacks his colleagues for stealing expense account monies by faking their reports with fictitious agents.' I wish my father had lived long enough to see the pathetic StB file that Frolik never actually saw, and had been alive to clear his own name. It was a dark shadow that followed him to death, and long beyond.

On the 27th, he attended the final bankruptcy court hearing, where he said: 'If I had not had a breakdown and had been in control of ongoing companies there would have been no bankruptcy.' Once all the hyperbole had died down, it transpired that he had claims of £258,164 and assets of £137,185, giving a shortfall of £120,979. He wrote to me on the 30th: 'It is marvellous to get it over.' He'd spent a night at Wormwood Scrubs Prison, saying, 'It was quite fascinating going back and not at all horrifying as one might have imagined. I had one of my best night's sleep (9 to 7) in a shared cell despite the extra noises there. I suppose I am becoming institutionalised after all this time. London (particularly the East End) looked as run down and filthy as ever and the people appeared miserable. Something has happened to this country. It is in a decline from which neither Jim's [Callaghan] exhortations nor North Sea oil will extricate it.'

On the 23rd May 1978, he wrote sad and despondent letters to both Jane and I. The state of African politics was getting him down, and he was worried about what would happen in South Africa. He wrote: 'Can anyone have any faith in the human race after the Nazis, Bangladesh, Vietnam, Ethiopia, Uganda and now the Congo again. When I was young I had such faith that goodness could win over evil, that people were honourable and once organised democratically could create a paradise. It will never happen. Men – and women – are greedy, feckless, cruel and brutal and need discipline to control them.' Even his 250 strawberry plants couldn't keep his spirits high. He wrote, 'I am sick to death with people and I am sure you know what I mean,' signing off with: 'I am thinking of you a lot and hoping you can get some happiness from the hard stone of existence.' This was the day his application for parole was to be heard, and he was stressed. He didn't know that the local review committee heard positive recommendations from the welfare department, the probation department, the prison wardens and the governor himself. As far as they were all concerned, parole should be granted. But somewhere between them and the parole board, or the home secretary, it was going to be denied – news we'd hear on the 19th September 1978, long after other prisoners had received their decisions. It seems my father's case had gone through some extra bureaucratic loops, which would form into his noose. June and July came and went with no news. The wait was agonising, and yet another expression of the cruelty we'd come to expect from British 'authorities'.

On the 13th August 1978, my father collapsed with another heart attack. He spent sixteen days at Lowestoft Hospital, where Sheila visited every day and Jane, Mathew and I would often see her. Sheila had been, metaphorically speaking, at my father's side through this whole imprisonment period. It was only now that he told us how bad he'd been feeling; he'd been trying to be stoic. From Lowestoft Hospital, he was driven in handcuffs to Wormwood Scrubs Prison hospital, where the conditions were notoriously draconian. A psychiatric consultant, Dr Tony Whitehead, later said, 'Conditions inside the Scrubs hospital are like those in a poor kind of mental hospital in the bad old days. It really is like an old Poor Law institution – wholly unsuitable for any kind of convalescence.'[5] A social worker, Rosalind Kane, wrote a critical report about the place and said, 'I came across endless men who tried to commit suicide because of the isolation, the lack of visits, and contact from families at a time when they needed them most.'[6] In Wormwood Scrubs Prison hospital wing, a person was allowed one half-hour visit every two weeks, and to send three letters a week – if the sadistic staff felt like facilitating them.

On the 6th September my father had a schematic attack, a cross between a heart attack and angina, which the so-called medical staff at the Scrubs ignored. It was only picked up days later when doctors from Hammersmith Hospital came to see him on a routine visit. They rushed him into Hammersmith where, on the 15th, my grandmother and Sheila happened to visit at the same time. My grandmother apparently told the *Daily Mail*: 'When I went in she was sitting holding his hand ... I don't think we spoke because there was nothing for me to say to her. She at least had the decency to leave. I believe Sheila Buckley was the cause of John's marriage break-up.'[7] On the 17th, radioactive dye was released into his heart to facilitate X-rays but, while this was being done, his heart stopped and was only revived after electric shocks were delivered through the cardiac catheter.

He was still terribly stressed waiting to hear news about his parole application, and the bad news that it had been refused came two days later, on the 19th, when he was sent back to the Scrubs hospital wing to wait for the urgent heart bypass surgery that was being delayed because of industrial strike action by the maintenance workers at Hammersmith Hospital. This was a really scary time for us all. He was lying in that horrific place, all alone except for the sadistic guards, knowing that his heart could give out again at any moment, and his parole had been refused by the faceless, cold-hearted 'powers that be'. It was literally like living inside a terrifying movie. We weren't with him, but the cruelty of the situation ran through our veins.

We all started campaigning for his release from prison on health grounds. We sent endless letters to the press and the Home Office, and were never off the phone. On the 31st October Sheila was sent a letter from the private secretary of Merlyn Rees, the home secretary, saying 'under the parole rules each subsequent parole review after the first must take place not less than 10 and not more than 14 months later … the Home Secretary orders a fresh review only in exceptional circumstances. The Home Secretary has now carefully considered Mr Stonehouse's case in the light of your letters, but I am afraid that he can find no grounds for asking the Parole Board to reconsider his case before the normal statutory date.'

Jane and Sheila gave a joint interview to the *Sunday Mirror* which was published on 15th October. A doctor at the hospital had told Jane that my father was in an 'extremely hazardous condition', and she described a visit she and Sheila had recently made: 'He is like something out of a horror film. Ghostly white as though Dracula has sucked the blood from his body. It was very emotional. We both held hands with him and tried to keep up his spirits. He was desperately low. But it was obvious to me that Sheila is his lifeline.' Jane said she already regarded my father and Sheila as married. In this visit, my father first revealed the truth about his experience in Blundeston Prison and he wrote to Jane about it when he was returned to Wormwood Scrubbs, saying he'd felt 'enormous strain caused by the constant humiliation from a majority of the staff'. Up to this time, as Jane told the *Sunday*

Mirror, 'he has always held things back, frightened to cause a fuss and spoil his chance of parole. Now he's got nothing to lose – except his life.'[8] My father thought his especially mean treatment was just because he was a public figure. For example, because of his bad back, he'd asked for a bed board to put under the mattress, but he would come back to his cell to find it had been removed for no reason, which meant he had to sleep on the floor.

On the 30th October Jane and I went to Oxford, where the home secretary, Merlyn Rees, was addressing the University's Fabian Society. During the Q&A sessions I accused him of withholding permission for parole, which he denied, telling us 'you girls are doing yourself no good by coming here'. Rees said: 'Ill health is not a factor in parole. The local board makes a judgement. If the parole board say he is to be paroled, it will come forward to me.' We knew that the review committee had approved my father's parole, so the problem had occurred further up the line of authority. Jane told the press: 'It was an act of desperation. If Joe Bloggs had done what my father had done he would be out by now.'[9] Jane wrote to Rees on the 6th November, asking what he'd meant by 'doing yourselves no good', and his assistant replied saying that, 'whilst, of course, the concern you are expressing cannot in any way jeopardise or delay your father's release, at the same time it will not alter the facts upon which decisions must rest'.[10] As it stood, my father was due for release in March 1981, but first he had to get through heart surgery scheduled for the following week.

My father's brother, Bill, who lived in New Zealand with his new wife, had a trip planned to the UK, and thought he'd get a health check-up in Harley Street. He was told that because their father had died of a heart attack at age 64, and because his 53-year-old brother was about to undergo heart surgery, it would be a good idea to have two heart bypasses as a kind of preventative measure. Bill, who was 57, had been checked in to have the procedure at Westminster Hospital. I was with my father at Hammersmith Hospital when Bill came to visit, bringing the autobiography of John Masters – the author of 25 books who'd initially had difficulty finding a publisher. It was a kind of 'don't give up' story. I left the brothers to catch up. Both had been trained by the RAF – Bill in Canada, my father in Arizona – and Bill had spent his working life as a pilot for the British Overseas Airways Corporation (BOAC). The brothers had a chance to talk before my father had four bypasses on the 7th November. Bill had two bypasses on the 9th. The first thing my father asked when we were allowed to see him was 'how's Bill?' We had to tell him that Bill had died on the operating table.

These were dark times. Bill's death and my father's precarious state of health added to the general sense of doom and gloom we all felt as a result of seeing England at its most cruel and cold-hearted over the four years since my father had carried out his 'psychological suicide' in November 1974. But there were a few good souls who cheered us up immensely. One was a Mrs D. Jones who lived near my parents in Kennington. She'd walked around the area collecting 221 names on a petition asking for my father's release on compassionate grounds due to his deteriorating state of health, and sent it to the prime minister, Jim Callaghan. She had an acknowledgement from 10 Downing Street, which she sent with a copy of the petition, recorded delivery, to my father on the 13th November while he was still in hospital. We didn't know who she was, but she brought a sorely needed ray of sunshine into our lives.

Another star in our eyes was our dear friend from Walsall, my father's former Labour Party agent, Harry Richards. With other supporters from the area, he started a 'fighting fund' which had reached £100, enough to send a letter to every MP in the House of Commons, which included the words: 'Society has had its pound of flesh from John Stonehouse – to leave him to die in prison would be inhuman and barbaric.' In a local paper, the *Sunday Mercury*, on the 19th, Harry is quoted as saying: 'It would have been easy for me to condemn him like many of his former close friends but if I had done that I would never have been able to live with myself after. If you do not stand by a friend when he is in trouble then you are not a friend at all.'[11] If only more people were like Harry, a gem of a man.

On the 12th November, the *Sunday Mirror* ran a story on page two with the headline 'For mercy's sake, Merlyn!' and began, 'Whatever is the matter with Mr Merlyn Rees? Why won't he do the decent, humane thing as Home Secretary and set John Stonehouse free from the rest of his prison sentence NOW?'[12] And in the *Daily Mirror* on the 18th, former Scotland Yard detective Ken Etheridge thought my father should be paroled and was quoted as saying: 'He has been punished. I do not really think the public would be offended if he was shown mercy.'[13] On the 20th, MP Kenneth Lomas submitted an Early Day Motion (EDM) calling for a debate on urging the home secretary 'on humanitarian, and medical grounds, to release John Stonehouse from prison immediately'.[14] My father's ex-parliamentary private secretary, Andrew Faulds, thought the word 'humanitarian' wouldn't help, so he made an amendment for that word to be cut. The EDM didn't collect enough signatures to force a debate but it did seem that the tide of public opinion was turning.

But elements in the press were not going to allow that to happen. On the 17th, *The Times* ran an extremely damaging editorial saying £600,000 had disappeared from the Bangladesh Fund. This old and erroneous story had been debunked by everyone in a position to know, including the government of Bangladesh, and now that had to be done again, by Michael O'Dell and MP Bruce Douglas-Mann. It got worse. On the 26th, this headline appeared on the front page of the *Sunday Express*: '£40,000 IN TRUNK STONEHOUSE DENIAL'. The story was based on an anonymous letter on House of Commons paper, addressed to Michael O'Dell, but which had 'some-how' come into the hands of the *Sunday Express*. The article started: 'John Stonehouse has been questioned over allegations that when he

leaves prison he intends to disappear again, using an assumed name
and taking with him a small fortune said to be hidden from the
police and Department of Trade investigators.'[15] The letter referred
to a trunk my father had left in a house in Sunningdale, Berkshire,
sometimes occupied by a man who my father had met in Brixton
Prison. My father had stayed at the house with Sheila a couple of
times before the trial, and as there was nothing of value in the trunk
it had been left there. The letter said the trunk contained banknotes,
letters of introduction in the names of Houston and Thomson, and
a blank passport. All that was a lie, but couldn't be proved because,
according to the anonymous author of the letter, and reported in the
Sunday Express, the trunk 'has mysteriously vanished'. Michael sent
a copy of the letter to the Official Receiver. This whole story came
on the back of *The Times* editorial of the 17th November, which
had also said: 'If there was any reason to suppose that he might be
released to enjoy the spoils of his crimes, that would be reason in
itself to deny him parole.'[16] In Michael O'Dell's letter in *The Times*
the following day, he'd said, 'It should be noted that the Board of
Trade inspectors indicated in their report that they did not consider
that there were any further monies unaccounted for.'[17] Jane told the
Sunday People, who had also acquired details of the story, that she
was there when the anonymous letter was shown to our father by
Michael O'Dell, and, 'My father simply regarded it as the work of a
scurrilous mischief-maker and took no more notice of it than that.'[18]
That was before we all realised it was going to become front-page
news. She added: 'he hasn't asked anybody to lift a finger to find
[the trunk] because he is totally unconcerned about it.' Jane wrote
to the editor of the *Sunday Express* on the 5th December asking
why they hadn't come to the family for comment before publishing
and said: 'We have been battling against stories like yours for over
4 years now. False and fanciful stories that have caused so much
harm.' Expecting an apology was like asking a hyena to say sorry
they ate your puppy – it wasn't going to happen. The closest we ever

got in similar circumstances was a short letter replying that it had been 'in the public interest' – a catch-all phrase that means they can do what they want.

People involved in this media concoction didn't want my father to have bail, and were using the notion of hidden money to prevent it. Who was behind it? The letter was anonymous. It was on House of Commons paper, which is easy enough to acquire and, although it might make the story more intriguing, it was a red herring. Only people associated with the house in Sunningdale knew about the trunk, and their only incentive to devise a story about it would be money, and the only place they'd get that from is the press. It's almost unheard of for a newspaper to print an anonymous letter, and for a weekly to do it on their front page must be unique in media history.

This mischievous story provided the *Sunday Express* with increased sales, but put us back to square one. My sister had written to the home secretary, Merlyn Rees, asking him to recommend the exercise of the Royal Prerogative of Mercy so my father could be released from prison. His private secretary, John Chilcot, replied on the 28th November, saying, 'the Home Secretary has decided that he would not be justified in recommending the remission of the remainder of your father's sentences.'[19] How much his decision was influenced by the malicious false story in the *Sunday Express* two days earlier, we shall never know.

Various MPs had written to the home secretary by this time and they got a standard letter back, copies of which they sent us, in which junior Home Office minister, Dr Shirley Summerskill, reassured them that 'his life cannot be said to be in immediate and predictable danger'. They were only going to release him if he were on the brink of death. Maureen Colquhoun MP wrote, saying, 'It is all quite appalling – and many MPs I have spoken to, feel he is being badly treated simply because he was an MP.'[20] The only MP to actually visit my father during the prison years was Bruce Douglas-Mann, with whom he'd campaigned for the independence of Bangladesh.

On the 5th December, our father wrote to Jane from Wormwood Scrubs: 'I have been feeling worse than at any time since the operation. I am suffering pain all over my body – everything aches, spreading from my chest and I walk like a cripple. At nights I still have sweats (although not as bad as before) and this is probably due to the continued infection in my left leg. Anyway I should be patient, they say it takes six months to get over such an operation … My back is hurting me so much when I sit down I am now standing up to write – and it's much better.' Being in his single cell was an improvement on the 'anti-hospital' ward, as he called it. Many people had written to him in support, but with an allowance of only three letters a week he felt guilty he couldn't reply.

1979 was an excruciating year, which we all spent just hoping my father would survive. On 9th January, he was again railing against the state of the country: 'Increasingly I realise the Trade Union leaders are greedy barons behaving as if their members were their feudal fiefs. Cynically (that's the way) they begin to behave "responsibly" in the one or two years before retirement so they can collect their "Companions of Honour" (CH) and peerages as with Jones and Scanlon. Moss Evans has a long way to go yet and meanwhile he intends to be a bully boy. As for the "statesmanlike" Len Murray, I heard him last night and thought I would puke: what he was saying was such patent nonsense.' But it was good to hear, 'My health is better. Am off most of the pills and Hammersmith hospital don't need to see me for another six months. My time is spent 23½ hours a day in my single cell with books and radio.'

The next week he was transferred to the hospital wing of Norwich Prison, but then put in the main prison, which he described as 'cold and forbidding and inhospitable. It was ghastly to be in a cell without heating for most of the day.' It was the coldest winter since 1947. But, as luck would have it, by 9th February he'd been transferred to the warmer 'Annex' and given a new job: 'It is really two jobs combined: Librarian and Education "Redband". The former means taking care of 3,000 books (indexing, issuing etc.) and the latter means rushing around in the evenings making sure the "classes" are organised properly.' He enjoyed sitting among so many books and said the selection was 'quite good considering there are only 100 inmates as the library's potential customers'. He wrote, 'The Annex as you would have seen is an old army barracks and fortunately the "prison" atmosphere is at a minimum. Everyone is much more relaxed than in the old-fashioned institutions. Life is therefore bearable and it is warmer!' The annex had hardly changed in years, and still had no window bars or locked doors. He wrote, 'In fact the only locked door I go through is to the library and I keep the key.' This whole set up was so much better than anything before, and it gave us hope. Above all, we were pleased to hear: 'The staff are much nicer than any I have come across before and they largely leave inmates alone.' But prison visits were always frustrating. As my father wrote, 'there is never enough time to talk properly! Remember those wonderful unlimited hours in the hospital.' It comes to something when recovering from open-heart surgery has an up-side. But, by 22nd March, he was not in a good way: 'Certain incidents have propelled me into a distant country called melancholia so please forgive me for writing so little this time.'

Having someone you love in prison is literally a nightmare. In dreams, I'd see Kafka-like scenes of people with pallid, puffy skin, shuffling down long corridors with their heads hung low, to the sound of metal doors slamming and keys jingling. The days were better, but if I heard the words 'The former …' on the radio or TV, my heart would stop because I'd expect to hear 'The former disgraced minister, John Stonehouse, died in prison today.' I did the only thing I could do – write letters. On the 25th April, my father wrote 'My dear Julia, You start your last letter (dated 23/4) apologising for not writing earlier but dear daughter you have showered me with meaningful letters in the past five weeks and I do not feel neglected at all. It is good to be kept in touch, to have a few lifelines to sanity. How one needs them!' I was very pleased to hear he was getting some help: 'A doctor from the old constituency (Dr Ralph Morton Brown) is campaigning for my release and has been supported in the press (not the nationals of course who ignore it) by the former mayor of Wednesbury (Mark Allen). I've had several very sympathetic and supportive letters from various people.'

When I visited my father on the 7th June, he made a record of how much time we had – one hour and 51 minutes. He'd been busying himself by building a lexicon of 1,000 new words. On the 9th, he wrote: 'Some of them are so expressive I wonder how I managed till now to do without them. "Ultracrepidarian" for instance which means "one who criticises beyond his knowledge". There are thousands of those around!' Sheila and he had been writing to each other using Chaucerian English and little-known words to avoid the warder-censors understanding what they were saying, and in this letter to me he wrote: 'Incidentally I must apologise for my parrhesia on Thursday but I had to let you know I am passible no longer. It is doubtful if I shall ever be resipiscent until this stercoraceous business is redressed. It would be a pity if it has to be post-exequial but somehow I feel we won't have to wait that long. Fortunately I am no longer a dysthemiac although my dyslogy is still badly frustrated. However the opportunities for positive action will be accrescent if I am callid.' The warders wouldn't have known this meant: 'Sorry to speak candidly on Thursday but I had to let you know I'm no longer able to suffer. It's doubtful I shall return to sanity until this shit business is redressed. It would be a pity if it has to be after I'm dead but somehow I feel we won't have to wait that long. Fortunately I'm no longer depressed although my ability to express ideas and reason is still frustrated by my mental disorder. However, the opportunities for positive action will continue to grow if I'm clever about it.'

In July we were told our father would be released in August. He wrote to me on the 29th July: 'Many thanks for your cheering let- ters and the lovely birthday card. You are great to keep my spirits up during this most extraordinary torture. Strangely, now it is nearing its end I feel the pain. It has a physical property. I can touch it. I can put it aside and other things contemplate but always I know it is there. It has a numbing effect. Partly the pain is my continued incredulity that men are capable in a country that aspires to civilization to inflict such cruelty on others. I can only suppose it is part of the circus of Government as it is surely evident there can be no positive good from it. I want you and Jane to know how much I have appreciated, admired and drawn comfort from your unflagging support over all this time.' In his last letter to Jane from prison, he wrote, 'I am numb and I need to rest.'

The newspapers were gearing up for his release. On the 6th August, the London *Evening News* ran the front-page head- line: 'Ex-MP does less than half sentence: STONEHOUSE TO BE FREED.' The report said: 'The news of his release was bro- ken today by his mother, Mrs Rosina Stonehouse, at her home in Southampton.'[21] They quoted my 84-year-old grandmother as saying about Sheila: 'I don't know what she hopes to get out of him. He's got nothing for her and he's too old for that sort of thing now.'[22] The next day, the *Daily Mail*'s front-page headline rang out: 'Ex-MP gets parole – and faces family row STONEHOUSE'S STORMY FREEDOM.' It told the world: 'He will leave Norwich Jail at 7.30am on Tuesday after serving less than half his seven-year sentence for theft, fraud and deception.' They quoted my grandmother as saying 'I never want to speak to her and I will refuse to see her. I know she wants to marry him, but he is far too old for her. She helped to ruin him – I'll never forgive her.'[23] On the following day, the *Daily Mail* continued the story with a headline on page three: 'That woman answers back'. Most of the page was taken up with photos of Sheila walking down the street after leaving work, and on the tube escalator, trying to avoid the reporters. Apparently, she said: 'She is a very old woman who has completely misunderstood the situation.'[24] The report continued 'And she in turn criticised Mrs Stonehouse – for publicising the fact that her son is to be released on parole next Tuesday.'[25] That was probably made up, but it kept the column inches dramatic, which is always the object of the reporter's exercise.

On the 8th August 1979, our father wrote to both Jane and myself, saying, 'Please do not have anything to do with the arrangements for my discharge.' To me he said, 'The circus is shattering and appalling. Please excuse me for being blunt but on *no* account must you or Jane or anyone come anywhere near the prison or Norwich on the day of my release. I mean this. Do *not* come under any circumstances. I shall not be able to leave the prison if you or anyone comes. We cannot add to the ballyhoo by having any such pressure.' We understood his concern. On a previous occasion, when Jane and I had picked him up from prison after he'd been given bail, we'd hired a professional driver to get away from the press cars and motorbikes, and it had been absolutely terrifying. We were taking him to meet up with Sheila in a remote location and couldn't have the press know where that was. We were driven at high speed, doing sudden U-turns and changes of direction, and although we soon lost the cars, the motorbikes stuck to us like glue. Eventually, we lost them too. Since then, my father had had three heart attacks – which the prison ignored, thinking he was malingering – and open-heart bypass surgery. Doing a repeat of the fast car escape would be dangerous to him, as well as to us.

He was finally released from Norwich Prison on the 14th August with a coat over his head, concealing his face from the press, and driven away by his solicitor, Michael O'Dell, who had to cross three counties before they could shake off the press. Since his arrest in Melbourne on the 24th December 1974, my father had experienced nothing but mental turmoil, and spent four years and seven months either preparing for trial, attending court, or behind bars.

17

Freedom

It would be 40 hours before Sheila could meet up with my father. First, Michael had to shake off the press and get my father to a safe house to spend the night. The next day, once reassured the press had been thrown off the scent, a friend of Sheila's picked my father up from a London street and took him to another pick-up point, from where he was taken to the house Sheila had borrowed from friends in London, a few days before. When he arrived, they hugged and sat on the sofa holding hands. Sheila said later that she felt very nervous. *Come Dancing* was on the TV with the sound down, but he turned it up, held out his hand and said, 'Come on, I want to dance with you.' He'd always been a good dancer. This broke the ice, and then they talked for the first time, properly, in three-and-a-half years. While he'd been in prison, Sheila had worked as a temp secretary using her middle and maiden name, Elizabeth Black. That had given her anonymity and if people said she looked like Sheila Buckley, she'd brush it off with, 'I know I look like her, everyone says that.' Now there would be no anonymity, and finding peace would be a struggle.

Two weeks later, on the 1st September, the entire front page of the *Daily Mirror* was taken up with a small, smiling 'before' photo of my father and an enormous, unsmiling 'now' photo, and one of Sheila. On page two there was a photo of the place where they'd been staying. He wrote to me from Hunstanton in Norfolk that day, saying: 'We are exploring the quaint villages of Northern Norfolk, every one of which has a 14th-century church, walking along the sand dunes by the Wash and even immersing in the North Sea. This Indian summer is a surprising bonus. We had the use of a cottage but survived there only 22 hours as the *Mirror* were hiding in the hedge on our return on the second day from a lovely trip to Thetford Forest ... That awful experience was on Thursday and they spread the terrible photograph all over the front page today. Is there no other news? Only one person knew we were there so we know who told the *Mirror*. It was a terrible breach of trust. Saddening.' The press photographers hounded them for months with their numbers slowly dwindling until there was just one, who seemed to live outside their front door. One day my father came out with a cardboard box over his head with two cut-out eyes and the words 'John Stonehouse' written across it, got in his car and drove away. The photographer took the photo and presumably showed it to the picture editors in Fleet Street. It seems even they realised that enough was enough because that photo was never published, and the photographer never seen again.

Having survived prison and heart surgery, my father was just pleased to be alive. He became easy-going and appreciative of the simple things in life. He and Sheila were homeless and moving from borrowed place to place while the owners were away. He looked for a job and applied for posts as a university lecturer, but nothing materialised and, anyway, his doctor had advised him to avoid stress. Not wanting to be idle, in January 1980, he started volunteering for a charity called Community Links in Newham, East London. He invited the press to see him there as a way of bursting the bubble of interest before it turned into an ongoing circus. The remit of the charity was to develop links within the community, encouraging mutual self-help, developing homes for homeless young people and single parents, and going door to door to collect unwanted items that others might need. He was asked whether he was doing this work to rehabilitate himself in the eyes of the public. He replied 'Frankly, I couldn't care less what is written about me, because 99 per cent of it is twisted and vicious.' He would work at Community Links for a year but found Newham depressing, writing to me in December, 'It is an extraordinarily dull area. In a place of real deprivation one could feel some animation but it is difficult in a place inhabited by seedy, apathetic characters who hardly stir to make their environment better. The ennui of the welfare state is not something the socialist pioneers anticipated: it creeps everywhere deadening human relationships.' Shortly after starting in Newham, he and Sheila had moved into a small flat at 157 Ashmore Road, in Queen's Park, North-West London, provided by the Brent People's Housing Association at a cost of £13 a week. Some people were reported as saying it should've gone to people more needy or worthy. Sheila continued to be the breadwinner.

In March of that year my mother married Dennis Flexney-Briscoe, a lovely, uncomplicated man, who enjoyed having a laugh and was never without new jokes. Like my father, he would extend a helping hand to anyone in need, and enjoyed doing *The Times* crossword. They moved to a house in Kennington and converted two floors to offices, from which my mother continued her public relations business, and Dennis started a marketing consultancy. They enjoyed working together to promote a wide variety of businesses and had a very interesting life, before retiring to a cottage set in a magnificent valley in Wiltshire. They would be married for 32 years – six years longer than my mother's marriage to my father. My parents met only once after he came out of prison. Jane was having the opening party for her painting show at an art gallery near the Connaught Hotel in Mayfair. My mother and Dennis met my father in the bar there, wanting to break the ice in private before entering the fray where photographers were expected. They made sure to keep their distance at the event, so no photo could be taken of them together.

My father and Sheila married in January 1981, by which time he was writing novels: *Ralph* would be published in 1982; *The Baring Fault* in 1986; and *Oil on the Rift* in 1987. In December 1982, Sheila gave birth to their son, James, and my father became a stay-at-home dad when Sheila went back to work. They'd moved to a house at 20 Shirland Mews, W9, by this time, where he'd be found organising papers on the table while trying to keep the crawling baby under control. He was a very good care-giver, keeping his cool throughout it all. Our favourite place to meet up was by the Serpentine in Hyde Park, where we'd picnic and catch up with family news while watching James run around. My father seemed generally very happy and relaxed during this period, although he would still get stressed when he gave print or TV interviews, forever trying to explain why his sentence had been so unjust. He'd been discharged from his bankruptcy in June 1980, and five years later became involved in a business that manufactured hotel safes. In late 1987, they were still living in London, but were planning to move permanently into the house they'd just bought in Southampton. They were looking forward to a peaceful new life of taking James for walks in the New Forest. But that was not to be.

On the 25th March 1988, my father went to Birmingham to appear on a late-night live TV debate show called 'Central Weekend'. The segment he was involved in was about missing people. As usual, he found himself trying to correct the interviewer's erroneous facts and tried to explain his psychiatric suicide. This brought on a minor heart attack and he collapsed, falling out of his chair. He was taken to Birmingham hospital, where he stayed overnight. In the very last letter to Jane, on the 30th March, he wrote, 'Central TV are very sorry! They sent me a big bunch of flowers. I cannot remember ever receiving a bunch before so I feel I must be nearing the end. Sort of advance funeral tribute.' The same day he replied to a letter of concern from Bill McCash, chairman of the Falcon Field Association – an association of ex-pilots who were trained by the RAF in Mesa, outside Phoenix, Arizona, of which my father was a member. He wrote in the jovial form of a pilot's report from 'Course 27 member, JTS': 'Re: incident 23:55 hours 25 March 1988. It was extremely embarrassing to have a duff landing at an on-air show with millions watching the air display. It was considered to be more than a prang and the show was brought to a premature end. However the ground crews were quickly on the scene and managed to avert a greater tragedy by keeping the engine ticking over … It is apparent that at some stage during its useful life this engine has been tampered with – probably being through dangerous and taxing assignments which overstretched its capacity … PS Technical note: The engine overhaul which was completed in 1978 included bypass additional (4) to the cylinders to improve fuel flow to the combustion chambers. This is now subject to a bush bundle malfunction.'

Two weeks later he was dead. He'd gone to the new house in Southampton to recuperate and finish his last novel, *Who Sold Australia?*. Sheila described his last minutes: '"He always felt cold and I tucked him up in bed and started to take off my make-up. Then I heard him say in a whisper: 'I feel terribly faint.' Then, 'Sheila, tell me you love me.' It was not the sort of thing he would ever ordinarily say, but I answered with all my heart. He was very happy and very calm. I would say it almost radiated from him." He died moments later.'[1] It was the 14th April 1988, and he was 62 years old.

My father was not only much maligned, but misunderstood right to the end of his life. My mother immediately sent a press release to the Associated Press and other news agencies detailing his political achievements, and saying we hoped they would not be forgotten in the obituaries. But, aside from listing the ministerial positions, his life's work was overlooked. The papers wanted drama, and even newspapers that had followed the story from day one got the details wrong. Several said that Sheila had been involved in the runaway plot from the start. The *Daily Express* on the 15th, said: 'It was two years later that police discovered the couple living in Australia.'[2] The *Evening Standard* said: 'His widow, Sheila, with whom he fled to Australia to start a new life under a fake name.'[3] The *Daily Telegraph* said: 'Stonehouse and his secretary, Sheila Buckley, plotted his disappearance off Miami Beach.'[4] Newspapers from all over the world covered the death, and they got it wrong too. According to the *South China Morning News*, 'Only last year Sheila Stonehouse, praised by many commentators for her staunch support of her husband throughout his troubles, divorced him on grounds of his unreasonable conduct'.[5] The *Hong Kong Standard* said my father had disappeared in November 1974, 'to evade an insurance fraud scandal'.[6] The inaccuracies were manifold, large, small, important and unimportant, and in every newspaper.

There were only 50 people at the funeral. My mother didn't attend, but sent a wreath of white roses with a card that read, 'Go in peace, Barbara'. Sheila placed a wreath of white carnations on the coffin, with a card saying, 'I love you, Sheila.' There was one ex-MP, Bruce Douglas-Mann. In her eulogy, my sister, Jane, said: 'He was a man of great courage and with the backbone to stand up for what he believed in.' In mine, I said: 'Making this world a better place because of our interaction with it is an aim we all should have. Yet, for most people, their sphere of interest extends only to themselves and their immediate family. It is a world of each man and woman for him or herself. This is the easy option, a comfortable life making critical comments from the cosy sofa. But if everyone were to have this self-centred attitude there would be no heroes and no life worth living. To me, my father was a hero – a source of pride and he taught me something invaluable: that the world can be changed if people talk enough and work together. His energy made changes and to know that change is possible providing one is prepared to do the enormous amount of work necessary to facilitate it is a vital cornerstone of my life. I can never say helplessly "what can I do?" because I know what I can do – like him, work with enormous energy at great sacrifice to myself. Until I am prepared to do just that, or until anyone else is, we are in no position to criticise this man who did just that for over 30 solid years. Over weekends and holidays, morning, noon and night. In a sense, he was killed by the human cruelty that he spent so many years trying to fight. He was wrong to suppose that his battle would ever be over because the monster turned when it saw he was down and lashed out, gleeful at finally being able to smash him to pieces. Those of us who experienced the daily horror of the 1974–5 period know only too well the profound ugliness that humanity can display and the only consolation is that now he is out of it and, at last, at peace. I send him my love and respect.'

18

The Famous File

In the file prepared on my father by the secret services of communist-run Czechoslovakia, the Statni Bezpecnost, known as the StB, there's not one single secret. Not one. I've analysed every document in this famous file, and as the daughter of the so-called 'foreign agent', some people are going to think I'm partisan and will edit what's in there, so I've no choice really but to tell you about everything in this file – thereby proving my father was not a spy.

I've heard the author of *The Defence of the Realm – The Authorized History of MI5*, Christopher Andrew, tell the British TV-viewing public that the file is over a thousand pages long, which sounds pretty big. What Andrew doesn't explain is that half the pages are blank. The StB archivists processed each piece of paper, envelope, file cover and miscellaneous item in the file by photographing both their front and back, and the reverse sides are invariably blank. My father's file contains 1,101 pages, but as that number includes 513 blank pages, 60 admin file-covers, blank forms and so forth, the file immediately reduces to 528 pages. Of these, sixteen pages are copies of a 1962 pamphlet for the London Co-operative Society presidential election, and some are just one-line memos or copies of other documents. When it all shakes down, the actual number of pages of interest is closer to 350, and these often relate to my father trying to sell VC10 planes to the Czech airline, CAS, or the twinning of his constituency of Wednesbury with the Czech town of Kladno.

Christopher Andrew does not seem to be aware that over the twelve-year period the StB held a file on my father they not once had our correct address. If he knew this, he might not confidently go about telling audiences about the system the StB devised to supposedly notify my father of meetings they wanted to hold with him. According to the file, they'd send my father a cutting from *The Times* newspaper, by post, showing the printed date. The meeting being called would take place a week from that date. The location was identified in the following way: by default it was Beal's Restaurant at 374 Holloway Road, London N7; but if they wrote the Roman numeral 'II' by the date on the news cutting, that indicated the meeting would take place at the Black Horse Saloon, 169 Rushey Green, Catford, London SE6. This clandestine, spy-like arrangement might have looked good to their masters back at Prague HQ, but the StB would never be able to contact my father at the only address they ever had for us, '22 Aldwyne Road, N1,' because we never lived there. The road is actually Alwyne Road, which a post delivery person would soon enough work out, but number 22 is a massive four-storey Victorian villa which, at the time these clandestine meetings were supposed to be taking place, was occupied by four families paying rent to the Northampton Estate – and we were not one of them.

The StB agents who compiled the file were professional liars. And they were not fans of the British because we betrayed them in September 1938 when, without the Czechoslovakian president Edvard Benes being invited, Britain, France and Italy signed a deal with Adolf Hitler, handing over a large part of Czechoslovakia to the Germans. This is known in Czech history as the 'Munich Betrayal'. The Czechs had a volunteer army of 1 million men ready to fight, but 'The Munich Agreement', as the British call it, showed them they would have no allies, and they surrendered. The British said it was 'appeasement', and hoped for 'peace in our time', but all it did was entrench Hitler in Eastern Europe, and make us enemies in Czechoslovakia. After suffering Nazi occupation during the Second

World War, the Czechs had to endure communism from 1948, under the authority of Russia. For the next 40 years the country lived a nightmare: the private business sector was totally banned; privately-held farmland was eliminated without compensation and replaced with collectivisation, with prosperous farmers being sent to gulags; religion was banned and the property of all religious orders confiscated; voluntary organisations were no longer allowed; the court system was purged; books were banned; and anyone who tried to leave was shot by the Border Guard (PS) – who were rewarded with a holiday and a watch for each dead body.

The Communist Party took control of the entire country, using the army, the uniformed Public Security (VB), the armed People's Militias (LM), civilian informants – of which 40,000 were recruited between 1969–89, and for good measure they instigated a system of volunteer snitches, the PS VB, who were secret police informants. Watching over them all was State Security – the StB – a secret organisation that was the main instrument of political terror, rooting out opponents of communism and suppressing civil and human rights. As well as employees, it's calculated that over 100,000 citizens collaborated with the StB.

The StB infiltrated all parts of society, including embassies, and their basic methods of control included kidnap, assassination, blackmail, intimidation and provocation. The Museum of Communism in Prague says: 'The StB literally "manufactured" class enemies, spitting them out on a conveyor belt to then smash them to bits. StB investigation methods included physical violence, brutal beatings, electrical torture methods, night-time interrogations, extended solitary confinement, and sleep, water, and food deprivation. Physical violence was accompanied by psychological terror, humiliation, threats of the arrest of family members, and even faked executions.'[1] Their physical interrogation methods included driving pins under the fingernails and kicking testicles until they burst. Psychological interrogation methods included the injection of large doses of the psychoactive drug scopolamine, after which anyone would admit to anything. The StB could send their victims to political trial based on false evidence, where the death sentences were meted out by the Communist Party rather than judges, or the lucky ones could get a lifetime in the uranium mines or gulags.

This was the charming organisation that the StB spies at the London embassy were part of, and the fact that commentators read their lies and swallow them, then repeat them as 'evidence', is completely absurd. The StB agents had to protect themselves and their families by playing the game of making up reports and filling the files, and falsifying documents was standard procedure. Some of them also tried to make cash out of the situation because after the currency devaluation of 1953 the Czech crown was worth peanuts. According to the defector Josef Frolik, his comrades used to joke that 'One half of Czechoslovakia is spying on the other half!'[2] and that was confirmed when Communist rule ended in 1989, and it was revealed the StB kept enough secret files on the citizenship to cover several football fields, piled many metres high. When Christopher Andrew accepts my father's StB file on face value he insults not only my father, but the Czech people who had to endure this tyrannical organisation.

❖

Inventing agents who don't exist was a feature of StB life in London. Soon after he was posted there, Frolik was taken to a club called La Campanina by Major Jan Koska who 'threw money around as if it was going out of fashion'. Frolik asked how the bill was going to be paid. Koska said, 'Don't worry about such trivia. The money will be arranged quicker than you can down that whiskey. Let me see now.' Koska looked around the room and said, 'You see that dope sitting on the bar stool there? … Well, he's going to be our contact for this evening.' Frolik then realised, 'Koska would write a report, saying he had made an interesting contact in the club and it had cost him so much money to make the man's acquaintance.' Also present was Robert Husak, Frolik's London boss, who features strongly in my father's story, and it's significant that he was party to this apparently routine method of extracting money from Prague in the form of financial rewards to 'contacts'. Frolik writes 'Thus I discovered that Koska, like little Fremr, was not averse to inventing agents and contacts in order to charge personal expenses to Intelligence Accounts. Later, for example, I heard that he had invented an English policeman who cost Prague £1,500 in bribes to cover Koska's drinking bills.' When Frolik returned to Prague in March 1966, he was chastised by his StB 'chief', Lt. Colonel Vaclav Taborsky, for having spent too much time 'fussing around with trade union leaders'. Frolik thought attack was the best form of defence and replied angrily: 'You know as well as I do what is happening over there in London. Half of your men are crooks lining their own nests. Look at Koska, for instance, padding expenses all the time, inventing and paying agents who don't exist. And you are covering up for these people!'[3] Taborsky avoided Frolik's gaze and, in a calmer voice, said to Frolik 'Let's forget it,' and changed the subject.

In his book, Frolik called the Czech ambassador, Dr Trhlik, 'a plotter and a pig, who continually tried to elbow his way closer to the trough, even if it cost the lives of others to do so'. He said his comrades at the embassy were 'not only double-agents, lechers, drunks and crooks, but also former torturers and even murderers. Diplomats in name only … each seeking his own pleasures, protected by his privileged position and living as well as any member of the London jet-set on the money supplied by the hard-working man-in-the-street back in the "People's Republic".' Going into specifics, he tells us that fellow agent Bohumil Malek was a 'dummy' who 'did not have one ounce of sense in his whole body', recounting how he picked up a typewriter and threw it at an irritating fly. Agent Fremr was another 'dummy', 'whose brain had become addled by too much whiskey. He was continually drunk and when he was, he was often seized by an unexpected aggressiveness.' The man tasked to 'watch over them' was Major Jan Koska, who Frolik describes as 'a snake – a reptile hated by every other member of the Intelligence Collective'.[4]

The StB agents at the London embassy were a nest of vipers but my father had to have meetings with Czechs from the embassy – some of them StB, unknown to him – because, in the early days, he needed to organise the twinning of his constituency Wednesbury with Kladno, and later when he was minister of aviation he was trying to sell them VC10 planes. It's pretty clear to see that the StB file blends the genuine meetings with invented meetings.

Having an StB file, in itself, is neither here nor there because every person from the West who travelled to Czechoslovakia during the communist era was checked out by the StB with a view to using them, and in this way acquired a file. In September 1957, my father went to Czechoslovakia as a board member of the London Co-operative Society, as part of a delegation. On this trip he visited Lidice – a place famous for having been obliterated by the Nazi SS in 1942 – and the nearby town of Kladno. His constituents had asked him to look out for a suitable town to 'twin' with Wednesbury, and as Kladno was also an industrial town, it seemed a good choice. He went to the Town Hall, established contact with the mayor, and the twinning began. There's still a street called 'Wednesbury' in Kladno today. Travelling to Czechoslovakia, in itself, had no particular significance because my father visited every European country from Turkey to Norway, and went to Strasbourg and Paris regularly, meeting European parliamentarians and diplomats in his capacity as a member of the European Assembly and the Council of Europe.

The StB decided to keep an eye on my father, and see what use he could be to them in London. It looks as if they followed him one day and watched him walk along Alwyne Road in Canonbury, London N1, and walk into a house. Usually in England, roads are numbered with the odd numbers on one side, and the even numbers on the other, but on Alwyne Road they run sequentially. An StB agent probably thought they saw my father walk into the house next door, number 22, when he actually went into number 21. Perhaps the agent held back because he saw uniformed police on the street, which was commonly the case because opposite our house there were three low-level apartment blocks which at the time was section housing for policemen. And because this part of the road is a cul-de-sac, he may have feared drawing attention to himself by walking past the house to check the number, turning around, and walking back. In any event, the agent wrote our address as '22 Aldwyne Road', making a mistake in the spelling of the road name, as well as getting the number wrong.

The StB agents in London referred to this address in reports back to Prague no less than 27 times, even once, in May 1961, to the leader of the StB, Minister of the Interior Rudolf Barak, one of the most powerful and dangerous men in Czechoslovakia at the time. (He was later arrested on the orders of the Politburo – proving that, in communist Czechoslovakia, nobody was safe.) The address is significant because it was supposedly used to call my father to meetings using *The Times* method of dated press cuttings and, surely, had my father been a spy, he would have given them his correct address – either at the outset of their so-called 'relationship', or when they all realised the wrong address was being used.* If, indeed, any press cuttings were ever sent to 22 Alwyne Road, they would end up in the mail of a fairly chaotic house occupied by four families, over-crowded housing being a feature of life in Britain following the damage caused by the Second World War. Sceptics might say, well, maybe someone at number 22, on seeing the envelope was

---

* Only once did the StB spell the road correctly, on page eight of a document dated 28th February 1963, but on page one they still spelled it 'Aldwyne', and on both pages they had the house number wrong as 22. In a document dated 4th November 1961, they reversed the usual meeting location numbers: default being Beal's Restaurant and 'II' indicating the pub in Catford.

addressed to Mr Stonehouse, delivered it next door, but it would then be opened by my mother, who routinely dealt with our mail in her capacity as my father's unpaid parliamentary secretary. I've asked her if she recalls any random press cuttings arriving at the house and she said that she does not and, anyway, she would have thrown them away because we had *The Times* delivered daily and would have no need of them.

We moved from 21 Alwyne Road in the summer of 1962, but the StB were still using the '22 Aldwyne Road' address in February 1963. They didn't seem to know where we were until almost two years later, December 1964, when they first mention a phone number for Potters Bar, Hertfordshire, where we'd moved to. The file first mentions Potters Bar as the place we lived in June 1966, but they never had a record of the address. And they'd be pretty stupid to use the phone because our phones were always bugged. I don't remember a time when they weren't. If my father was a spy, he would surely have warned the StB about the phone bugging, but there's not one word about phone bugging in this file.

Our house at Alwyne Road was a meeting place for anti-colonial political fighters and my father and his friends were always under surveillance. All the talk over the years about MPs not having their phones bugged is laughable. Of course they were. When it started, it was quite primitive. We'd pick up the phone and hear nothing but a few taps. One day my mother picked up the phone and heard a conversation between Duncan Sandys – who was a minister in the Conservative government of Harold Macmillan – and another man. When my mother realised who he was she said, 'I know you're Duncan Sandys and recognise your voice because my husband is in the opposition party. We know our phones are being tapped and it looks as if yours are too.' Both men immediately put their phones down. Of course, it's impossible to know whether it was Duncan Sandys' phone being tapped or that of the man he was talking to. As time went on, we'd hear a recording going 'Scotland Yard Police,

Barbara leaving Brixton
Prison by a back door,
6th August 1975.

Photo by Bill Cross.
© ANL/Shutterstock

After release from Brixton Prison on bail, 28th August 1975.

Photo by Hulton Deutsch. © Getty Images

Arriving at
Kennington
police station for
daily signing as a
condition of bail,
29th August 1975.

© Daily Mail/Shutterstock

Sitting alone at the Labour Party conference, Blackpool, 30th September 1975.

Photo by Graham Wood. © Getty images

Outside committal proceedings, 13th October 1975.

Photo by Graham Morris. © ANL/Shutterstock

Leaving the House of Commons after making his statement, 20th October 1975.

Photo by Ken Towner. © Evening News/Shutterstock

With solicitor
Michael O'Dell at
magistrates' court for
committal proceedings,
5th November 1975.

© Keystone Press /
Alamy Stock Photo

With Beatrice and Dr Frank Hansford-Miller
at an English National Party event,
Trafalgar Square, London, 9th April 1976.

Photo by Bill Cross. © ANL/Shutterstock

Sheila arriving at the Old Bailey,
29th April 1976.

Photo by Peter Cade. © Getty images

Gerald Scarfe, *The Sunday Times*, 8th August 1976.
© Gerald Scarfe

Keith Waite,
Sunday Mirror,
8th August 1976
© Renee Waite

"OH DEAR—HERE WE GO AGAIN"

Jane, to left, Mathew
and Julia at press
conference about
father's health
issues in prison,
8th August 1978.
© Keystone Press /
Alamy Stock Photo

Julia with John and James, Hyde Park, London, 1984.

John with James, Hyde Park,
London, 1984.

Michael Heath, *Mail on
Sunday*, 17th April 1988.

Plán nového spojení:

S KOLÓNEM je sjednáváno pravidelné spojení vždy na závěr každé
schůzky,kdy je určen čas a místo s jedním náhradním termínem.

V případě ztráty spojení je nutno s KOLONEM schůzku vyvolat.

Vyvolání schůzky z naší strany:

Zasláním dopisu na adresu KOLONA 22,Aldwyne Road,London N.1.v němž
bude výstřižek novin The TIMES,ze stránky přinášející zahr.polit.
zpravodajství,výstřižek musí obsahovat horní lemovku stránky,kde
je název listu,datum a slovy den týdne.
Schůzka je za týden od dne vyznačeného na lemovce(př. The TIMES
Wednesday 21th Of October.1961 - schůzka je ve středu 28.10.1961).
Místo č.1 restaurace "Beal´s" v 1 patře Grill Room - 374 Holloway
Road.London N.7.
Čas 12.30

Vyvolání ze strany KOLONA:

Stejným způsobem zašle výstřižek na jméno ŘO na čs.ZÚ vLondýně.
Místo schůzky č.2 - je v restauraci "Black Horse Inn, 169 Rushey
Green v saloon baru.
Vyvolání schůzky na místo č.2 se provede naprosto stejným způso-
bem jako na místo č.1 s tím rozdílem,že v horní části výstřižku se
udělá znamení "II",rovněž den a čas stejný.

Kontakt třetí osobou:

Kontakt třetí osobou bude proveden na místě vyvolané schůzky nebo
na místě schůzky sjednané nynějším ŘO a bude proveden novým ŘO
pomocí hesla.
Heslo: "Pane KOLÓN přináším Vám pozdrav od Harolda POULTERA!"
            Základem hesla je jméno Harold Poulter,heslo bude pro-
            neseno v angličtině.

Možnost schůzky s KOLONEM v třetí zemi(Skandinavie nebo severní
Afrika) bude prověřena a dodatecne projednána.

StB document showing our address as '22 Aldwyne Road'.

© Archiv Bezpečnostnich Složek. Fond Foreign Intelligence Main Directorate –
Operative Files (I. S – svazky): personal file reg. no. 43075 I. S, code names 'Kolón',
'Twister', including MTH 21968 I. S. File number 43075_43075_000_0393

Our house at
21 Alwyne Road, London N1,
showing number 22 next door.

© Julia Stonehouse

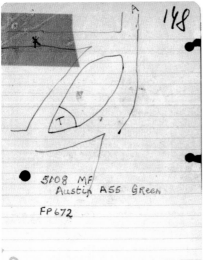

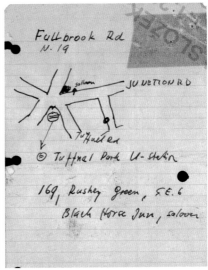

Map in StB file supposedly showing Wells Street, and said to be in John's handwriting.

© Archiv Bezpečnostnich Složek. Fond Foreign Intelligence Main Directorate – Operative Files (I. S – svazky): personal file reg. no. 43075 I. S, code names 'Kolón', 'Twister', including MTH 21968 I. S. File number 43075_43075_000_0388

Reverse of map showing 'Fullbrook' Road in 'Tuffnel' Park.

© Archiv Bezpečnostnich Složek. Fond Foreign Intelligence Main Directorate – Operative Files (I. S – svazky): personal file reg. no. 43075 I. S, code names 'Kolón', 'Twister', including MTH 21968 I. S. File number 43075_43075_000_0387

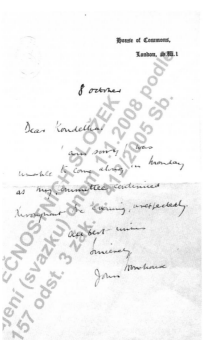

At London Airport before leaving for Czechoslovakia, leading a delegation to sell British aircraft to East European countries, 21st September 1965.

Photo by Tony Wallace. © Daily Mail/Shutterstock

LEFT: One of two examples of John's handwriting in the StB file – the letter to Koudelka, 8th October 1958, regarding meeting to discuss twinning of Wednesbury and Kladno.

© Archiv Bezpečnostnich Složek. Fond Foreign Intelligence Main Directorate – Operative Files (I. S – svazky): personal file reg. no. 43075 I. S, code names 'Kolón', 'Twister', including MTH 21968 I. S. File number: 21968_43075_000_0006

Seasonal Greetings and All Good Wishes

Christmas card from StB file with 'deary Kolona' added in another's handwriting, and ink.

Chief of CIA counterintelligence, James Jesus Angleton, Washington DC, 24th September 1975.

Photo by Harvey Georges. © AP/Shutterstock

MI5 officer Peter Wright in Sydney, Australia, 1st December 1986.

© AP/Shutterstock

Scotland Yard Police'. My father once heard a man say 'get that cat out of here', and when he became postmaster general he went to the MI5 underground phone-bugging operation in Holborn and asked, 'Where's the cat?' They asked back, 'How do you know we have a cat?' and looked at each other in shock.

The system the StB said they devised to call my father to meetings was supposed to be a two-way system, whereby my father could likewise send the StB a cutting from *The Times*. But there are no envelopes from him in the file, which they would have kept as 'proof' of his involvement. There are two cuttings from *The Times* with the same date, 22nd November 1960, which have articles about communist subversion on the Indian borders, and NATO as the fourth nuclear power – both of which the StB could have cut out for their own information-gathering purposes. The only other cutting from *The Times* which had a date, 18th February 1965, is hand-written on in a stranger's handwriting, and this is about my father's ongoing fight to stop the communists in the London Co-operative Society (LCS). The heading is: 'New Group Aims to Reform London Co-Op – Ending Control by Communists – Mr J. Stonehouse's Move'. It says: 'Mr Stonehouse said he believed that communists, having failed in the trade unions, were making a special effort to infiltrate Co-operative societies.' The StB knew very well that my father was actively anti-communist. There are no other dated cuttings from *The Times*. There are four scrappy non-dated cuttings, and two cuttings from a Swedish newspaper – again about the London Co-operative Society. That's all the newspaper cuttings in this StB file, and they provide no evidence that my father was involved in this clandestine *Times* method of arranging meetings.

The StB agents at the embassy in London couldn't go with a 'communist sympathiser' narrative to explain to their masters in Prague why my father would act as an agent for them because they knew he had an active dislike of communism and was in a long-term battle to prevent or curtail their infiltration of the LCS. And *I* know my father understood the nasty nature of communism and had not one iota of tolerance for it, because he made a point of taking me to see Janacek's *From the House of the Dead* – not because I would enjoy this depressing opera based in a gulag, with an entirely grey stage set, but because he could give me a long lecture afterwards about the perils of totalitarianism.

In his ministerial career in the Labour governments led by Prime Minister Harold Wilson, my father had access to plenty of secrets about commercial and military planes, new technology, and secret communication networks. His positions were, in order, parliamentary secretary at the Ministry of Aviation, parliamentary under-secretary of state for the colonies, minister of aviation, minister of state for technology, postmaster general and minister of posts and tele-communications. In this entire StB file the only document that could be called 'technical' is a small-format four-page leaflet produced by the Ministry of Technology and the Royal Aircraft Establishment about carbon fibres for the reinforcement of structural plastics. The information in it was already in the public domain, as shown by the references in the leaflet: two articles – from *The Engineer* dated May 1966 and *Nature* dated February 1967; and a book dated 1964. The Czechs could have picked this leaflet up from anywhere and, having been to the Farnborough Airshow myself a few times, I sug-gest they got it there.

Also not in this file is anything along the lines of new technol-ogy. In March 1967, when he was minister of technology, my father instructed the director of the royal radar establishment (the technol-ogy research department of the Ministry of Defence) at Malvern to find an alternative to the imported cathode ray tubes that were costing the Ministry of Defence a fortune. A working party was set up to achieve it. This led to the discovery of liquid crystal displays by Professor George Gray, to highly lucrative UK patents, and the development of flat screen technology. If my father was a spy, one might expect there to be some reference to this groundbreaking work in the StB file, but there is not. Indeed, there is absolutely nothing in this file to indicate my father was handing secret or sensitive information to a foreign power.

When interviewed in 1977 for Thames TV, Josef Frolik told the rather surprised interviewer, Peter Williams, that of the 40–45 people working at the Czech embassy in London only five were not spies. In Frolik's time, 27 were StB intelligence officers, about ten were military intelligence and others state security or part-timers on special assignments.[5] The spies didn't advertise themselves as such and went under various diplomatic guises including consuls and attachés. One such person was Vlado Koudelka, who my father met thirteen months before the StB claim to have recruited him. It's the first meeting recorded in my father's file, and may well have happened. Instead of using a code name as they did later, the report of this meeting, unsigned but presumably by Koudelka, is headed 'Stonehouse', and says they 'talked about the exchange of delegations between Wednesbury and Kladno – I will handle the Ministry of Foreign Affairs'.[6] Over the twelve-year period that the StB kept a file on my father, there are only two items in my father's handwriting, one of which relates to this meeting: it's a short note on House of Commons paper, dated 8th October, and says 'I am sorry I was unable to come along on Monday'. A short follow-up letter, dated 18th November 1958, is typewritten and signed, and suggests they meet the next day for lunch at the Hungarian Restaurant in Regent Street. The twinning of the towns of Wednesbury and Kladno proceeded from this time.

The second, and last, document written in my father's handwriting is 450 words long, of which 130 words are brief notes on an interview given by a US diplomat, and the rest are biographical notes on two African politicians. There's nothing secret in any of this information, yet the StB have taken the trouble to forge the cover note that accompanies it. All it says is, on one line, 'from Paul Barnes' and on another, 'Harold Poulter Esq.'[7] 'Paul Barnes' was the cover name the StB devised for my father and 'Harold Poulter' was the cover name for any StB agent concerned. It's not in my father's handwriting, but by fabricating this five-word cover note, they're trying to make this inconsequential 450-word document seem very clandestine and important. It's possible the document itself found its way into the file via Will Owen's StB handler. Owen was a Labour and Co-operative Party MP who admitted to passing non-classified information to the Czechs for money.* Although usually categorised under the 'Labour Party', the Labour and Co-operative Party are a separate group within it, and as my father was also a Labour and Co-operative Party MP, Owen and he had reason to be in contact over Co-operative Party matters within the House of Commons. It's possible that some of the other documents in this file came via Owen, especially as Owen was 'handled' by Robert Husak, and then by Josef Kalina, both of whom were StB agents in London who wrote reports that appear in my father's file.

Another document in the file is five typewritten pages from a report my father was writing about the financial aspects of colonialism, in which he says: 'Due to the domination of the economy by European Companies Africans could not control more than one

---

* In January 1970 Will Owen MP was charged under Section 1 of the Official Secrets Act 1911 for communicating information calculated to be useful to an enemy, and receiving money from Czech intelligence agent, Robert Husak, for doing so. Owen pleaded not guilty to all charges, saying that while Husak had indeed paid him £2,300 over a period of nine years, none of the documents handed over to him were classified. For the prosecution, an officer from Special Branch told the court that Owen had confessed that he couldn't be sure that he'd not told Husak classified information over one of their lunch-time meetings. The prosecution could not provide any documentary evidence, and nothing incriminating was found at Owen's home. Judge Stephenson told the jury that suspicion was not enough to convict, and Owen was found not guilty in May 1970. Although cleared of passing classified information, Owen had admitted to handing the Czechs non-classified documents.

seventh of the total commercialised production in the private sector.' He also quotes figures from the United Nations Economic Bulletin for Africa, and writes 'Under Belgian colonial control the resources of the Congo were developed primarily in the interests of corporations and financial concerns; and to a lesser extent for the welfare of the white settlers.'[8] My father was very clear that colonialism was about financial gain, and asked questions in the House of Commons about this, including on the government interest in British Petroleum. As the government had a majority holding in BP, and those profits flowed back to UK government coffers and UK shareholders, it suited them to keep white settlers in positions of colonial government and power so the financial activities could continue unimpeded. Financial gain was underpinned by land-grab and white settlement which, in turn, was rationalised by rampant racism on the part of whites in Africa and the UK. My father challenged all elements of this exploitation on an almost daily basis, making himself enemies in the British and Colonial establishments.

On the face of it, the most damning item in the StB file is a letter addressed to my father dated 4th June 1959, from the Colonial Office, sent on behalf of the secretary of state of the colonies, Alan Lennox-Boyd. It says, further to my father's letter of 30th April, asking if the Czechoslovakians could have a consul in Lagos or a trade delegation to Nigeria, the answer was 'No'. Nigeria was not yet independent, so at the time all enquiries of this nature had to go through the Colonial Office. Without knowing any background to this, it may look damning – why is my father trying to do the Czechs a favour? However, my father was a hornet in the hair of the Colonial Office and just about the last person in the House of Commons they were going to accommodate. My father knew that when he sent the request. In the month before that 4th June letter from the Colonial Office, my father had asked the secretary of state for the colonies no fewer than 22 challenging questions. They included these, on the very same day the Colonial Office wrote their reply: on African land being made available to Africans – 'Can he say whether arrangements will be made for loans to enable co-operative farms to be developed on the unused land in the highlands?'; on the imprisonment of Africans in the Hola Camp in Kenya – 'Is the Under-Secretary aware that the composition of this tribunal gives no cause for faith that there will be a full investigation?'; and 'if he will give details of the detention camps now in use in Kenya, and the number of detainees in each establishment at the latest convenient date?'; and 'Is the Under-Secretary aware that we continue to receive allegations about past and present ill-treatment of these detainees? In view of the considerable improvement in the political situation in Kenya, has not the time come for these men to be released or to have charges brought against them?'; on hospital conditions for Africans – 'what action has been taken with regard to the conditions at the African Hospital in Lusaka?'; and on African political freedom – 'if he will make a statement on the banning of the Uganda National Movement and the Uganda Freedom Movement and on recent events in Uganda.'

Alan Lennox-Boyd had reason to fear my father because my father knew all about what the Colonial authorities were doing in Africa, and they'd been sparring about it for a long time. In 1958 my father asked for an independent inquiry into the conditions at Kamiti Prison in Nairobi. On 18th December 1958, Lennox-Boyd refused that request, but allegations of British brutality continued, so a demand was made for an independent inquiry into conditions in all the prisons and detention camps in Kenya. On 20th January 1959, Lennox-Boyd replied that an investigation was 'not justified'. My father then placed on the Order Paper of the House of Commons a motion asking again for an independent and public inquiry which gathered over 100 Labour and Liberal signatures but the Conservative Lennox-Boyd didn't respond. So the Labour Opposition forced a debate, and on 24th February, the under-secretary, Julian Amery, said 'The Government of Kenya and the Prison Service in Kenya is perfectly capable of keeping its own house in order and is doing so.'

A week later, eleven Africans were beaten to death by warders at Hola Detention Camp. My father contributed to a 1959 book, *Gangrene*, in which he said about this incident 'They were acting, apparently, with the full approval of the Governor, the Kenya Government, the Colonial Secretary, and the Under-Secretary.'[9] In a chapter called 'From the Documents on Hola', my father named the eleven victims and detailed the injuries that led to their deaths. He despised Lennox-Boyd and wrote in *Gangrene*, 'Mr Lennox-Boyd has shown an intense loyalty to his officials and the Ministers in Kenya. Personal loyalty to such persons is not enough. The British Secretary of State for the Colonies owes a higher loyalty – to human justice and human dignity.'[10]

In 2012, after decades of trying, a small group of elderly Kenyans were given permission to take the British government to court. For years, successive British governments had tried to block these charges with the falsehood that no papers from that period of time still existed, and those lies are documented in the book *The History Thieves* by Ian Cobain. He also describes what they were trying to hide: 'They detailed the way in which suspected insurgents had been beaten to death, burned alive, raped, castrated – like two of the high court claimants – and kept in manacles for years. Even children had been killed.'[11] Papers have emerged showing that Lennox-Boyd knew what was happening to tens of thousands of detainees in those camps. Lennox-Boyd was lying in the House of Commons, and my father knew he was lying, and Lennox-Boyd knew my father knew that. Any letter from my father regarding the Czechs, or indeed anyone else, was going to be met with an attitude of non-cooperation. My father would have known that, so while on the face of it, this letter to Lennox-Boyd seems as if my father was doing the Czechs a favour, the opposite is true. The last person Lennox-Boyd was going to look positively upon was my father. If the Czechs asked him to write the letter, my father would have known the answer was going to be 'No'. Perhaps that was the idea, because my father was vehemently anti-communist and helping them spread that ideology in Africa was the last thing he would want to do.

The file contains a postcard-type Christmas card with a photo of my sister and I dating from 1960 or 1961. Under the photo of me blowing a balloon and my sister holding her ears as if it's about to burst, it's printed: 'Seasonal Greetings and All Good Wishes' and under that, in handwriting, 'Barbara and John' and 'Jane' and 'Julia'. Maybe my father sent it to the embassy in the normal course of seasonal pleasantries, or maybe there's more to it. In his book, *The Deception Game*, Ladislav Bittman describes the operations of Department D, 'Prague's bureau of black propaganda', and talks about the methods of collecting raw data for making forgeries, including this: 'Intelligence officers abroad, authenticated as diplomats or representatives of various governmental organizations ... send out a large number of Christmas greetings to their foreign counterparts and to important persons in general. As etiquette dictates, their greetings are duly answered, the answers signed, and the signatures sometimes written on letterhead stationery.'[12] If our Christmas card was part of this deception, they would have been disappointed because it had no useful signature, but they still filed it away under 'Kolon's children'. The interesting thing about this Christmas card is that someone has written at the bottom, in a different-coloured blue ink, 'deary Kolona'. Over the period of the file, the StB allocated my father four agent names: 'Root' which they used only once, Kolon, Katalina, and Twister. The word 'Kolona' is 'Kolon' with the grammatical suffix 'a' – which is one of the suffixes added to names in the Czech language. The word 'deary' is not Czech or Slovak, and is a word of endearment found in an English dictionary but which would never be used by an English person, unless they sold violets on the streets of 19th-century London. In other words, an StB agent has added these words to make it appear that it's from an affectionate and friendly agent who recognises himself as 'Kolona'.

The agents liked to promote to Prague the notion of friendliness, saying in one report that a 'motive for cooperation' was my father's 'brotherly relationship with comrade Kugler'.[13]

The StB pumped up the file with anything they could lay their hands on, to make it look as if the file had something in it. From 1960, there's an eight-page typed list of the proposed membership of the Monckton Report into the future of East African colonial countries – all of which was public knowledge, and could have been prepared by anyone. It doesn't have my father's name, yet alone signature on it. Again from 1960, there's a typewritten itinerary of a trip my father took to East Africa – which could have come from anyone in the Labour Party. There's a letter dated 12th October 1960 from an assistant of Joshua Nkomo, of the National Democratic Party of Southern Rhodesia, addressed to the Czech embassy, and with no reference to my father. Nevertheless, the StB chose to put it in his file. Indeed, throughout the file there are reports written in Czech on all kinds of political issues, probably gleaned from the newspapers or Hansard, and the aliases for my father are not incorporated into the typewritten text. Only later has an alias been handwritten at the top of the page, as if someone was allocating them in retrospect to an appropriate-looking file.

There's a letter in the file dated 18th December 1959 which is a carbon copy of a letter to my father on plain, unheaded paper, stamped 'Ernest Marples' instead of a signature. This relates to a debate in the House of Commons on 9th December, when MPs were asking Marples, the minister of transport, about nuclear marine propulsion. Mr Awbery MP asked if the UK was in a position to compete with Western Germany, and my father asked, essentially, how the UK shipbuilding industry will be affected, and whether the minister was going to make a further statement. The letter in the file is a reply to these parliamentary questions and it is carbon copied and stamped because these were not personal letters, they went out to several people at the same time. It was just before the Christmas recess and Marples says: 'Invitations to tender will be issued by my Ministry very shortly', and, 'I would, of course, have announced this in the House had it been possible. But the decision has only just been taken; I am therefore announcing it to the Press.'[14] So, this is a letter following normal parliamentary procedure where a minister, as a matter of courtesy, gives the interested MPs an update to their questions. This is no secret, as the press are imminently going to be informed, and it had no urgency to it as, two years later, other MPs were pressing Marples to tell them when the tendering process will be complete. Nevertheless, it's a curiosity as to how it came to be in the file, and why. If my father gave it to the StB, there was nothing in it they couldn't have read in the newspapers the next day, so why even bother giving it to them? It's a worthless piece of paper, but somehow it got in this file, and there's the mystery. Maybe someone took it off my father's desk at the House of Commons.

A two-page report typewritten in English is headed in handwriting 'Od Lee' – 'From Lee' – and given that 'Lee' was the StB code name for the backbench Labour MP Will Owen, I think it's fair to assume it came from him. In 1969 Frolik told the secret service that Lee was handing them information for cash, and he was arrested in January 1970, admitting he'd done wrong. This document predates any of that, 1st November 1967, and records a lunch between Owen and my father at which they discussed events at a Labour Party Defence Committee meeting. At the end, Lee says, 'Stonehouse was seeking to impress, in view of the criticism of NATO.' What this document shows is that while the Labour Party were emphasising the weakness of NATO, my father was doing the opposite. This goes against what the StB were reporting back to Prague. In a document dated February 1963, they say they have 'no compromising material, the only fact is that he's passing information willingly, damaging British interests'. But emphasising the strength of NATO is not 'damaging British interests', and I wonder why the StB had to get a report of a conversation from 'Lee' if 'Katalina', as the StB called my father at this time, was actually one of their agents. Surely, he could have just told them directly what he thought or, better still, given them a handwritten report? That's what they said they were paying him for.

There's only one other political document in the StB file and that's a two-page typed minutes which appears to be from a Labour foreign affairs committee of 1960, which my father attended, along with Barnett Stross who Frolik also accused of being an StB spy. At the meeting, apparently, Stross said that he was in Prague two weeks earlier talking to 'leading officials' who believed that 'Germans are absolutely unfit to have arms.'[15] While the Czechs probably opened a file on Stross, that in itself is not proof of anything, and I'm not saying the document came from him. One possibility is that this document made its way into the file via Will Owen, who admitted to handing Labour Party material over to the Czechs. The report itself is short and contains nothing that can't be read in the newspapers, and certainly no secrets – and there's nothing to indicate it came from my father.

I've now described every single document in the English language in my father's StB file. The Czech portion of the file, which is the major part, is written in a certain style that I've been told is typical StB – using a lot of words that, when examined closely, don't actually say very much. It's not 'gobbledygook', and I don't have a suitable word to describe it, but it's a peculiar blend of verbosity, obfuscation and repetitive totalitarian bureaucracy. There's no criticism of comrades in the StB file, which is understandable given they never knew who their enemy might be, or how other people were connected. The safest thing was to say nothing negative, which also helped to reassure Prague that everything was fine, which seemed to be important.

Many of the documents are just admin bulk – CV-type reports on my father, drafts of documents with rows of dots that will be handwritten or typed in for a later version. There's a huge amount of repetition generally. Then there are evaluation reports, mostly consisting of how my father can be useful in the future. Indeed, much of what's in these files is about the future – what will happen in the future rather than what happened: they *will* have a meeting; they *will* pay him; they *will* get photos, etc. Maybe they thought that if they prevaricated long enough the personnel in Prague would change, and nobody would remember what they'd said about what was going to happen.

Josef Frolik said in his book: 'I know of no other place in the world, outside of Austria and West Germany, where access to the Government apparatus, Parliament, the trade unions and scientific institutes was *at that time* so complete and on such a scale as in Great Britain'[16] (emphasis Frolik's own). Britain was a remarkably open society. Every word said in the House of Commons was available at the time in the form of printed copies of Hansard, which could be picked up the following day for a couple of shillings at Her Majesty's Stationery Office in Holborn. Someone from behind the Iron Curtain would find some of the information in those papers very revealing, especially when it's to do with defence. Plus, our newspapers are very open, and scientific, military and trade journals were available on subscription or in libraries – a mine of information for communist spies. The StB seem to have spent their time gathering publicly-available information and packaging it as insider 'agent' information. That's what their reports back to Prague consisted of – information that communist Central Office in Prague couldn't dream of as being public knowledge.

Some documents in the file are one-line memos, usually referring to other documents, which are themselves repetitions of other documents, just changed a little so the emphasis is on one subject rather than another previously highlighted. They made a huge deal out of every document. For example, the typewritten itinerary of my father's trip to Africa – basically a list of names they could have got from a dozen sources if they wanted to – is translated and spun into: 'This will also provide opportunities for our trade policy penetration after gaining independence in the current year.'[17] Everything is made to seem more significant than it is.

Comparing the English documents with the reports written about them, it's possible to see that the StB are masters of spin. Every word gets a little turn, a little exaggeration or change of emphasis or even direction, until by the end of a paragraph a complete 180-degree turn has been achieved. It's quite impressive really. The spin is always positive, and leading towards the notion that my father was worth keeping as an agent. I'm reading this and thinking, 'Yes, you need to justify your existence and, while you're at it, pocket some cash.'

If the StB were anything like the KGB, it's quite likely that the people reading these reports in Prague knew they were made-up nonsense. In his autobiography, *Next Stop Execution*, the Russian KGB defector Oleg Gordievsky says of his boss, Viktor Grushko, 'He wanted nothing to do with the huge reports that people kept sending in from foreign stations: even though he was head of the department, he never read them, knowing that most of what they said was invented.' Writing about his time in London, Gordievsky says 'officers often exaggerated their successes and up-rated the importance of their contacts'.[18]

My father's recruitment, according to the file, took place in January 1960, and Robert Husak's report of the event was very descriptive. He's referring here to the fact my father accepted £50 – according to Husak – at Christmas: 'After receiving the money, in that first moment he lost his self-confidence and consciously accepted the position of subordinate. He was not accustomed to this position and apparently rebelled internally. I helped him to move through this depression and he sensed that I understood him well and I saw boyish gratitude in his eyes.' Husak reports that his understanding and tact led to their friendship and, 'he had complete confidence in me'. Husak notes that, 'There is no space in the operative record to describe psychological moments,' but says, 'Kolon accepted my leading role and in terms of that personal relationship he became an agent.'[19] Husak must have been very pleased with himself – he'd just invented an agent over which he claimed to have control and, at the same time, justified where the £50 went, which was probably into his own pocket. Husak says: 'We agreed to explain Communist principles to him and help him with advice and criticism in preparing his book on British democracy. It wants to address the system of non-corruption, i.e. the de-politicisation of public life and especially the youth. The book will be controversial, but formulated to draw the attention of the British public to a politician fighting to deepen democracy and thereby enhance the moral prestige of Britain abroad.'[20] Prague might have bought this nonsense, but my mother doesn't. At this time, January 1960, my father was engaged in a battle with communism within the London Co-operative Society, of which he was a board member – a bitter battle that would ensue over the next few years. He knew very well what communist principles meant, and he detested them – and that is no exaggeration. My mother typed up all my father's paperwork, including reports and books, and she tells me that no such book was planned at any time. Husak's fantasy report continues, 'I am confident that I will help to get him into the leadership of the Labour Party over a period of ten years.' Husak's laying plans for his long-term pocket money stream.

According to the defector Frolik, standard procedure included this: 'working on the precept that had been drummed into us in Prague ... we ensured they received money from us and *signed* for it' (his italics), and the 'receipt is carefully filed away'.[21] In my father's file, there's a reference to him being given £25 in February 1960 which 'he signed' for, but there's not a single signed receipt, or unsigned receipt, in his file.

The StB agents liked having good lunches on expenses, paid for by Central Office in Prague, at the best restaurants in London, including the San Frediano, White Tower, Prunier, Boulestin,

Bentley's, Hatchetts, The Vine, Marquis and Frascati, but they could only justify these expenses if they said they were meeting an 'agent'. Their reports of meetings always began with a description of the efforts they made to make sure they weren't being followed, sometimes with details of the circuitous route they took to get there. They did this even when the destination they were heading for was routinely frequented by people who would notice a famous British politician meeting shady characters from the Czech embassy – like journalists, politicians or the British secret service.

An example of an invented meeting is recorded in the file as having taken place between my father and StB agent Captain Robert Husak on 29th December 1965 at the Grill Room at St Ermin's Hotel, 2 Caxton Street. This was literally the last place in the entire country that a UK politician would agree to meet his communist StB 'handler', because in the 1960s it was the main watering hole for all the branches of the British secret services. It was the place where the Special Operations Executive (SOE) was formed in the 1930s, and was for years later used by the Secret Intelligence Service (SIS), which became MI6, whose HQ was nearby at 54 Broadway. It was the HQ for Section 'D' of SIS, and home for the Statistical Research Department of SOE. The Government Communications Headquarters (GCHQ) were around the corner in Palmer St, MI9 were in Caxton Street, and the Chief of SIS had his office at 21 Queen Anne's Gate, with further offices in Artillery Mansions on Victoria Street and in the basement of St Anne's Mansions. Military intelligence, MI8, had a listening post on the roof of what was the passport office in Petty France. The hotel was used by MI5, and the Naval Intelligence Division. Even as late as 1981, it was the natural meeting place for the St Ermin's Group – a right-wing Labour Party group including Denis Healey, that organised to prevent Tony Benn taking over the Party. St Ermin's was also a ten-minute walk from the old Scotland Yard police headquarters, the Foreign Office and the Houses of Parliament. It even had an extension of the division bell so the many MPs and Lords who frequented the hotel's restaurant and bars could be alerted when they had to return to parliament to vote. In this most unlikely of places, Husak says he had a clandestine meeting with my father. He reports it was 'perhaps the most interesting meeting during my entire stay in London'. Apparently he told my father they 'are fully aware of fact that he was now a minister, and therefore want to pay maximum attention to the perfect conspiracy of contact and ensure the "cover story" provides the possibility of a full explanation for his contact with them'. My father was reported by Husak to have said 'there must be no scandal'.[22] The idea that my father met Husak at St Ermin's Hotel is ludicrous. The more credible scenario is that Husak wanted a nice lunch on expenses and felt it would be cute to walk into 'the lion's den', as it were, and observe the secret agents as, no doubt, they observed him.

In 1961 the StB reported paying my father £250 in document 000_0389. His code name at the time was 'Kolon'. They say, 'Kolon said he was going to be at Sadler's Wells Theatre on the evening of 30th June. We agreed he would leave his car at Wells Street, about 3/4 km from the theatre. The street is quiet in the evening, the entrance to the park, and movement on it is easy to control. Kolon himself made a drawing – see attachment, where we should put the money and gave us the description and dates of the car. New station wagon, Austin A55, green, number 5108 MF, key number FP672.'[23] Indeed, the adjacent document, 000_0388, is a page taken from a notebook showing a map, and it has those car details on it. But it's not written in my father's handwriting. Depending on how it's approached, Wells Street is about three kilometres from the theatre, but there's no park on it. The map shows roads going around an oval-shaped central section, presumably buildings, with the letter 'T' marked at one end, and four roads leading into that oval area at somewhat haphazard angles, one marked with an 'A' and another with an asterisk. No road names are given. Wells Street itself is straight, and nowhere along its kilometre length does it have the road configuration as shown in the map, so identifying from this map where the car was supposed to be parked would be difficult to say the very least. The report describes events at 9.30pm when agent 'Kugler' attempted to put the money in the car while 'Hanousek' kept watch from a distance. There was a 'technical failure' because the key my father had supposedly given them from the 'bundle' on his key ring was the wrong one. Kugler tried the doors and then worked out it was the key to the back-hatch. He put the package of money between the gear stick and the 'overhang of the front seat'. According to the report, 'Shortly after 10pm, Kolon came to the car alone and immediately left without looking for money in the car.'[24] Given that finding the car on Wells Street from the map would be nigh on impossible, and given that the map was not, as they said it was, drawn by my father, I think it's fair to say this entire scenario was also fake.

The Wells Street map has a file number, 148, and on the reverse of this page taken from a notebook there is another map, this time with no file number and no reference to it within the file documents. Again, it is not in my father's handwriting. It identifies a location in 'Fullbrook Road, N19' (actually spelled Fulbrook) showing the streets around Tuffnel Park (actually spelled Tufnell) underground station or, as it's marked on the map, 'U-station' (as in the German 'U-Bahn'). And there's a mark indicating the location of a pub, spelled incorrectly as 'salloon'. Under the map are the words '169 Rushey Green Lane, Black Horse Inn, saloon' – which is location 'II' of *The Times* system of calling meetings. The map shows a location in north London, while the Black Horse Inn address is in Catford, south London. Given that this map bears no relation to any text in the file, it seems likely that the purpose here was to link a supposed regular meeting place, the pub in Catford, with my father – who was supposed to have drawn the map on the other side.

'Hanousek' was the StB's alias for Premysl Holan, and a year later he was involved in another purported money exchange, this time for

£100. To make it look genuine to the masters in Prague, they pretended that my father had cancelled the meeting, then rearranged it. To support this notion, the file contains an envelope dated 19th June 1962, addressed to 'Mr Premys Holan 60 Maitland Court Lancaster Gate W2' (in capitals) and another, a day later, to 'P Holan Esq' (in lower case letters), this time accompanied by a note saying 'P.H. Thursday impossible suggest Tuesday In haste P.B.'[25] The initials 'P.B.' probably stand for 'Paul Barnes', the cover name the StB devised for my father. None of these documents are in my father's handwriting, even given that he could be expected to try and disguise that.

Captain Robert Husak apparently thought he was the James Bond of the StB. Joseph Frolik describes him as 'a handsome young playboy-gangster', and recounts a story of him seducing a top-level German secretary at NATO HQ and 'obtaining classified information in return for his services'.[26] My father met Husak at a cocktail party for a visiting delegation at the Czech embassy. He wrote: 'I was approached by a tall, handsome and suave Czech who seemed to know me, although I did not have any recollection of meeting him. His manner did not attract me to him. In the hubbub of the cocktail conversation he was trying to push his luck with me … when he started trying to make a date for lunch, I allowed myself to be pushed forward in the party melee, and so hoped to avoid any commitment. But as I moved forward he pushed an obviously prepared note into my hand with his name on it, "Husak", and begged me once more to have lunch with him. I did meet him for lunch but took the precaution of putting in a full report of our conversation through the Ministry's Intelligence Officer.' That officer was David Purnell. My father continues, 'I saw Husak at several diplomatic functions afterwards and when I was involved in negotiations on the possible sale of VC10s to CSA, the Czech Airline, Husak turned up as an interpreter for the Czech Minister.'[27] In the course of his ministerial job, my father had to communicate with the Czechs, and the Czech trade negotiators were required to accept the involvement and oversight of the StB. On 21st September 1965 my father left Heathrow Airport, spearheading a government drive to sell British Aircraft to Iron Curtain countries, and it was arranged for a VC10 exhibition flight to take place in Prague the following year.

It was in connection with VC10 sales that my father agreed to meet Husak on 9th August 1966, thinking he was going to get an update on the trade situation. Husak had suggested they meet at the Carafe Restaurant, off Lowndes Square. This was no clandestine meeting as far as my father was concerned, because he arrived in his ministerial car, and Lowndes Square was not an appropriate location for spy-and-handler meetings because it's close to many embassies and frequented by diplomats. It's also a four-minute walk away from the Special Forces Club at 8 Herbert Crescent – a favourite hang-out of the secret services. But Husak had big plans for this meeting. In his report he says, 'I wanted pictures taken of me,' so at the last minute he suggested a change of venue to the Chelsea Room at the Carlton House Hotel in Cadogan Place, around the corner, where another StB agent was waiting to take the photos clandestinely. These photos, of my father and Husak walking to the Carlton House Hotel, are the only photos in the StB file. The only tape recording referred to in the StB file also relates to this lunch meeting. There's no actual tape, but Husak was supposed to have taken a tape recording of their conversation at lunch. The file states, using the code name 'Twister' for my father, that: 'Unfortunately, the recording is very poor quality because the restaurant was noisy. The clearer part (only partially) is basically just a monologue by Hanc [Husak's alias], while Twister's voice usually disappears completely.'[28] Elsewhere in the file we're told Husak didn't mention the name of the agent in the tape. By having photos taken, and deliberately botching a recording, Husak was trying to cover his back because after the lunch, according to him, he gave my father £1,500 in the back of a taxi. That was supposed to be £500 back-pay for three years. In the ten years during which my father was supposed to be spying for the Czechs, a total of £4,280 came out of the accounts department in Prague. It looks like Husak got most of it, and Hanousek and Kugler did pretty well too, but most – not all – of the StB agents seem to have had their fingers in the 'spy' pie.

The file shows that the Czechs intended to prevaricate over the purchase of the VC10s. In February 1967, Husak wrote a report about a lunch meeting, saying: 'Right from the start he turned to me with a question: are you going to buy the VC10s or not? I answered in the spirit of your telegram to Petrane. The conversation then focused mainly on the problem of business law, which is the decision.'[29] From this, it seems they'd made a decision in Prague to use 'business law' as a delaying tactic. The next month, one of the three first secretaries at the embassy, Colonel Josef Kalina, reported a meeting in which my father said if they didn't want to buy the VC10 planes, that would be fine because the UK will sell them to Austrian Airlines instead. Kalina's title as 'first secretary' was a cover for the fact that he was the residency chief of the StB, with eighteen personnel under him. His alias was 'Karhan'.

I've seen so many newspapers and websites repeat the notion that my father became a traitor for the money, yet his StB file contains entries that conflict with that idea. In October 1962 the file says: 'His parliamentary salary of £1,750 a year is enough for him to reach a decent level for him and his family, including a decent apartment and a car.'[30] In March 1967, Husak reports to Prague that my father's salary is now £7,000 a year and, knowing he couldn't spin the 'he does it for the money' line, writes 'later when he drank a little more, surprisingly, he emphasised that money is just a "minor" reason for his cooperation with us, the main point is his ideological views. And from this point of view, his cooperation with us has lasted.'[31] That is pure invention. According to the file, the first payment was made to my father over lunch at Hatchetts restaurant on the 21st December

1959, with Robert Husak reporting on the 10th that he would give him '£50 for Christmas present for questions in parliament'.[32] I've been able to contrast and compare the subject of 'cash for questions' through the whole period of this file because every word my father ever said in the House of Commons is online at api.parliament.uk, and there's no proof of any such arrangement.

There is only one instance over a twelve-year period where the file mentions a specific question in the House of Commons. It concerned a visit to the UK by the foreign minister of Spain which, at the time, was still ruled by the fascist General Franco. On the 29th June 1960 my father asked: 'Is the Foreign Secretary aware that the over-whelming mass of the British people of all political parties …' (he's interrupted by Tory MPs shouting 'No') '… despite the shouts from the benches behind him, are very unhappy indeed about this visit and its implications? Will he take this opportunity of denying that there is any prospect of any defence arrangements being entered into between this country and Spain, and any question of Spain being admitted to the North Atlantic Treaty Organisation?' When he was a teenager, my father's parents had taken Spanish refugee children into their home in Southampton because of the peril the children faced in Guernica, and other towns in northern Spain, where Franco's fascism was opposed and Franco's air force had been dropping bombs, as part of the Spanish Civil War in the late 1930s. As a child I'd been taken by my parents to see Picasso's painting *Guernica*, and fascist Spain was a live issue in our household. My father asking questions about Spain's potential entry into NATO was completely in character, and needed no prompting from the StB. On 1st July, the StB file records that the *Daily Mail* and *Daily Express* had reported what my father had said in the House of Commons, but they say he asked the question because he'd been instructed to do so by agent Kugler on the 20th June: 'I showed him a cutting from the *Daily Express* dated 18.6 about the Spanish Foreign Minister … and Kolon agreed to ask questions if they were short.'[33] The 'reward' was £30. Someone who believes the word of a communist agent might think this proves my father took 'cash for questions', but anyone who knew my father would say he would have known of the intended visit anyway, and had his question lined up already. All this report really proves is that the StB were capable of back-dating a report and extracting cash from Central Office in Prague.

The file shows that the StB were constantly complaining they were getting nothing from him. In June 1961 they were saying 'the results for the last six months were minimal', and 'he had been without contact for several months'.[34] In November, Captain Sochor reported: 'some of his questions are not successful', saying they 'plan to deepen Kolon's compromise', noting 'he isn't a "foodie", and doesn't drink much'.[35] Sochor says he 'hands in hand-written reports with no espionage value',[36] but I've already discussed the only, single, hand-written 'report' – it's 450 words long and there's nothing to indicate it was written for them, and it certainly had 'no espionage value'. Underneath a report dated 8th December 1961, there's a handwritten note by someone who appears to be overseeing things: 'Kolon is too accustomed to receiving fees from us without us making them dependent upon the quality of the reports. The source of the difficulty with cooperation is that we want high-quality information, which he is too lazy to get.'[37]

In January 1962, the StB complain that my father 'did not provide essentially any quality information',[38] and in July say, 'Kolon did not produce any interesting information' and 'he could show more of his own initiative'.[39] In a February 1963 report, the words 'he did not show enough initiative'[40] were underlined twice, with three exclamation marks added to the side. In March 1965 agent Robert Husak (alias 'Hanc') says 'I've been calling his apartment since I came from Prague. The phone is either answered by his wife or not by anyone.'[41] In October he says he couldn't make contact with him at the Labour Party Conference – although they were 'close a couple of times'.[42] In January 1966, after being unable to reach my father by phone, they 'accidentally met'. In May 1967, Husak writes that he wants to discuss 'the inertia of the present connection and the transition to submit written reports in any form'.[43] In July 1968, the Czechs were having a hard time making contact; they said that was because they didn't know the phone number. Later that year agent Pravec went twice to the House of Commons, supposedly to make contact, but could only report that, 'he looked at me in the gallery during PM's question time'.[44] Pravec reports in May 1969 that, 'Attempts to contact him were unsuccessful. However, they provided a good picture of Twister avoiding cooperation in every way possible. In the meantime, I called his apartment eight times over 14 days, but always without results.'[45] The following month, 'just for peace of mind', Pelnar says he 'went to the House of Commons three times between 16–19 June at question time, but Twister was never there'.[46] I've seen it written that contact between my father and the StB ceased when Frolik defected, but it's clear from the file that making contact was an issue for the StB long before Frolik started his holiday on 23rd June 1969, which landed him in the welcoming arms of Richard Helms, the director of the CIA.

On 20th January 1970, agent Karel Pravec (alias 'Pelnar', who defected to the CIA in 1980), wrote a seven-page report summarising the situation. Underlined in the report is the statement: 'We've not had contact for one and a half years,' and it also says that they 'tried to contact him by phone more than 20 times. His wife constantly said he wasn't at home, despite calling when they were sure he was at home, for example, very early in the morning.'[47] Pravec says that despite giving him money, 'his intelligence results were still practically worthless'.[48] On the 19th October, Major Vaclav Cepelak writes that, 'since the last assessment nothing has changed in the case',[49] and by the 5th of November, he's had enough and writes: 'Because of the fact that the use of compromising material against this person is questionable, I suggest the Twister file is sent permanently to archive.'[50] And that's where the file ends.

There's not a single piece of paper in the StB file that in any way proves my father was a spy. On the contrary, the file proves he wasn't. It seems obvious to me what happened: the StB had to justify their cosy existence in London by inventing 'agents' and they benefitted from this by pocketing the cash they were supposed to be giving those agents. This is, indeed, exactly what Josef Frolik said they did at the London embassy.

19

The Mountain and the Molehill

The molehill was the inconsequential file created by the StB at the Czech embassy in London, and it grew into a mountain, that turned into a volcano spurting pyroclastic flow, that rushed down into the surrounding sea of media, causing a tsunami which engulfed my family. Some of the garbage swept onto the desks of three prime ministers – Harold Wilson, Jim Callaghan and Margaret Thatcher – and wasted their time, along with that of their cabinet secretaries.

The nonsense began in 1969 when Joseph Frolik, an StB agent of seventeen years standing, defected to the CIA. He'd worked for two years as a Labour attaché at the Czech embassy in London and told the CIA he was '90 per cent sure' my father was spying for the StB, although he'd never had any dealings with him or seen his file. The media love to call Frolik a 'spymaster', but he was no such thing. He was a low-level operative who followed people around London trying to find the dirt on them, but once in the hands of the CIA, he was treated like a rock star. In his memoirs, *The Frolik Defection*, he gives details of how he was directed by a CIA agent to wait for a boat, with his wife and son, at a precise location on the Gulf of Burgas, on the Bulgarian shore of the Black Sea. The boat arrived, with two CIA agents, who took Frolik to Istanbul where a US Air Force plane was waiting for them at a US Air Force base in the suburbs. Frolik takes up the story of their arrival in Washington: 'Surrounded by CIA men and the Secret Servicemen who had been assigned to guard me, I was hustled through customs to meet no less a person than Richard Helms, the head of the CIA himself.'[1]

Soon after landing in Washington, Frolik was flown to London with a CIA agent, to be debriefed by MI5. He spent a week in the UK talking to members of the secret service, including Peter Wright, Martin Furnival Jones and Charles Elwell. On 4th August 1969, Elwell interviewed my father at 10 Downing Street in front of Harold Wilson and his parliamentary private secretary (PPS), Michael Halls, who took notes. My father went through all his dealings with the Czechs, including approaches by StB agent Robert Husak that he'd reported to David Purnell, his ministry's intelligence officer, and to George Wigg, Wilson's security liaison with MI5 and MI6. He met Elwell several times again so Elwell could go over the details, including the facts that my father had not accepted free holidays, party invitations, or presents of alcohol, and his passport showed no trips to Czechoslovakia other than those declared. By coincidence, Charles Elwell was from the family of a large tool-making firm in my father's constituency, Elwell's, and when my father was in Kladno he'd taken some of the firm's tools, by way of promoting manufactured goods from his constituency.

Frolik was debriefed in America by the CIA for three years, then encouraged by them to write his memoirs, which they first translated, then cut down, omitting the material embarrassing to them. They thought the British market would be more appropriate, given that Frolik had been based in London and had named three Labour MPs, one of whom – Will Owen – had been put on trial. The CIA passed the manuscript to a British ghostwriter, Charles Whiting, and in November 1973 Frolik moved to Yorkshire so they could work together. The publisher Leo Cooper was approached, and Whiting told him that Frolik had already been over to the UK four times since his defection, helping the British secret services with their enquiries. Cooper checked with the secretary of the D-Notice committee, Admiral Farnhill, to make sure he wasn't going to break any security laws.* MI5 would go on to make their own cuts of the manuscript. Cooper records that, 'Frolik volunteered right from the off about Stonehouse,' and according to David Leigh, author of *The Wilson Plot*, 'News of Frolik's planned disclosures began to seep around Fleet Street.'[2] Leo Cooper was married to the author Jilly Cooper, and I expect they had many journalistic contacts to 'seep' this information to. One of them was Bernard Levin, a columnist on *The Times*, to whom Cooper told this: 'Frolik's material would make your hair stand on end.'[3] Levin didn't take up the story, but another *Times* journalist, Christopher Sweeney, did. That's how my father came to choke on his cornflakes on the 25th January 1974, when he read 'Defector reveals MPs' part in spy ring'.[4] Although his name was not mentioned here, so many parliamentarians had already heard the gossip about him he knew they'd make the connection. He was helpless: innocent but with no way to prove it.

I've often read that my father wasn't properly investigated by MI5 at the time of the Frolik accusation, but the investigating officer, Charles Elwell, was no pushover. Indeed, few people at MI5 were as fanatic at chasing down communists as him. Christopher Andrew writes that: 'Shortly before Elwell retired, [in May 1979] he "abandoned bureaucratic niceties" and fired off a minute to the DG and DDG [director general and deputy director general] complaining that the Service was not paying enough attention to the threat of subversion: "The Communist threat has become more insidious because of the 'blurring of the edges between Communism and democratic socialism'".'[5] Once retired, Elwell became involved in anti-communist think tanks and was the author of *British Briefing*, a newsletter that attacked left-wing MPs and trade unionists and

---

* A D-Notice was a request from the UK government to newspaper editors and broadcasters not to publish or convey information to the public that was deemed a threat to national security. Although advisory, it was invariably complied with. Today, a similar system is in place under the title DSMA-Notice (Defence and Security Media Advisory Notice).

was circulated to politicians and reporters. Each issue carried a note asking readers 'to refrain from mentioning it, or its existence, or from direct quotation'. Elwell met his wife, Ann, at MI5, and she spent most of her career at the covert Information Research Department (IRD) within the Foreign and Commonwealth Office, which was tasked with disseminating non-attributable anti-communist briefings to a select group of politicians, journalists, broadcasters and opinion leaders.*

Although Elwell had no proof my father was a spy, he might have used him as a pawn in the larger game of bringing Wilson into disrepute – for having appointed him, and then keeping him in a ministerial position after the spy accusation had been made. Elwell certainly had the establishment friends to spread the rumour to, while his wife had the media contacts. Gossip became rumour, and that became a dark, enveloping cloud of suspicion. It seems that many people in Fleet Street and the corridors of power, and members of the exclusive gentlemen's clubs frequented by establishment figures, had become aware of the accusation years before Frolik publicly named John Stonehouse as a spy in the *Daily Mirror* on 17th December 1974. I've seen it said that my father didn't have many friends in the Labour Party, but that was not the case in 1969, when Frolik first started the rumour. By June 1970, my father was out in the political cold, and not offered a shadow ministerial position by Wilson when

---

* The IRD was founded in 1948 by Labour Foreign Minister Ernest Bevin, who thought that 'The most effective method of countering Soviet propaganda was to provide specific information refuting the misrepresentations made by the Soviet Government.' (Ref: Ernest Bevin, Cabinet Meeting (48), 2nd Conclusions, 8th January 1948, The National Archives File CAB 128/12/2, page 16.) It provided scripts for 'The Voice of Britain', a radio station based in Cyprus that promoted British policy in Arabic and English, as well as suggesting authors and themes for books that Bodley Head published under their 'background books' series, which the IRD underwrote by purchasing 15,000 copies of each which they distributed to Foreign Office posts around the world. The authors were often unaware that a 'see-safe' arrangement with a secretive Foreign Office department was behind their success.

Labour lost the election. Perhaps Wilson saw an association with him as too dangerous, given that Wilson himself was under attack from the right-wing establishment. And even an unsubstantiated rumour of being a spy is politically hazardous because spying is treason and guaranteed to incur the wrath of every person in the country – right-leaning or left. Certainly something had changed Wilson's mind about my father since 1968 when his government recommended my father's appointment as a life-long privy counsellor.

Frolik wasn't a good witness: he'd never seen the file or had any direct contact with my father; he lied about other British politicians and trade unionists, and changed his story all the time. One person who was well aware of this was John Hunt, cabinet secretary to three prime ministers – Edward Heath, Harold Wilson and James Callaghan. On the 3rd June 1975 he wrote a long memo to Ken Stowe, PPS to Prime Minister Harold Wilson, updating him on the Frolik situation, prior to the publication of Frolik's memoirs in July. The purpose of this memo was to inform the prime minister of issues that might arise in the form of Parliamentary Questions following publication. Hunt referred to the article in *The Times* on 25th January 1974, in which it was announced that Frolik was writing the book. This article started off my father's year of madness, because he knew the book would regurgitate the false accusations of 1969, and take him out from under the cloak of suspicion and into the firing line. In a charmingly understated fashion, Hunt tells Stowe that, 'We have obtained a sight of the text through somewhat unorthodox channels.' Contrary to Frolik saying 'the book is intended to be an authoritative account of the methods, techniques and targets of a communist Intelligence Service', Hunt reports that 'it is in fact an exaggerated and tendentious account of Frolik's own career in the Czech intelligence service with the emphasis on the period (1964–6) when he served as Labour attaché at the Czech embassy in London. The book contains several references to politicians and other persons in public life. Few of them are named, but we can identify some of them.' He writes 'There is a reference to an unnamed homosexual Labour Minister who was "greedy for money" and another reference to an unnamed Labour MP involved "in some sort of homosexual trap in Czechoslovakia". Both are believed to refer to Mr Stonehouse, and if these references are noticed the press may make the same deduction.'[6] Hunt has either got things mixed up here, or the manuscript changed, but either way it was Will Owen MP who Frolik talked of as always 'greedy for money', and my father who – without naming him – 'had been involved in some sort of homosexual trap'.[7] I know from examining every page of the famous file, there never was a homosexual honeytrap, nor a heterosexual honeytrap or, indeed, any other form of compromise.

Frolik had made an allegation against the left-wing Labour MP Michael Foot, and Prime Minister Harold Wilson was informed by the director general of MI5, Sir Michael Hanley. Harold Wilson sent a reply through Robert Armstrong on the 4th July 1974: 'The Prime Minister has his reservations about the story. He thinks it unlikely that Mr Michael Foot was in Brighton for the TUC conference in September 1965, because he had no interest in the trade unions until he was appointed Secretary of State for Employment earlier this year.'[8]

Frolik dedicated an entire chapter in his book to what he called 'The Heath Caper'. Because the musically talented prime minister Edward Heath wasn't married, some people assumed he was gay – including the StB. Hunt wrote to Stowe: 'The book contains an extraordinary story of a plot to compromise Mr Heath. It says that he was not markedly heterosexually inclined, and that, although the Czechs had no evidence on which to base their assumptions it seemed worth trying to compromise him. The plot was to invite him to play the organ and then put him in a position where he would be open to blackmail and forced subsequently to feed the Czechs with top-level information. The book says that two years were spent in preparing the trap but at the last moment British counter-intelligence warned

Mr Heath of what was afoot. This story appeared in rather jocular form in the Atticus column of the *Sunday Times* on 20th January, 1974, and Mr Heath then told me that he had never received any invitation to play the organ in Czechoslovakia and that consequently the suggestion that he had been warned off by the Security Service did not arise.'[9]

The BBC's security correspondent, Gordon Corera, investigated this story in June 2012 by examining the StB archives in Prague and tracking down the ex-StB spy who Frolik said was behind the plan – Major Jan Mrazek. Supposedly, the plan was to get Heath to meet the Czech organist Reinberger in London, then lure him to Prague and entrap him in a homosexual honeytrap. With the help of archivists of the Czech security service and a translator, Corera examined hundreds of pages in the Mrazek files and correspondence between Prague and London. There was no file on Heath himself. In all this, there was no hint of a 'Heath caper', yet alone evidence. When Corera found Mrazek living twenty miles from Prague, then a man in his eighties, he said the Heath blackmail plan was 'absolutely nonsense'. But Mrazek did have one recollection about Heath. Corera says: 'He tells me that he was present at a meeting after the end of the Cold War when Heath told a Czech minister that the story had been created by a "British right-wing organisation" in order to undermine his position as leader of the Conservative party in the early 1970s.' Corera says that 'In the Cold War, hidden hands were frequently involved in memoirs written by defectors such as Frolik. Such books could be useful vehicles to score points and reveal who might have been on the other side's payroll. And in the case of Frolik's book there is evidence that people with links to the shadowy nexus between the intelligence world and politics were involved.' Corera interviewed Frolik's publisher, Leo Cooper, who told him, 'he was sure the security and intelligence services had a hand in the book. He also recalls right-wing MPs, linked to the intelligence services, asking him if Frolik had material which could be useful for Margaret Thatcher in her campaign for the leadership of the Tory Party – although he recalls this being "dirt" about Labour and the Trade Unions.' Corera adds that: 'There is no suggestion that Mrs Thatcher was aware of, or involved in any of these machinations.' Mzarek himself thought that George Kennedy Young was involved. Corera explains that he was 'a former deputy chief of MI6 turned Conservative candidate who was particularly active on the right of the party, notably in trying to take control of The Monday Club – a right-wing Tory party pressure group. Mrazek met Young in the 1960s and believes this is why he was singled out to have been behind the Heath Caper. Young certainly disliked Heath intensely – as did others on the right who believed he had sold out and needed to be replaced.'[10]

Frolik went public with the spy allegation on the front page of the *Daily Mirror* on 17th December 1974, when my father was still missing, presumed drowned. It began: 'Missing MP John Stonehouse was a contact for a Communist spy ring.'[11] This caused such a furore that the prime minister, Harold Wilson, was obliged to refer to it later that day in the House of Commons. He said: 'Publicity has recently been given to allegations that my right hon. Friend the Member for Walsall, North was spying for the Czechoslovak Intelligence Service at the time he held ministerial office. These allegations were first made by a Czechoslovak defector in 1969. With my approval, the security service investigated these allegations fully at the time. In the course of its inquiries it interviewed the defector, and it questioned my right hon. Friend about his contacts. Following its investigations the security service advised me at that time that there was no evidence to support the allegations. I am today advised that no evidence to support these allegations has come to light at any time since then. There is no truth whatever in reports that my right hon. Friend was being kept under investigation or surveillance by the security service at the time of his disappearance.' Frolik was upset to be called a liar in such a public way, and about Wilson's additional comment: 'One must always face the possibility that defectors, when leaving a country where they previously were and finding their capital – intellectual capital, of course – diminishing, try to revive their memories of these matters.'

Frolik was stung by these remarks, which undermined his credibility and threatened his position with the CIA, upon whom he was totally dependent not only financially, but for his day-to-day security too.* A few months later, on 18th May 1975, Frolik was visited in Florida by a CIA agent and an MI5 officer called Mr Shipp, who'd gone there to ask him some questions. But Frolik was still so upset he wouldn't talk. Two years later, on 16th March 1977, he wrote to

---

* On the 18th November 1975, the CIA introduced Frolik to the Senate Committee of the Judiciary as 'one of the most senior Eastern intelligence agents to defect to the West since World War II'. He was there to give evidence at the closed session hearings on 'Communist Bloc Intelligence Activities in the United States.' He named John Stonehouse as an agent, saying, 'Subject is under investigation today for embezzlement, fraud and insurance fraud.' Frolik regaled committee members with stories including how a Canadian hockey team had been made so exhausted by the sexual exploits of clandestinely recruited Czech prostitutes the night before the 1959 World Hockey Championships finals, they lost the next day to the Czechs. He told them how Czech agent Mrs Zizka had been assassinated in 1962 by an StB and a KGB agent because she and her husband were about to defect, being an alternative version of events known to the New York police – that her husband killed her and then drove from Manhattan at 110 miles an hour, pursued by the police who, when he crashed, shot him in the shoulder, before Mr Zizka shot himself in the head. Frolik said, 'I cannot prove that this is true,' but that he'd heard it from 'numerous people in the Czech service'. Then he scared the committee rigid by telling them that the KGB directed and coordinated the Czech secret services, that more than half the people in the Czech embassy in Washington were spies, as were Czechs at the UN, not to mention that Czech spies were masquerading as American citizens and naturalised immigrants, and they had agents in various Government agencies as well as in organisations such as the American Civil Liberties Union. (Ref: 'Communist Bloc Intelligence Activities in the United States,' 94th Congress, Committee on the Judiciary, United States Senate, 18th November 1975.) Frolik's performance in front of the paranoid anti-communist Senators no doubt helped ensure the continuance of the CIA's very generous budget.

Czech émigré Josef Josten in London, referring to the Shipp visit, and the House of Commons statement by Wilson: 'Three months later he [meaning Wilson] sent to the United States a high official M15 who conveyed to me the personal apology of the same Mr Wilson.'[12] This implied that Wilson had changed his mind or lied to the House of Commons, and that my father was, indeed, a spy.

But it was all a misunderstanding. The Shipp visit is recorded in a 1978 letter from Cabinet Secretary John Hunt to MP Patrick Mayhew: 'If Mr Wilson had asked for an apology to be conveyed there would have been a record of that instruction; there is none. The officer concerned is quite clear that he received no instruction and that he did not convey an apology from the Prime Minister. He did however express his personal regrets that the Prime Minister had referred to the possibility that defectors, finding their intellectual capital diminishing, tried to revive their memories of certain matters. His reason for doing this was that he found Frolik so angry about the statement that he was unwilling to grant the interview, and he therefore sought to mollify him. Soon after his return to this country the officer recorded what he had done and noted that he had described that particular remark by the Prime Minister as "unfortunate" (the American case officer who had been present at the interview recalled that a somewhat stronger adjective than "unfortunate" had been used). I think there was a genuine misunderstanding, and that Frolik assumed that an official would not have spoken in this way unless he had been authorised to do so.'[13]

Frolik had not been told about this 'misunderstanding' and nor had the recipient of his letter, Josten – and he'd started talking in London about the 'personal apology' Frolik had supposedly received from Wilson, via Shipp. The news reached the ears of three right-wing Conservative MPs, two of whom were ex-MI6: Stephen Hastings, Cranley Onslow and Peter Blaker. Armed with this new information or, rather, misinformation, the triumvirate headed for the House of Commons and demanded a full inquiry into the Frolik allegations, particularly against Stonehouse. On the 14th December 1977 at 4.55pm Hastings opened the batting: 'The matters that I wish to raise concern the security of this country.' By the time they'd finished, Frolik had been mentioned no less than 53 times. Hastings told the Chamber he had new evidence 'of recent date – about a week ago to be precise – and it concerned the letter from Frolik to Josten'. He impressed upon the MPs that Frolik was reliable and should be taken seriously, saying that Frolik had met trade union leader Ernie Roberts and describing the events that had occurred 'one evening, after they had had a lot to drink'. Then MP Hugh Jenkins interrupted to say, 'On a point of order, Mr Speaker. I happen to know Mr Ernie Roberts, and I also happen to know that he is strictly teetotal. The story that he had had a lot to drink must be inaccurate, unless, of course, he was drunk on lemonade.'

The next day, the 15th December, *The Times* reported the call for an inquiry. The prime minister could anticipate questions being asked in the House of Commons on the subject, so that day his cabinet secretary, John Hunt, prepared a background note for him in which he refers to *The Frolik Defection*: 'In many respects the book was an "improvement" on the account of his activities which Mr Frolik gave when he defected; and, when asked about the differences, he said that passages which were inconsistent with what he had originally reported (to the security service and to the CIA) could be ignored.'[14] So it appears that even Frolik didn't believe his own book. In the House of Commons, Callaghan said: 'What has been happening recently is that Mr Frolik has been embroidering the original stories that he told when he was debriefed some years ago. It is a way of keeping himself in the public eye, and from time to time he manages to get some press interest and to catch one or two Conservative members.' Stephen Hastings had retorted, unrepentant, 'I make no apology whatsoever for raising this matter.'

The security services knew that Hastings et al. were wrong about the Frolik-Josten letter being 'of recent date – about a week ago to be precise'[15] because they had, somehow, acquired a copy of it in April 1977 – eight months earlier. And they knew that what was in it was based on a 'misunderstanding'. In January 1978, the prime minister, Jim Callaghan, was reassured, via his PPS Ken Stowe, to learn from Robert Armstrong, permanent under-secretary of state at the Home Office that, 'In his speech in the House of Commons on 14th December, Mr Hastings was relying mainly upon a transcript of a conversation between Frolik and Stott of the *Daily Mirror*, which was widely available in Fleet Street'[16] (then the centre of the UK press industry). Stowe had attached a compliment slip to Armstrong's letter before forwarding it to the prime minister, which said: 'What is clear is i) that Frolik keeps on embroidering the same story and ii) that the security service (right-wing bias and all!) can find no substance in it.'[17]

The triumvirate of right-wing MPs was now joined by another Conservative MP, Patrick Mayhew, and he wasn't going to rely on some letter, he was going straight to the source. So it was that in June 1978 Mayhew visited Frolik in America and recorded two three-hour conversations with him. On the 26th June 1978, the prime minister, James Callaghan, wrote to Mayhew saying: 'Thank you for your letter of 19th June about John Stonehouse. I note that you interviewed Josef Frolik in Washington earlier this month, that with his consent you recorded this on tape and that you are ready to make the entire record available to me. I should be grateful if you would do this as soon as possible so that I may consider whether what he says provides grounds for further investigation and, if so, what form this investigation should take.'[18] The next day, Mayhew's secretary duly delivered the tapes to Number 10. On the 30th June, Mayhew wrote to the prime minister telling him that he was going to inform Mrs Thatcher, then leader of the opposition, about his conversations with Frolik. On the 11th July, Mayhew writes again to Callaghan about the six hours of taped conversations with Frolik – which he expected 10 Downing Street to transcribe: 'Two weeks have now elapsed since you received the tapes of my interviews with Frolik, for which you asked, and more than three weeks since I sent you my letter of 19th June summarising why I believe that the matters affecting John Stonehouse that arise from these interviews ought to be the subject of independent inquiry. I now think it right to tell you that unless I earlier learn from you of your decision in this regard I shall table a question on 13th July' – two days later.[19] As well as having Mayhew on his back, Callaghan had to write to Cranley Onslow on the 28th June, thanking him for his letter of 7th June 'about the allegations that John Stonehouse was a Czechoslovak agent'.[20] On 2nd July Onslow wrote to the prime minister again, laying on more pressure.

Callaghan met Mayhew on the 12th July in the prime minister's room at the House of Commons. It was 8pm, and I expect Callaghan would have preferred to be having dinner. Minutes were taken, and Callaghan told Mayhew that he'd only received the transcript of the Frolik interviews that day, and Mayhew replied that he 'fully understood that the Prime Minister was very busy', that 'he was quite clear that there was nothing in what Frolik had said in relation to trade union leaders which was worth further investigation', and that 'He was concentrating on the Stonehouse aspect which, in his view, did need independent investigation.' Mayhew told Callaghan that Frolik told him that, 'much of his book that had been published had been written for him by a crooked publisher'. When Callaghan asked Mayhew what his opinion was on meeting Frolik, Mayhew replied that he wasn't the shady character he'd expected, and that, 'Obviously he was someone who had committed frightful crimes but he thought he was genuine in what he was now saying.' Callaghan asked: 'does Frolik say he <u>knew</u> Stonehouse was a spy?' (his emphasis). Mayhew replied: 'No: he said that Husak told him that he was going to approach Stonehouse – and said that he did so – and Frolik says that he does not know whether Stonehouse gave Husak any information.'[21] Having pretty much destroyed his own argument,

Mayhew then says 'but', and turns to what was said by another StB defector, Frantisek August. The meeting was left with Mayhew telling Callaghan that he'd be putting down a Parliamentary Question for the 20th July, eight days later, after the prime minister had been to the Bonn Summit in Germany. Mayhew was still being pushy and demanding.

By the 18th, the long transcript had been fully examined, and a letter to Mayhew drafted. It says: 'I note that you say that you do not consider that it calls for investigation in the context of national security of any person other than Stonehouse, and I agree with you about this. [2] As regards Stonehouse the tapes add nothing at all to what the Security authorities already knew. I can quite understand that some of it may have been new to someone who had to rely on published material, but the Security Service had long sessions with Frolik on four occasions between 1969 and 1975, and several sessions with August.' Point [3] then explains about the interview of Frolik on 18th May 1975 in Florida by the MI5 agent, Shipp (without mentioning him by name), saying 'he did not convey an apology from the Prime Minister. What is more he made it quite clear to Frolik that he defended the Prime Minister's statement that there was no evidence to support the allegations against Stonehouse. He did however describe as unfortunate the Prime Minister's reference to the possibility that defectors, finding their intellectual capital diminishing, tried to revive their memories of certain matters. His reason for doing this was that he found Frolik so angry about this slight that he was unwilling to grant the interview, and he therefore sought to mollify him.' Point [4] is that 'Frolik told you that he had denounced Stonehouse to the Americans even before he left Communist territory. This seems to be true: very soon after Frolik's defection and before he arrived in the United States, he said that although he had not seen any reports emanating from Stonehouse he was 90 per cent sure he was an agent of the Czech Intelligence Service. A few days later however he made a further statement in which he said that it was his impression that Stonehouse was either an agent or a confidential contact, though on this occasion he emphasised that his knowledge was tenuous.' Point [5] was about Frantisek August: 'August told us in the spring of 1975 that he had seen a file, which he firmly believed to have been about Stonehouse, in the 1950s. When August was first questioned by the Security Service in 1969 he said he had no knowledge of the recruitment of a British Minister. In the 1975 interview he asserted that he had reported in 1969 that Stonehouse had been recruited in the 1950s and had then referred to a file he had seen in Prague and which he believed to be that of Stonehouse, but there was no trace of this in the records made at the time. Confusion of this kind is common when defectors are interviewed over a number of years. It was not until November 1974, just after Stonehouse's disappearance had been reported in the press, that Frolik said, for the first time without any qualification (and also without evidential proof), that Stonehouse had certainly been a Czech agent and been paid.' The prime minister ends by saying, 'I have decided that no purpose would be served by an independent inquiry' and, rather to Mayhew's chagrin, I imagine, 'your tapes add nothing to our knowledge'.[22]

Frantisek August (alias 'Adam') is often linked with both Frolik and my father. He worked at the London embassy between December 1961 and October 1963, just before Frolik did his term there between 1964 and 1966. Like Frolik, August defected in the summer of 1969 – because they were both worried about their position following political manoeuvrings in Prague. As the letter to Mayhew explained, August was first interviewed by the security service in 1969, and at that time had no knowledge of the recruitment of a British minister, but in the spring of 1975 – when my father was all over the international newspapers and TV – he suddenly remembered that Stonehouse had been recruited in the 1950s, and started saying he'd

seen a file in Prague which he believed to be that of Stonehouse. The
security service weren't buying it because August had said none of this
in 1969. According to August, he met my father in the late 1950s
and had a 'debriefing' session with him in Czechoslovakia, but as my
father wasn't recruited until 1960 – according to the StB file – who is
to say this wasn't just a conversation, if it happened at all. August is
the source of the notion that my father was also a KGB spy, and that
really emanates from August's main thesis that everyone was a KGB
spy. That was his USP, and the CIA loved all that. By the time August
published his 1984 memoirs, *Red Star Over Prague*, he'd abandoned
his Stonehouse fantasy and had not one word to say about him.

'The Frolik Affair Meeting' was held between James Callaghan
and Margaret Thatcher, along with Callaghan's PPS Ken Stowe,
in the prime minister's room at the House of Commons on the
18th July at 9pm. The prime minister began by referring to Mayhew
wanting to put a Question down that day, but Mrs Thatcher immediately intervened and said that she 'had asked that the Question
should be withdrawn because the Prime Minister would not have
had time while at Bonn to attend to these matters'.[23] Callaghan must
have taken a sigh of relief. Now he could get on with some work.
Poor Stowe, on the other hand, had to meet Mayhew at 9.30pm to
go over the whole thing again in Mrs Thatcher's office at the House
of Commons, at her 'invitation'.

Frolik knew nothing about John Stonehouse yet he managed to
waste the time of a great many people who had better things to do.
MI5 didn't seem to think much of Frolik, but his allegations were
kept alive by the press and various right-wing elements in the British
establishment. The man who published his book, Leo Cooper, made
the most appropriate observation about him: 'It was all teasing. Frolik
always knew somebody who had seen a dead donkey.'[24] The fact that
so many people were fooled by him, or pretended to be for their own
purposes, says more about them than about Frolik himself.

20

Secrets and the Security Services:
MI5, MI6 and the CIA

*'There is absolutely no doubt at all that a few, a very few, mal-
contents in MI5, people who shouldn't have been there in the first
place, a lot of them like Peter Wright who were right-wing, malicious, and with serious personal grudges were giving vent to these
and spreading damaging malicious stories about some members of
that Labour government.'*

John Hunt, cabinet secretary, 1973–79

There was nothing my father could have done to avoid being branded a spy. Although he was completely innocent of the charge, circumstances conspired to allow the miasma of suspicion to fall on him. I don't entirely blame the press for this, because they were fed the idea by people within the secret services – by which I do not mean the 'official' MI5 or MI6, but rather certain rogue elements within those organisations, who were themselves encouraged by the paranoia of the CIA.

During the Cold War it was not possible, as a government minister, to avoid having contact with countries behind the so-called Iron Curtain. Political biographies make it clear that politicians of all parties were taking trips to Eastern Europe or Russia, attending receptions and meeting delegations at their embassies, or bumping into personnel from those embassies on the diplomatic circuit. And some of those personnel were spies. They didn't advertise it, so a politician wouldn't have known the difference between a regular commercial attaché and a spy who hid behind that official title.

If a politician suspected he'd been approached by a spy, it was expected he would report it. When my father was minister of state at the Ministry of Technology, he went to Czechoslovakia to sign a technological agreement and, following an approach, he reported the events to George Wigg, who Harold Wilson had appointed to act as liaison between the Labour government and MI5/MI6. One night, after dinner with other members of the delegation, my father had entered his hotel suite to find Robert Husak and another man sitting, sinisterly, in the dark. Husak had a bottle of wine with him, and introduced the man as a fellow diplomat about to be sent to London. They talked and drank until 1am, then left. My mother remembers my father telling her that he took this as a crude attempt to recruit him, saying it was very clumsily done, with them trying to get him drunk. The next day, when the delegation went skiing, Husak's friend came up alongside my father on the slopes; nothing much was said. In July 1968, this character turned up at a dinner party in Hampstead at the London home of the Czech Ambassador, and tried to talk to my father, who avoided him. The guest of honour at this dinner was Dr Ota Sik, the deputy of the leader of Czechoslovakia, Alexander Dubcek, who tried to introduce liberal reforms and in so doing incurred the wrath of the Russians, who reacted a month later by invading with tanks and bringing in another twenty years of repression.

My father had first been made suspicious of Husak when he'd approached him at a Czech embassy reception, and pressed him for lunch, which they subsequently had. My father reported what had happened to the security officer at his ministry, David Purnell. The authors of *Smear! Wilson and the Secret State*, say this: 'MI5 … although tipped off about the meeting by Stonehouse, did nothing to warn him about Husak's identity and let him continue the meetings, using him as a kind of bait.'[2] Apparently, this is what MI5 had done to another Labour Party minister, Charles Loughlin. When my father later reported the events in Czechoslovakia to George Wigg, he expected Wigg to pass that information to the security service. Presumably they knew that Husak was an StB agent, so why didn't they tell my father and warn him? That omission could make a government minister vulnerable to the pernicious interest of the StB – a situation the secret service are tasked to avoid, surely?

On 12th March 1970, Tony Benn asked the Ministry of Technology's security officer, David Purnell, to come and talk to him about the impending trial of the MP Will Owen, who denied passing classified information to the StB but had admitted passing them non-classified information and being paid for it, after being identified by the defector Josef Frolik. Benn didn't want the date of the trial to clash with the visit of the Czech minister of technology, who was due to visit Benn in London in April. That would be too embarrassing. Purnell told Benn what information was likely to come out in the trial, including that Owen was handled by Husak – as recorded in Benn's diary: 'The Czech diplomat in question, who is going to be named, is Robert Husak, and apparently he and John Stonehouse used to talk informally and personally while John was at Mintech. Purnell told me he had a record of all these discussions and it appeared that John's name might come out at the trial and the press were going to make a big thing of it. Purnell said he would like to go and see John Stonehouse if I had no objection, and I said I had none. I don't think anything improper will emerge but one can imagine what the press will make of it.'[3] After this conversation, Benn thinks that nothing 'improper will emerge', which indicates that Purnell, being aware of the 'record of all these discussions' thinks there was nothing untoward in them. Indeed, MI5 left my father to get on with his job, which implies they weren't worried he was passing information to the Czechs – that he was not, in fact, a spy. This appears to be the first time the security services thought it appropriate to let my father know that the man with whom he had been discussing the sale of VC10 planes was an StB agent.

My father had been appointed a privy counsellor almost two years earlier, in June 1968, and I'd expect the Security Service to have made additional security checks before giving him clearance to act as an advisor to the Queen at Privy Council meetings. But no doubts were raised about him then, otherwise his elevation to this highly trusted position would not have gone ahead. Indeed, it's significant that none of the StB agents or defectors seem to have known about my father's role as a privy counsellor, implying once again that their knowledge was superficial and not first-hand.

My father was a pawn in a much larger game of chess. In *Smear! Wilson and the Secret State*, Stephen Dorril and Robin Ramsay say this: 'By the time that the Frolik allegations had winged their way across the Atlantic in 1969, MI5 had had Stonehouse under surveillance for some years, ever since he reported the first approach from Husak. They knew on the ground that the stories about Stonehouse were fiction, but the Frolik allegation provided them with a weapon to use against Wilson.'[4]

Harold Wilson was in the sights of the chief of the CIA's Counterintelligence Division, James Jesus Angleton, because Wilson had been involved in – although not responsible for – sales of jet fighters to the Soviet Union.* Also, Wilson had taken twelve trips to Russia during the 1950s, either through his position at the Board of Trade or when working for the trading company Montague Meyer.

---

* Under Labour Prime Minister Clement Attlee, and president of the Board of Trade (1947–51) Stafford Cripps, the British government sold Rolls Royce Nene jet engines to the Soviet Union, who reverse-engineered them to make the Klimov engine that became part of the MiG-15 fighter aircraft – responsible for bringing down between 139 and 1,106 American planes in the Korean War of 1950–53 (depending on which side's account is believed). Harold Wilson followed Cripps as president of the Board of Trade, from April to October 1951. Prior to that, from 1947, Wilson had been secretary for overseas trade.

He'd been buying timber so Britain could rebuild all the houses that had been blown up during the war: we needed timber and didn't have any; Russia had half the wood in the world. Wilson acquired it for the UK and while some would consider that a valuable act in the national interest, the CIA had to make something of it. The CIA and MI5 were also suspicious of Wilson's friends who traded with the East. Some people in the security services on both sides of the Atlantic also believed the far-fetched notion that the former leader of the Labour Party, Hugh Gaitskell, had been assassinated by the KGB to allow space for Harold Wilson as leader. How this rumour got started is a matter of debate. Although usually attributed to KGB defector Anatoli Golitsyn, it may have begun with Peter Wright, assistant director of MI5, who told Golitsyn, who told the CIA's Cleveland Cram, via whom it reached Roger Hollis, the director general of MI5. However it arose, the rumour undermined Wilson in the security communities on both sides of the Atlantic, with Golitsyn its chief advocate and James Angleton its master weaponist. Angleton pounced on Frolik's idea that my father worked for the StB because, as a Wilson appointee, he could use it against Wilson.

It was generally agreed, then and now, that Peter Wright, assistant director of MI5, was out of control, paranoid, inconsistent and badly informed.* He wrote about an approach from Angleton in 1964: 'Angleton came to offer us some very secret information from a source he would not name. This source alleged, according to Angleton, that Wilson was a Soviet agent.' Interestingly, Wright also

---

* Peter Wright spent much of his time in 'the service' trying to prove that the director general of MI5, Roger Hollis, was a KGB spy. He got this notion after being given a small exercise book detailing allegations of MI5/MI6 penetration which had once belonged to MI5 officer Ann Glass (who Wright misnamed Ann Last), the wife of Charles Elwell – the MI5 officer who interviewed my father at 10 Downing Street following Frolik's allegation. When Ann Glass left MI5, she'd left the book behind. On the last page it was written: 'If MI5 is penetrated, I think it is most likely to be Roger Hollis or Graham Mitchell.' (Ref: Peter Wright, *Spycatcher*, page 189.)

says: 'I knew from bitter experience that Angleton was more than capable of manufacturing evidence when none existed.'[5] Even the CIA would come to realise how much time and energy Angleton's paranoia had wasted the agency, especially looking for 'moles' that didn't exist. Coincidentally, Angleton resigned on the very day my father was arrested in Australia, the 24th December 1974, after *The New York Times* revealed that the CIA had been involved in counterintelligence operations against anti-Vietnam-war protestors, and other liberal groups.

Peter Wright had become more renegade than usual after 1972, when he learned that MI5 were not going to honour the fifteen-year Admiralty pension he'd been forced to give up when he joined 'the service'. He knew he'd have to find a source of income after he retired, so he went to a London hotel to meet a businessman who said he was interested in security: 'His colleagues were a ramshackle bunch. They were retired people from various branches of intelligence and security organizations whose best years were well behind them. There were others, too, mainly businessmen who seemed thrilled to be in the same room as spies, and did not seem to care how out of date they were.' The would-be employer said: 'We represent a group of people who are worried about the future of the country.' He wanted information: 'Anything on Wilson would be helpful. There are many people who would pay handsomely for material of that sort.' Several other groups had formed with the objective of bringing down the Wilson government including GB75, which was started by the founder of the SAS, Colonel David Stirling, and Unison, a group set up by George Kennedy Young, former deputy director of MI6. One of Young's big ideas was that non-white immigrants should be subjected to compulsory repatriation. After August 1974, Unison was supported by General Sir Walter Walker, ex-commander of NATO Northern Europe, and morphed under him into Civil Assistance, an organisation he claimed had 100,000 members who were willing to break any general strike called by the unions which he considered

riddled with communists. Standing behind all this right-wing sedi-
tion was Cecil King, the owner of the *Daily Mirror* who, according
to Wright, 'made it clear that he would publish anything MI5 might
care to leak in his direction. It was all part of Cecil King's "coup",
which he was convinced would bring down the Labour Government
and replace it with a coalition led by Lord Mountbatten.'[6]

MI5 itself was a hotbed of anti-Wilson sentiment. Wright wrote
that in early 1974, 'I was in my office when two colleagues came in.
They were with three or four other officers ... "Wilson's a bloody
menace," said one of the younger officers, "and it's about time the
public knew the truth." ... The plan was simple. In the run-up to
the election which, given the level of instability in Parliament, must
be due within a matter of months, MI5 would arrange for selec-
tive details of the intelligence about leading Labour Party figures,
but especially Wilson, to be leaked to sympathetic pressmen. ...
Soundings in the office had already been taken, and up to thirty
officers had given their approval to the scheme.' Wright wrote that,
'A mad scheme like this was bound to tempt me. I felt an irresistible
urge to lash out. The country seemed on the brink of catastrophe.
Why not give it a little push?'[7] In the end, Wright decided not to
help – by photocopying papers in the director general's safe – because
he was near to retirement and worried he'd lose the little pension he
did have. But all these renegades were still in MI5 and prepared to
cause whatever trouble they could for Wilson, and the 1969 spy
allegation gave them ammo: they hoped that by causing a scandal
with Stonehouse, they could bring down Wilson.* In *The Wilson
Plot*, David Leigh writes about November 1974, when my father
was missing: 'They must have hoped he had defected'[8] – because a

---

* When Peter Wright was questioned on the issue of an MI5/6 plot to bring down
Wilson, following the 1987 publication of his book, *Spycatcher* – which Margaret
Thatcher tried to get banned – he suggested that his co-author, Paul Greengrass,
had misunderstood him and that he himself hadn't checked the proofs. More likely,
Wright was feeling remorse at revealing what his ex-colleagues had been up to.

defection would have proved the spy theories favoured by the MI5 rogue elements working against the Labour Party at the time.

The CIA weren't satisfied that the Frolik allegations were being taken seriously enough in the UK. James Jesus Angleton was convinced that Britain was crawling with communists and didn't want to be caught out again. He'd made the devastating mistake of trusting MI6's liaison officer in Washington, Kim Philby, who was a KGB spy.* The pair had been friends for years, and the charming Philby listened while Angleton told him all the CIA's secrets. Aside from their 36 official meetings in Washington – the records of which Angleton burned after Philby's defection to Moscow – they had booze-fuelled lunches once a week, usually at a restaurant called Harvey's, spoke on the phone three or four times a week, went fishing, and relaxed at Angleton's home. As a direct result of Angleton's misjudgement of character, hundreds of foreign CIA operatives died, including waves of anti-communist activists sent into Albania. The CIA couldn't figure out how the communists acquired advance knowledge of the dates of operations, and the coordinates for the drop zones, and were waiting to shoot them. The Albanian communists had been told by the KGB, who had been told by Philby, who had been told by Angleton. Angleton became consumed by a paranoia that was matched by that of MI5's Wright, and they determined that my father's 'case' shouldn't be dropped, and with the help of their British

---

* During the 1940s, 50s and 60s, at least five KGB spies were working in the British secret services and the Foreign Office: John Cairncross (MI6); Guy Burgess (Section D/MI6 then Foreign Office); Donald Maclean (Foreign Office); Kim Philby (MI6); and Anthony Blunt (MI5). Cairncross confessed in 1952 but wasn't prosecuted; Burgess and Maclean defected to Russia in 1951 before they could be caught, with Philby following in 1963; and Blunt confessed in 1964, but was given immunity from prosecution and allowed to continue working as Surveyor of the Queen's Pictures until his spying history was made public in 1979, upon which he was stripped of the Knighthood he had since acquired. The fact that none of these spies were identified in situ or put on trial didn't give the CIA much confidence in the British secret services.

right-wing friends, and press contacts, they'd ensure suspicion fell on my father, and stayed there.

One of their 'foot soldiers' was right-wing activist Geoffrey Stewart-Smith, who wrote to Czech émigré Josef Josten on the 19th December 1974, knowing that Josten had helped Frolik write his book. This was two days after Harold Wilson had said in the House of Commons there was no evidence my father was a spy or had been a security risk and in the letter Stewart-Smith offered Frolik and Josten money if they could provide any hard evidence that he was a spy. They couldn't. His letter came into the hands of Frolik's publisher, Leo Cooper, and he recorded that it said: 'I am sure you are aware of the potential political significance of the fact of the public reaction if we could prove that Wilson was lying to the House of Commons – a British Watergate cover up?'[9]

According to David Leigh in *The Wilson Plot*, the *Sunday Express* journalist, William Massie, said that after Harold Wilson's election defeat in 1970 'a CIA officer and an MI5 officer met him together and showed him transcripts of the raw debriefing tapes made in Langley by Josef Frolik. These "revealed", of course, that a senior Wilson minister, Stonehouse, had been a Soviet Bloc agent. They went on to tell him how Wilson had refused to let Stonehouse be interrogated, and had deliberately hushed the matter up. The implication was that Wilson too, had something to hide. As we have seen, it was the second attempt made by Intelligence men to "expose" the Stonehouse story and thus discredit Wilson. The two Intelligence officers added that President Johnson had already been warned to treat Wilson with "circumspection". Massie's newspaper was – not surprisingly – unwilling to print the story. But Massie told his editor, and others. It began to circulate underground in Fleet Street.'[10]

❖

One regular conduit for misinformation from the rogue right-wing elements in MI5/6 to the reading public was the satirical political magazine *Private Eye*. Under cover of hilarity, they continuously threw aspersions on Wilson, his political secretary Marcia Williams, and his friends including Joseph Kagan and Rudy Sternberg. My father was another of their targets. On the 14th May 2009, the *Guardian* published an article, '*Private Eye* "may have been used by MI5"', which said: 'Journalists who worked for *Private Eye*, the satirical magazine, believe that it may have been used by the security services to spread smears against the Wilson government in the mid-1970s. The most remarkable circumstantial evidence for this comes from the diaries of Auberon Waugh. His savage fortnightly flights of fancy were rarely taken seriously at the time, but a rereading of his diaries published in the magazine between 1974 and 1976 reveals allegations which are uncannily similar to the ones being regurgitated in the current MI5 controversy. For most people they were the first public intimations of the rumours. Mr Waugh, whose pieces regularly combine fact with rumour and personal prejudices, said yesterday that he had made up most of his stories. However, he added: "I think the *Eye* was probably used by MI5, but I only knew two people who were connected with it." … Mr Richard Ingrams, who was editor from 1963 to 1986, said: "Looking back, it's obvious that the *Eye* could have been used by MI5, but it's hard to be concrete."'[11]

Private Eye publishes every two weeks. On the 20th September 1974, two months before my father disappeared, *Private Eye* published: 'Delicacy and good taste prevent me from mentioning the names of two Labour MPs who are at present under investigation by the Special Branch.'[12] On the 15th November, five days before he disappeared, *Private Eye* ran a gratuitous and humourless character assassination, 'Bungler Dashed', and in their next issue two weeks later, on 29th November, they continued with 'Bungler Dashed (2)', and two weeks after that, on 13th December, 'Bungler Dashed (3)'. At this point, my father was still missing, presumed drowned. On the 10th January 1975, two weeks after my father was discovered in Melbourne, the *Eye*'s Auberon Waugh invented the notion that on 17th December 1974 Wilson had announced in the House of Commons: 'there is not a shred of evidence for believing John Stonehouse was a Czech spy apart from the first-hand testimony of his Czech spymaster.' On the 4th April the cover headlines were 'Stonehouse Arrested', and 'Missing Member Held', with a picture showing the back of three men at a urinal, one appearing to be wearing a police helmet, and the man in the middle saying, 'Can't you see I'm having a nervous breakdown?' All this negativity had a profound effect on my father, not to mention the family, and it no doubt had an influence on the readers' opinion of my father.

Private Eye's Auberon Waugh told friends that he'd tried unsuccessfully to join MI5 after he left Oxford University in 1960, and in this whole sorry saga this seems to be a theme running through it, of men wanting to associate themselves with the world of spies. It's a kind of James Bond complex. They love secrets, intrigue, being 'in the know' – having information other people can't get hold of. It's what makes them special. With the older generation, it has the ring of derring-do, characteristic of the comics they read as children with men having comradely army-like adventures as they did in the 'Eagle' comic, or 'Boy's Own'. It's a kind of vicarious machismo, usually played out in the safety of comfy armchairs in London's exclusive men-only private clubs like the Garrick or Whites. It's a form of elitist escapism, with the added advantage that a man can feel he's doing his patriotic duty in besmirching the 'spy' MI5 don't have the evidence to convict – John Stonehouse.

Meanwhile, the man himself never gave away any secrets. In public he spoke about 'cant and humbug' but didn't go into details. In the February 1976 House of Commons debate on 'Foreign Policy and Morality', he said, 'We should investigate other areas involving activities of our own secret service and foreign affairs officials,' by which he meant a closed-session select committee. But he only talked in general terms, about 'secret donations that have been made by British Governments to foreign political parties to enable them to win certain elections', and, 'I know of examples, which I should like to give to a select committee.' He knew things, but never spilled the beans. What he knew made him disenchanted with the whole political system, and if he'd spoken about the specifics people might have had some sympathy for his internal conflicts. But he kept his mouth shut through it all. And that's because he was a patriot, not a traitor, and certainly not a spy.

21

Fake News

Having lived in the belly of the beast, I don't see much difference between the way the British media handled information and the way the communist secret agents did. They both made things up or twisted the truth, either blatantly or in small, subtle steps. It's like they were twisting a Rubik's cube one square at a time – a quotation mark moved here, an omission there, an exaggeration here – and with all these small steps, information ends up 180 degrees in the opposite direction of truth. However, they differ in two respects. First, the information in the StB file was accessible to only a few people at the Czech embassy in London, not even to Frolik for example, plus a few people in Prague, while the whole point about media is to spread the word far and wide. Secondly, the StB files are remarkable in that agents never criticise their colleagues. One woman got mentioned for sending a bit of paper to the wrong department but, other than that, the agents kept their opinions of each other to themselves. In the file, at least. That's because they were all in mortal danger of being fingered by their colleagues and ending up down a uranium mine or worse. They seem to have had some kind of code of practice where they didn't criticise each other in the hope they could escape this tyrannical regime with their lives. The British media, on the other hand, criticise everyone, and everything, on a regular basis. There's a reason for that – money. Negative press stories attract attention, just as indignant anger in posts online attracts 'clicks'.

When we got every newspaper on every day for two years the family became very attuned to lies, not only in our story but in others' too. We knew how particular journalists approached their subjects and could even tell which legal advisor had been on duty overnight. It was like we had press X-ray vision. Over time, I've lost that skill, and now I'm like everyone else – I believe what I read. Most of it, anyway. Believing the press is a trap that's easy to fall into. Even though I know – logically – that some of what I'm reading is fake news, I can't identify the truth from the lies any more. It's rather scary.

All this is on top of the rather more mundane aspect of 'fake news' where the newspaper or media outlet simply omits aspects of a story that are not dramatic. In our case, this was seen very clearly in the reporting of the trial. Every accusation of the prosecution became a headline story, while the defence of that accusation was ignored. This is what's known as 'unbalanced reporting' and it is endemic.

Fake news is absorbed not only by the general reader, but becomes source material for writers of books, then those books become a source of information for journalists, and the fake news is thus embedded and perpetuated. On the face of it, the biography of Michael Sherrard QC, the DTI inspector who spent two years examining my father's businesses in detail, would seem to be a good source of information. But even his book is stuffed with factual inaccuracies, including the story that he was arrested at his apartment because someone thought he looked like Lord Lucan, complete with an invented dialogue between my father and the police. The following sentence has three inaccuracies: 'Early in 1974, faced with exposure and ruin, both in finances and of reputation, he fled to America where he faked his death, leaving his clothing on a Miami beach and a suicide note for his grieving wife and daughter.' But it was late 1974, 20th November; he left his clothes with Helen Fleming at the beach cabana and; far more importantly, he did not leave a suicide note. Had there been one, my father might not have been charged with life insurance fraud because everybody knows insurance isn't paid out in the case of suicide, especially one confirmed by a 'note'. Sherrard writes that, once in Melbourne, 'as Donald Clive Mildoon, he set up home with Sheila Buckley, his secretary'. No he didn't. 'Mildoon'/Stonehouse had been arrested five weeks before Sheila arrived in Australia. Sherrard says that he was appointed 'to inquire into London Capital Group Ltd, a business in which Stonehouse had been deeply involved. He had arranged to change its name from that of a charity, the British Bangladesh Trust.'[1] No, he hadn't. The British Bangladesh Trust (BBT) was never a charity. Sherrard is confusing it with the Bangladesh Fund charity which closed on 8th January 1972, before the BBT was first discussed.

Sherrard continues in his 2008 biography: 'The purpose of the Stonehouse investigation was to see if there was any impropriety in the way that the charity's funds had been used in the light of the complex transfers of money between the companies with which Stonehouse was associated.'[2] This conflicts with what he said in his 1977 DTI Report: 'Although not strictly within our terms of reference, we kept a weather-eye open for any evidence of improper dealings with the funds of that charity or the possible mixing of such funds by Mr Stonehouse but our work did not reveal any hint of wrongdoing in this connection.'[3] So was 'the purpose' of the DTI investigation to look into 'any impropriety' in charity funds or did Sherrard just keep 'a weather eye' on the subject? Either way, after finishing his DTI Report, in 1977, Sherrard was invited to the House of Commons to a meeting with the attorney general, the solicitor general, and the director of public prosecutions, held in 'a tiny, windowless room' with 'dingy panelled walls' and one chair – 'a shabby arm-chair with springs bulging below the seat', on which sat the attorney general. Sherrard told this 'full legal panoply of state' that, 'We thought that he had not actually robbed the charity.'[4] 'Bad press' in the form of a baseless rumour that began a week after my father disappeared in 1974 had such long legs that it ran for years and gained the interest of the 'full legal panoply of state' three years later. And it's still online today that he misappropriated £600,000 of charity money. Anyone who thinks bad press doesn't really have much impact has not had the misfortune to experience it.

Under English law, newspapers can say what they like about a person when they're dead and can't be sued because the dead person no longer has a reputation to damage so can't be defamed by libel or slander. When my father actually died, some of the more outrageous stories began to appear in print. Three days after his death, on the 17th April 1988, *The People* ran with 'STONEHOUSE "GAVE" CONCORDE SECRETS TO RUSSIA'. This was a completely unfounded story for which there has never been a scrap of evidence. Given that the concept for the Tu-144, or Concordski as it came to be known, was published in 1962, long before my father was involved in the Ministry of Aviation, and it had many entirely different engineering systems to Concorde, and a habit of crashing, it was an unlikely story even before the famous StB file revealed there was nothing to it. The source, according to the newspaper, was MI5, who 'continued to believe that Stonehouse was a spy'. The former *The People* editor, Richard Stott, had met Frolik and is quoted as saying, 'Frolik never had any direct evidence. But he remained convinced that Stonehouse was a spy because of what he heard inside the Czech embassy in London.' Going with Frolik's 'homosexual' reference, *The People* say: 'He fell victim to a classic "honey trap" operation which exploited his bisexualism.'[5]

Inaccurate reporting is not just about getting the facts wrong accidentally. It can be about twisting the facts so it makes the reporter look knowledgeable, 'in the know', or creating a 'reality' that simply does not exist. Ultimately, it's all about making money. One master of this dark craft was Chapman Pincher who, on 2nd January 2006, wrote a piece entitled 'STONEHOUSE WAS A SOVIET SPY' for the *Daily Express*. The whole article was a plethora of unsubstantiated rumour and out-and-out lies, but a particularly annoying paragraph was this, referring to them apparently meeting after my father had come out of prison: 'When I asked him about the spying allegations he smiled and said: "Why don't we both fly out to America and interview Joe Frolik," indicating (deliberately I suspected) that he had met the defector and knew him well enough to call him Joe.'[6] This is outrageous because Pincher knew perfectly well that my father had never met Frolik, yet he would go so low, in journalistic terms, as to say that my father implicated himself. Everyone who discussed Frolik *ad infinitum* called him 'Joe', because that's what he called himself. If this conversation happened at all, my father would have been saying, in essence, let's go to America and confront Frolik once and for all, but Pincher manages to twist things into an admission of guilt on the part of my father. My father had been dead eighteen years, and Pincher was still squeezing him dry. What had begun as an unsubstantiated rumour in 1969 had morphed, 37 years later, into an admission of guilt, on the part of the accused, no less!

And it carries on. Theo Barclay, a barrister by profession, wrote in *The Times* on 22nd February 2018, 'While on holiday in his mid-thirties in 1959, the married MP was approached by a mystery temptress. Later recalling the one-night stand, he said the vixen sent "sensations of joy into every crevice of his brain." She spurred him on to "one last magnificent thrust" before he rolled over, looked up and – to his horror – spied a camera in the ceiling that had filmed the whole encounter. From then on, fearful of his infidelity being exposed, he was on the StB's payroll.' When Barclay writes 'Later recalling the one-night stand' he is, in fact, taking text from a novel my father wrote called *Ralph*, and turning it into an admission of guilt from the author's *actual life*. Barclay knows perfectly well that this scenario and its quotes come from the pages of the fictional work *Ralph*, but he presents it in *The Times* as my father being caught in a real-life honeytrap. He has added the word 'last' before 'thrust', and invented a 'camera' being 'spied', but the infinitely more important point is that he's turning words *from a novel* into *an admission of guilt*.

The article additionally contains the highly damaging claim that 'he passed plans for a new bomber aircraft to his handler'.[7] Among the inaccuracies in Barclay's 2018 book *Fighters and Quitters*, is his reference to the speech my father made in the House of Commons on 20th October 1975, in which Barclay uses two quotes that did not come from that speech at all. The speech is readily available online so there really is no excuse, and he makes things worse by 'topping' his quotes with comments about the Speaker, and 'tailing' it with a quote from someone remarking on the real speech, not the words Barclay uses in their place.*

I thought Barclay turning words from a work of fiction into an admission of being a real-life spy was crossing a line, so I made a complaint to his professional body. Even though I sent the Bar Standards Board five supporting documents they replied that they couldn't see there was evidence that Barclay had deliberately or intentionally made the leap from fiction to fact. Apparently, Barclay can write what he likes with impunity. Nobody has ever apologised to the Stonehouse family for their peddling in misinformation. The reason for that is fairly obvious: an apology admits fault, which could have legal repercussions.

On 15th January 2006, two years before the StB file on my father was released for public view by the Czech secret service archives in Prague, the *Mail on Sunday* ran a four-page article based on 'a copy of the file … stored on microfiche, which has now fallen into private

---

* The two quotes Barclay purports on page 47 of his book *Fighters and Quitters* to have been spoken by my father in the House of Commons come from page 182 of *Death of an Idealist* by John Stonehouse (although Barclay's quote omits the crucial word 'too' from a sentence in which my father includes himself: 'Members around me were robots too, voting on issues which they did not bother to understand …'), and from a letter dated 26th January 1975, to Edward Short MP, published in First Report from the Select Committee on the Right Honourable Member for Walsall, North, Session 1974–75, HMSO, 11th March 1975, page 10. The quote Barclay 'tails' the speech with is from pages 534–535 of Bernard Donoughue's book *Downing Street Diary*, London, Jonathan Cape, 2004.

hands'. It's hard to take too seriously material that is potentially stolen or incomplete, and is certainly from an unofficial source, but that didn't stop the newspaper giving it the title 'STONEHOUSE WAS A CZECH SPY'. It goes into some detail about the 'arrangements for meetings' in which 'letters would be sent regularly to the MP's London home, containing a clipping from the foreign news pages of *The Times*, always with the date intact'.[8] What it doesn't say, because the journalist didn't bother to check, is that the MP never lived at the only address the StB ever had for him. Among the plethora of inaccuracies was the usual fantasy that, after his disappearance, he'd 'settled in Melbourne, Australia, with his mistress Sheila Buckley' – proving once again that known facts are no impediment to 'a good story'. The next day, the 16th January, Chapman Pincher of the *Daily Express* jumped on the renewed-interest bandwagon with a re-run of the completely groundless Concorde allegations: 'Minister sold our Concorde secrets to KGB'. The opening sentence told the readers: 'He was a traitor in our midst, a high-ranking government minister who sold the nation's secrets to spymasters behind the Iron Curtain.'[9]

As well as being branded a communist spy, my father has been accused of being a fascist sympathiser. In September 2019 Ferdinand Mount, once head of the Number 10 Policy Unit under Margaret Thatcher, reviewed a book about Enoch Powell in *The London Review of Books*, in which he accused my father of being 'an ally' of Powell, slipping in, with no explanation, that he joined the English National Party when he returned from Australia. Reading this with no background, it would be all too easy to think my father was really a racist or even fascist (Hitler is quoted in the following column). I feel I need to put this accusation into context because there is no way my father was 'an ally' of Powell. On 17th February 1968 the *Express & Star*, a West Midlands-based local paper, ran a half-page article asking seventeen MPs from the area, including Powell, what they had to say about the racial tension then being caused after many Asians came to the area, having been affected by Kenya's 'Africanisation' policy. Ernest Prince, the reporter, introduced the seventeen short quotes by saying: 'The number of "dependants" coming here to join Commonwealth immigrants allowed in with work permits now far exceeds what was envisioned. Many loopholes for the dodgers are becoming apparent … like the "24 hours in Britain and you're free to stay" one which was plugged two days ago.'[10] Within this broader immigration policy topic, one of the questions of the time was whether Sikh men could wear turbans, instead of uniform caps, when working for the transport company. My father was probably insensitive to the fact that the turban is a religious requirement, rather than a cultural preference, although he was soon put right and was involved in the negotiations that led to Sikhs wearing turbans in the standard navy-blue uniform colour. His whole take on immigration was that people should integrate, mix culturally, and this is why he said: 'The Sikh community's campaign to maintain customs inappropriate in Britain is much to be regretted. Working in Britain, particularly in the public services, they should be prepared to accept the terms and conditions of their employment. To claim special communal rights (or should one say rites?) leads to a dangerous fragmentation within society. This communalism is a canker; whether practised by one colour or another it is to be strongly condemned.'[11] Powell used this quote in his infamous 'Rivers of Blood' speech in Birmingham on 20th April 1968. Sixty years later, Ferdinand Mount writes: 'Stonehouse had denounced as a "canker" the campaign by local Sikh bus conductors to be allowed to wear their turbans at work'[12] – completely omitting the full quote, where my father said that 'communalism is a canker; whether practised by one colour or another'. My father can be blamed for being ignorant at the time about the religious nature of the turban, but he can be praised for helping solve the problem once informed. Also, he can be blamed for being naïve enough to think different cultures can easily integrate if they try to be less communally-minded, but he cannot be accused of being 'an ally' of Powell, because he was not.

Someone reviewing this book in the future may pick out my words above – 'my father can be blamed for being ignorant' – because that is what people do: they take things out of context. Ferdinand Mount wrote: 'He later resurfaced in Australia, then returned to England, where he joined the English National Party before being jailed ...' but Mount is old enough to know that my father represented that Party for four months, and that the English National Party of 1976, which disbanded in 1981, was a harmless jolly band of people promoting Morris Dancing in schools, and a devolved English parliament to counter preferential demands of the Northern Ireland Assembly and proposed Scottish and Welsh assemblies. That ENP had nothing whatever to do with the racist ENP that emerged with that name decades later, but Mount doesn't explain this because he's promoting the story that my father was 'an ally' of Powell and slipping in an ENP reference supports his narrative.

Information is the blood flow of society, but when it is abused by exaggeration or contrived omission an insult is made to the society that information is meant to inform. My family have been very much wronged by all sorts of writing – including that by Czech spies and British journalists – and for us it is too late. But I implore contemporary and future journalists to beware the temptation to be lazy and skip original document research, or twist words into untruth for sensationalism and 'clicks'. That is not, after all, what their readers expect, and pay for.

Ever since the 1969 spy accusation first found its way into the parliamentary gossip mill and onto the pages of the press, my father has been utterly misrepresented and maligned. At the same time, he was a cash machine for the many journalists who know that the more dramatic their stories, the better they sell. For some, especially during the 1970s, their negativity was designed to gain right-wing political advantage. But beyond this, my father was, and still is, presumed guilty of being a communist spy and that gave people licence to punish him when he was alive, and trash his memory now he's dead. Nobody likes a traitor. My family are only glad of one thing: we didn't go through these experiences during the internet age. The Orwellian 'hate', 'hate', 'hate' was palpable in the 1970s, and I can't imagine how that would feel now.

If anyone is suffering from the delusion that the internet brought 'fake news' into the world, I can tell them from personal experience, there's nothing new about fake news. Commentators today complain that social media has trapped people in 'information bubbles', but the negative Stonehouse information bubble came about because when one journalist came out with a bad story about my father, other journalists didn't check those 'facts', print our denials, or simply present a more balanced view. They instead absorbed that original negative story, and then amplified it with more lies and misrepresentations. The problem with a misinformation bubble such as ours is that it so easily morphed into 'the truth', then 'common knowledge', and then 'history'. Unbalanced reporting has always been a form of brainwashing; we didn't have to wait for the internet for that.

Notes

Proceedings in the House of Commons and reproduced in Hansard, as well as select committee reports contain parliamentary information licensed under the Open Parliament Licence v3.0. Documents in The National Archives, as well as personal correspondence from The Home Office contain public sector information licensed under the Open Government Licence v3.0.

Chapter 1

1. John Stonehouse, *Death of an Idealist*, London: WH Allen, 1975, page 172.
2. Ibid, page 173.
3. Ibid, page 179.
4. Ibid, page 181.
5. Ibid, page 181.
6. Sheila Stonehouse, 'Why I loved this man', by Diana Hutchinson, *Daily Mail*, 15th April 1988, page 12.
7. Geoffrey Robertson, *The Justice Game*, London: Chatto & Windus, 1998, page 68.

Chapter 2

1. London Co-operative Society Archive: 306, No. 2 Sub-Committee reports (Sept. 1960–Aug. 1961) 30th January 1961 'The development of the food trades department'.
2. *The Grocer*, 6th April 1963.
3. John Stonehouse in 'Crossroads' News Sheet No. 1 of The Co-operative Reform Group, 1963, 'Comment', pages 2, 4.

Chapter 3

1. John Stonehouse, *Prohibited Immigrant*, London: Bodley Head, 1960, pages 186–7: quoting Clyde Sanger in *Central African Examiner*, quoting *Rhodesia Herald*.

2. *The Birmingham Post*, 27th February 1959, page 1.

3. *The Birmingham Post*, 21st March 1959, page 1.

Chapter 4

1. Fred Wenner, 'Yard mystery of Stonehouse fund', *Daily Mail*, 2nd December 1974, page 22.

2. Michael Sherrard, *London Capital Group (formerly British Bangladesh Trust Limited): investigation under section 165 (b) of the Companies Act*, London: H.M.S.O., pages 353–4.

3. 'Should Mr Stonehouse Be Paroled?', *The Times*, 17th November 1978.

4. Michael O'Dell, 'Mr Stonehouse and parole', letters section, *The Times*, 18th November 1978.

5. Bruce Douglas-Mann, letters section, *The Times*, 21st November 1978.

6. Geoffrey Levy, 'He faked his death, fled Britain with his lover and was spared spying charges … So was Labour minister John Stonehouse – the real Reggie Perrin – a spy?', dailymail.co.uk, 8th January 2011, accessed 17th November 2020.

Chapter 5

1. 'John Stonehouse got U.K. millions,' *Express & Star*, 18th March 1967, page 20.

2. Michael Sherrard, *London Capital Group (formerly British Bangladesh Trust Limited): investigation under section 165 (b) of the Companies Act*, London: H.M.S.O., page 66.

3. Ibid.

4. Peter Pettman quoted by Richard Milner and Anthony Mascarenhas, 'Five questions on the British Bangladesh Trust', *Sunday Times*, 19th November 1972.

5. Michael Sherrard, *London Capital Group (formerly British Bangladesh Trust Limited): investigation under section 165 (b) of the Companies Act*, London: H.M.S.O., page 62.

6. John Stonehouse, *Death of an Idealist*, London: WH Allen, 1975, page 141.

7. Michael Sherrard, *London Capital Group (formerly British Bangladesh Trust Limited): investigation under section 165 (b) of the Companies Act*, London: H.M.S.O., page 71.

8. 'Accomplice's letters trapped Stonehouse', *Sunday Times*, 29th December 1974, page 3.

Chapter 6

1. 'Note for the record' of meeting between Callaghan and Mayhew, prepared by Ken Stowe, 12th July 1978, The National Archives File PREM 16/1848, page 2.

2. Cabinet Room 'Notes for the Record' by James Callaghan, 12:45 14th July 1978, The National Archives File PREM 16/1848, Document 11, page 2.

3. Christopher Andrew, *The Defence of The Realm*, London: Allen Lane, 2009, page 707.

4. Ibid, pages 707–8.

5. Josef Frolik, *The Frolik Defection – Memoirs of an Intelligence Agent*, London: Leo Cooper, 1975, page 97.

6. Ken Stowe to Harold Wilson, 4th July 1977, The National Archives File PREM 16/1848.

7. John Hunt to Mr Wood for the attention of Prime Minister James Callaghan, 15th December 1977, 'Line to Take' attachment, 'Allegations about Czech Intelligence Service contacts with trade unionists and with Mr John Stonehouse', page 1, The National Archives File PREM 16/1848.

8. 'Note for the record' of meeting between Callaghan and Mayhew, prepared by Ken Stowe, 12th July 1978, The National Archives File PREM 16/1848, page 1.

9. Gordon Corera, BBC, 25th June 2012, https://www.bbc.co.uk/news/magazine-18556213, accessed 29th June 2019.

10. Christopher Andrew, *The Defence of The Realm*, London: Allen Lane, 2009, page 708.

11. Robert Armstrong to Margaret Thatcher, 7th July 1980, The National Archives File PREM 19/360, Document 1, page 1.

12. Robert Armstrong to Margaret Thatcher, 11th September 1980, The National Archives File PREM 19/360, Document 3.

13. Clive Whitmore (PPS to PM) to John Halliday (Home Office), 6th October 1980, The National Archives File PREM 19/360, Document 7, page 1.

14. Ibid.

15. Christopher Andrew, *The Defence of The Realm*, London: Allen Lane, 2009, page 708.

Chapter 7

1. Christopher Sweeney, 'Defector reveals MPs' part in spy ring', *The Times*, 25th January 1974, page 8.

2. Michael Sherrard, *London Capital Group (formerly British Bangladesh Trust Limited): investigation under section 165 (b) of the Companies Act*, London: H.M.S.O., pages 135, 177, 185, 186.

3. Ibid., page 133.
4. Ibid, pages 3, 105.
5. Ibid, page 26.
6. Ibid, page 278.
7. 'Diplomatic Bag', *Private Eye*, 20th September 1974, page 3.
8. Judge Eveleigh, Sentencing Statement, Friday 6th August 1976 at the Old Bailey, The National Archives File J 82/3714, page 77.

Chapter 8

1. 'Where is the Missing MP?', *Daily Mirror*, 27th November 1974, page 1.
2. Alan Rainbird, 'The Real John Stonehouse', *Sunday Times*, Letters and Correspondence, page 15.
3. Sheila Buckley, 'The truth about John and me', *Woman* magazine, 30th October 1976, pages 9–11.
4. Piers Akerman, 'Slab of Concrete Murder Clue to Lost MP', *The Sun*, 12th December 1974, page 7.
5. D.E.R. Moore to Mr Winters, 29th August 1975, The National Archives File FCO 53/435, Document 347.
6. 'Disclosed – facts of lost MP's insurance', *Sunday Express*, 15th December 1974, page 1.
7. Richard Stott, 'Stonehouse Security Sensation', *Daily Mirror*, 16th December 1974, page 1.
8. Richard Stott, 'MP was Named as Spy Contact', *Daily Mirror*, 17th December 1974, pages 1–2.
9. David Thompson, 'Wilson: Defector Did Name Lost MP', *Daily Mirror*, 18th December 1974, page 2.
10. Stewart Steven, 'The spy and Mr Stonehouse', *Daily Mail*, 18th December 1974, page 6.

Chapter 9

1. John Stonehouse, *Death of an Idealist*, London: WH Allen, 1975, page 195.
2. John Stonehouse, *My Trial*, London: Star Books, 1976, page 194.
3. Caroline Gay, witness statement 5th June 1975, pages 2 and 3, The National Archives File J 267/707.
4. Detective Senior Sergeant Hugh Morris, witness statement, 23rd October 1975, page 2, The National Archives File J 267/707.
5. Detective Sergeant John Coffey, witness statement, 23rd October 1975, pages 11, 7, 6–7, The National Archives File J 267/707.
6. Detective Senior Sergeant Hugh Morris, witness statement 23rd October 1975, page 4, The National Archives File J 267/707.

7. *Daily Mail*, 27th December 1974, page 3.
8. Detective Sergeant John Coffey, witness statement, 23rd October 1975, page 7, The National Archives File J 267/707.
9. John Stonehouse, *Death of an Idealist*, London: WH Allen, 1975, page 213.
10. Detective Sergeant John Coffey, witness statement, 23rd October 1975, page 1, The National Archives File J 267/707.
11. Ibid, page 11.
12. Detective Chief Superintendent Kenneth Etheridge, witness statement regarding interview of Sheila Buckley 29th–30th January, 13th March 1975, pages 4–5, The National Archives File J 267/707.
13. Ibid, pages 6–7.
14. Ibid, pages 7–8.
15. Ibid, pages 8–11.
16. Sheila Buckley, 'The truth about John and me' (Part 2), *Woman* magazine, 6th November 1976, page 18.
17. Detective Chief Inspector Barbara Tilley, witness statement, 8th January 1975, pages 1–2, The National Archives File J 267/707.
18. Detective Sergeant John Coffey, witness statement, 23rd October 1975, page 9, The National Archives File J 267/707.
19. Ibid.
20. Detective Senior Sergeant Hugh Morris, witness statement, 23rd October 1975, page 4, The National Archives File J 267/707.

Chapter 10
1. Paul Hopkins, 'Why I Came to Hate England', *Daily Express*, 27th December 1974, page 1.
2. Janice Morley, 'I'll fly out if he wants', *Daily Mail*, 27th December 1974, page 2.
3. 'Surprise! Surprise! John Stonehouse lives', *Daily Mail*, 27th December 1974, page 6.
4. Harry Longmuir and Peter Birkett, 'Yard Ready to Fly Stonehouse Home', *Daily Mail*, 28th December 1974, page 1.
5. John Dale and Jon Ryan, '"Blackmail? Well, massive pressure"', *Daily Mail*, 28th December 1974, page 1.
6. Clem Davenport, witness statement, 15th January 1975, pages 2–3, The National Archives file J 267/707.
7. John F.W. Mulcahy, witness statement, 4th July 1975, page 5, The National Archives file J 267/707.
8. Detective Inspector David Townley, witness statement, 30th October 1975, page 2, The National Archives File J 267/707.

Chapter 11
1. Tony Benn, *Against the Tide Diaries 1973–76*, London: Arrow Books, 1991, page 272.
2. Maurice Edelman, 'Conduct unbecoming', *Daily Mail*, 28th December 1974, page 6.
3. Ibid, page 6.
4. Peter Burden, 'Come home Stonehouse', *Daily Mail*, 2nd January 1975, page 13.
5. Harry Longmuir, 'What "S" wrote to Stonehouse', *Daily Mail*, 6th January 1975, pages 1–2.
6. Paul Hopkins, 'My Dirty Trick, By Stonehouse', *Daily Express*, 6th January 1975, page 1.
7. Ibid.
8. Auberon Waugh, *Private Eye*, 10th January 1975, Edition 340, page 20.
9. J.M. Hay of British High Commission, Canberra, to P.G. de Courcy-Ireland of Foreign and Commonwealth Office, 28th January 1975, The National Archives File FCO 53/433.
10. A.R. Clark, 4th February 1975, The National Archives File FCO 53/433, Document 98.
11. Sir Thomas Brimelow, 6th February 1975, on A.R. Clark, 4th February 1975, The National Archives File FCO 53/433, Document 98.
12. Public Library of US Diplomacy, 20th January 1975, Canonical ID: 1975CANBER00425_b.
13. John Stonehouse letter to Edward Short, Leader of the House of Commons, 13th January 1975, First Report from the Select Committee on the Right Honourable Member for Walsall, North, Session 1974–75, London: HMSO, 11th March 1975, pages 8–9.
14. Public Library of US Diplomacy, 14th January 1975, Canonical ID: 1975LONDON00579_b.
15. John Stonehouse letter to Edward Short, Leader of the House of Commons, 16th January 1975, First Report from the Select Committee on the Right Honourable Member for Walsall, North, Session 1974–75, London: HMSO, 11th March 1975, pages 9–10.
16. John Stonehouse letter to Edward Short, Leader of the House of Commons, 13th January 1975, First Report from the Select Committee on the Right Honourable Member for Walsall, North, Session 1974–75, London: HMSO, 11th March 1975, page 8.
17. 'Stonehouse "Like Maniac"', *Evening News*, 16th January 1975, page 1.
18. Edward Short letter to John Stonehouse, 21st January 1975, First Report from the Select Committee on the Right Honourable Member for Walsall, North, Session 1974–75, London: HMSO, 11th March 1975, page 10.

19. Bernard Levin, 'John Stonehouse: call off the Labour pack', *The Times*, 21st January 1975, page 14.

20. Andrew Alexander, 'Wrong time and place?', *Daily Mail*, 29th January 1975, page 8.

21. First Report from the Select Committee on the Right Honourable Member for Walsall, North, Session 1974–75, London: HMSO, 11th March 1975, pages 3, 7.

22. John Stonehouse letter to George Strauss, 18th February 1975, First Report from the Select Committee on the Right Honourable Member for Walsall, North, Session 1974–75, London: HMSO, 11th March 1975, pages 12–13.

23. Quoted in letter from E.J. Bunting, Australian High Commission, London, to Select Committee, 27th February 1975, in First Report from the Select Committee on the Right Honourable Member for Walsall, North, Session 1974–75, London: HMSO, 11th March 1975, page 13.

24. Note to letter from E.J. Bunting, Australian High Commission, London, to Select Committee, 27th February 1975, in First Report from the Select Committee on the Right Honourable Member for Walsall, North, Session 1974–75, London: HMSO, 11th March 1975, page 13.

25. John Stonehouse, 'The Man I'd Been Was A Broken Useless, Pathetic Sham. He Had To Die', *News of the World*, 16th March 1975, page 3.

Chapter 12

1. Trudi Pacter, 'How I helped Stonehouse, by wife he betrayed', *The Sunday Express*, 17th April 1988.

2. Betty Boothroyd, *Betty Boothroyd: The Autobiography*, London: Arrow Books/The Random House Group, 2002, page 153.

3. Sheila Buckley, 'The truth about John and me' (Part 2), *Woman* magazine, 6th November 1976, page 50.

4. Ibid, page 62.

5. Ibid, page 65.

6. Ian Ward, 'Stonehouse Had Secretary's Clothes Sent On', *Daily Telegraph*, 12th February 1975, page 3.

7. Ibid.

8. Harry Longmuir and Rupert Massey, 'The love trap triangle', *Daily Mail*, 13th February 1975, page 8.

9. Judge Eveleigh, Summing-Up at the Old Bailey, Monday 2nd August 1976, The National Archives File J 82/3714, page 21.

10. Ibid, page 22.

11. Judge Eveleigh, Summing-Up (continuation) at the Old Bailey, Wednesday 4th August 1976, page 34, The National Archives File J 82/3714.

12. Ian Ward, 'Secretary's secret Copenhagen days with Stonehouse', *Daily Telegraph*, 25th February 1975, page 15.

13. Sheila Buckley, 'The truth about John and me', *Woman* magazine, 30th October 1976, page 10.

14. 'He needs me now says Mrs Stonehouse', *Daily Mail*, 22th March 1975, page 1.

15. Richard Stott, 'MP in New Spy Probe', *Daily Mirror*, 24th March 1975, page 1.

16. Sheila Buckley, 'The truth about John and me' (Part 2), *Woman* magazine, 6th November 1976, page 18.

17. Peter Deeley, 'Mrs Stonehouse talks about "John's cracking point": The Runaway MP', *The Observer*, 8th June 1975, page 5.

18. Sheila Buckley, 'The truth about John and me', *Woman* magazine, 30th October 1976, pages 8, 11, 23.

19. Ibid, pages 23 and 28.

Chapter 13

1. John Stonehouse letter to Edward Short, 26th January 1975, First Report from the Select Committee on the Right Honourable Member for Walsall, North, Session 1974–75, London: HMSO, 11th March 1975, page 10.

2. J.S. Dixon to Mr C.P. Scott, 13th February 1975, The National Archives File FCO 53/434, Document 107, page 1.

3. Telex from O'Leary, 17th February 1975, The National Archives File FCO 53/434, Document 111.

4. J.S. Dixon to Mr Hawley, 28th February 1975, page 1, The National Archives File FCO 53/434.

5. John Stonehouse letter to Swedish prime minister, 4th March 1975, in 'Second Report from the Select Committee on the Right Honourable Member for Walsall, North, Session 1974–75', London: HMSO, 6th May 1975, page 2.

6. Second Report from the Select Committee on the Right Honourable Member for Walsall, North, Session 1974–75, London: HMSO, 6th May 1975, page 1.

7. G.L. Scullard, British Embassy, Washington, to Robin Blair, 2nd April 1975, The National Archives File FCO 53/434, Document 175.

8. J.S. Dixon to G.L. Scullard, 8th April 1975, The National Archives File FCO 53/434.

9. Telex from J.S. Dixon to Port Louis, Mauritius, 19th March 1975, The National Archives File FCO 53/434, page 1.

10. James telex to Port Louis, 12th April 1975, The National Archives File FCO 53/434, Document 186.

11. Downing Street letter, 12th April 1975, The National Archives File FCO 53/434, Document 192, page 1.

12. Fourth Report from the Select Committee on the Right Honourable Member for Walsall, North, Session 1974–75, London: HMSO, 10th June 1975, pages iii, x.

13. John Stonehouse letter to George Strauss, Chairman of the Select Committee, 30th May 1975, Fourth Report from the Select Committee on the Right Honourable Member for Walsall, North, Session 1974–75, London: HMSO, 10th June 1975, page vi.

14. Barbara Stonehouse quoted in Peter Deeley, 'Mrs Stonehouse talks about "John's cracking point"', *The Observer*, 8th June 1975, page 5.

15. Cabinet Minutes 10 Downing Street, 9th June 1975, 11.30am, The National Archives File CAB 128/56/26, pages 1–2.

16. A.A. Bartholomew, letter to Deputy Director General, Social Welfare Department, Melbourne, 11th June 1975, in The National Archives File J 82/3714.

17. John Stonehouse, *My Trial*, London: Star Books, 1976, page 47.

Chapter 14

1. 'In the streets of indifference, the Rt Hon Member for Walsall North returns after nearly 11 months …', *Daily Express*, 8th September 1975, page 9.

2. 'Lawyer who helped MP dies', *Daily Mail*, 6th October 1975, page 10.

3. John Stonehouse, *Death of an Idealist*, London: WH Allen, 1975, pages 152–3.

4. Ibid, pages 154–5.

5. Ibid, page 158.

6. Ibid, page 72.

7. Justin Long, 'Stonehouse attacks DPP', *The Financial Times*, 6th April 1976, page 12.

8. Public Library of US Diplomacy, 8th April 1976, Canonical ID: 1976LONDON05424_b.

9. Geoffrey Robertson, *The Justice Game*, London: Chatto & Windus, 1998, page 66.

10. *The Times*, *Daily Telegraph*, *Guardian*, and *The Sun*, 28th July 1976.

11. Judge Edward Eveleigh, The National Archives File J 82/3714, 6th August 1976, 'Sentence', Pages 75–6.

Chapter 15

1. Geoffrey Robertson, *The Justice Game*, London: Chatto & Windus, 1998, pages 65, 68–9.
2. Judge Eveleigh, the Old Bailey, Friday 6th August 1976, The National Archives File J 82/3714, pages 80–81.
3. Judge Eveleigh, Summing-Up at the Old Bailey, Tuesday 3rd August 1976, The National Archives File J 82/3714, pages 17, 56.
4. Ian Ward, 'Stonehouse Had Secretary's Clothes Sent On', *Daily Telegraph*, 12th February 1975, page 3. (In later editions titled 'Stonehouse shipped secretary's clothes three months ago', page 15.)
5. Richard Stott, 'The night Stonehouse danced with Sheila's undies', *Daily Mirror*, 31st October 1975, page 5; Paul Hopkins, 'Runaway MP's "petticoat polka"', *Daily Express*, 31st October 1975, page 3.
6. Ian Henry Ward, Statement 14th July 1975, page 7, National Archives File J 267/707.
7. John Stonehouse quoted in Judge Eveleigh's Summing-Up at the Old Bailey, Wednesday 4th August 1976, The National Archives File J 82/3714, page 23.
8. Ian Henry Ward, Statement 14th July 1975, page 7, National Archives File J 267/707.
9. Robert Rowland Hill quoted in Judge Eveleigh's Summing-up (continuation) on Wednesday 4th August 1976 at the Old Bailey, The National Archives File J 82/3714, page 34.
10. Judge Eveleigh, Summing-Up at the Old Bailey, Monday 2nd August 1976, The National Archives File J 82/3714, page 24.
11. 'Runaway MP "not insane"', *Guardian*, 22nd July 1976.
12. Judge Eveleigh, Summing-Up at the Old Bailey, Monday 2nd August 1976, The National Archives File J 82/3714, page 23.
13. Dr Gibney quoted in Judge Eveleigh's Summing-Up at the Old Bailey, Wednesday 4th August 1976, The National Archives File J 82/3714, page 27.
14. Judge Eveleigh, Summing-Up at the Old Bailey, Wednesday 4th August 1976, The National Archives File J 82/3714, page 27.
15. Dr Gibney quoted in Judge Eveleigh's Summing-Up at the Old Bailey, Wednesday 4th August 1976, The National Archives File J 82/3714, page 27.
16. Judge Eveleigh Summing-Up at the Old Bailey, Wednesday 4th August 1976, The National Archives File J 82/3714, page 27.
17. Dr Heywood quoted in Judge Eveleigh's Summing-Up at the Old Bailey, Wednesday 4th August 1976, The National Archives File J 82/3714, page 29.

18. Judge Eveleigh, Summing-Up at the Old Bailey, Wednesday 4th August 1976, The National Archives File J 82/3714, page 30.

19. Professor Watson quoted in Judge Eveleigh's Summing-Up at the Old Bailey, Wednesday 4th August 1976, The National Archives File J 82/3714, page 30.

20. Dr R.D. Laing quoted in Judge Eveleigh's Summing-Up at the Old Bailey, Wednesday 4th August 1976, The National Archives File J 82/3714, page 32.

21. Kenneth Clarke, 'I'd Cover for Him Again if I Had To, Says Mrs Buckley', *Daily Telegraph*, 21st July 1976.

22. Ann Morrow, 'Like a head girl, with Alice band and freckles', *Daily Telegraph*, 21st July 1976.

23. James Lewthwaite, 'Flight From Ruin', *The Sun*, 29th April 1976, page 5.

24. Michael Sherrard, *London Capital Group (formerly British Bangladesh Trust Limited): investigation under section 165 (b) of the Companies Act*, London: H.M.S.O., pages 37–8.

25. Judge Eveleigh, Sentencing Statement, Friday 6th August 1976 at the Old Bailey, The National Archives File J 82/3714, pages 77–8.

26. Sheila Buckley, 'The truth about John and me', *Woman* magazine, 30th October 1976, page 8.

27. Judge Eveleigh, Sentencing Statement, Friday 6th August 1976 at the Old Bailey, The National Archives File J 82/3714, pages 77–8.

28. Judge Eveleigh, Summing-Up at the Old Bailey, Monday 2nd August 1976, The National Archives File J 82/3714, page 10.

29. Regina v. Stonehouse 4265/R/76, Appendix 1: Sequence of Events, The National Archives file J 82/3714, page 3.

30. Ibid, page 4.

31. Geoffrey Robertson, *The Justice Game*, London: Chatto & Windus, 1998, page 66.

32. Judge Eveleigh, Summing-up at the Old Bailey on Tuesday 3rd August, The National Archives File J 82/3714, page 51.

33. John Stonehouse quoted in Judge Eveleigh's Summing-Up at the Old Bailey, Wednesday 4th August 1976, The National Archives File J 82/3714, page 14.

34. Judge Eveleigh, Summing-Up at the Old Bailey, Wednesday 4th August 1976, The National Archives File J 82/3714, page 14.

35. John Stonehouse quoted in Judge Eveleigh's Summing-Up at the Old Bailey, Wednesday 4th August 1976, The National Archives File J 82/3714, page 15.

36. Judge Eveleigh, Summing-Up at the Old Bailey, Monday 2nd August 1976, The National Archives File J 82/3714, page 13.

37. Lord Salmon, in 'Director of Public Prosecutions v Stonehouse: HL 1977', References: [1978] AC 55, [1977] 2 All ER 909, (1977) 65 Cr App R 192, Coram: Lord Dilhorne, Lord Edmund-Davies, Lord Diplock.

38. Judge Eveleigh, 5th August 1976, The National Archives File J 82/3714, page 63.

39. Paul Hopkins, 'Why I'll Divorce John', *Daily Express*, 6th August 1976, page 1.

40. Ian Henry Ward, Statement 14th July 1975, pages 8–9, National Archives File J 267/707.

41. Judge Eveleigh, Sentence Statement at the Old Bailey, Friday 6th August 1976, The National Archives File J 82/3714, page 76.

42. 'Notification of Result of Application to the Full Court', 24th and 25th January 1977, The National Archives File J 82/3714. Also, 27th January 1977: 'The application for leave to appeal upon the remaining counts having been abandoned by counsel in Court'.

43. Letter from Francis E. Eteng, Senior Medical Officer, Blundeston Prison, to Criminal Appeal Office, pages 1–2, 21st December 1976, The National Archives File J 82/3714.

Chapter 16

1. Mrs J. Thompson, Home Office, to Julia Stonehouse, Correspondence Reference PDP/S 11825/1/3, 3rd June 1977.

2. Michael Sherrard, *London Capital Group (formerly British Bangladesh Trust Limited): investigation under section 165 (b) of the Companies Act*, London: H.M.S.O., pages 271, 38, 201 and 177.

3. 'Loose Minute' from G. Clark to H.C. Gill, 11th November 1977, The National Archives File BT 299/346, page 1.

4. 'Loose Minute' from H.C. Gill to Mr W. Cook, Postscript 10th November in 9th November 1977, The National Archives File BT 299/346.

5. Tony Whitehead quoted in Martin Walker, 'Why Stonehouse fears prison hospital', *Guardian*, 17th November 1978.

6. Rosalind Kane quoted in Martin Walker, 'Why Stonehouse fears prison hospital', *Guardian*, 17th November 1978.

7. Rosina Stonehouse quoted in Frank Thompson, 'No meeting for the women who love Stonehouse', *Daily Mail*, 16th September, page 3.

8. Tony Frost, 'Sheila Buckley's Plea for Mercy', *Sunday Mirror*, 15th October, page 3.

9. James Meikle, 'Stonehouse: plea by girls', *Oxford Mail*, 31st October 1978, page 1.

10. S.S. Bampton of Home Office to Jane Stonehouse, 15th November 1978.

11. Harry Richards quoted in Peter Whitehouse, 'Release him ...', *Sunday Mercury*, 19th November 1978, page 16.

12. 'For mercy's sake, Merlyn!', *Sunday Mirror*, 12th November 1978, page 2.

13. 'Let Stonehouse go – top cop', *Daily Mirror*, 18th November 1978.

14. Mr Kenneth Lomas, Early Day Motion No. 65, 'Notices of Questions and Motions: 21st November 1978', No. 15, Hansard, page 1087.

15. Michael Dove, '£40,000 in Trunk Stonehouse Denial', *Sunday Express*, 26th November 1978, page 1.

16. 'Should Mr Stonehouse Be Paroled?', *The Times*, 17th November 1978.

17. Michael O'Dell, 'Mr Stonehouse and parole', letters section, *The Times*, 18th November 1978.

18. 'Stonehouse in £40,000 Riddle', *Sunday People*, 26th November 1978.

19. J.A. Chilcot, Private Secretary to Home Secretary, Home Office, 28th November 1978.

20. Maureen Colquhoun MP, to Jane Stonehouse, 15th December 1978.

21. David Meilton, 'Ex-MP does less than half sentence Stonehouse To Be Freed', *Evening News*, 6th August 1979, page 1.

22. Rosina Stonehouse quoted in David Meilton, 'Ex-MP does less than half sentence Stonehouse To Be Freed', *Evening News*, 6th August 1979, page 1.

23. Rosina Stonehouse quoted in Raymond Rogers, 'Stonehouse's Stormy Freedom', *Daily Mail*, 7th August 1979, page 1.

24. Sheila Buckley quoted in Tim Miles, 'That woman answers back', *Daily Mail*, 8th August 1979.

25. Tim Miles, 'That woman answers back', *Daily Mail*, 8th August 1979.

Chapter 17

1. Sheila Stonehouse quoted in Diana Hutchinson, 'Yes, it WAS worth it – I'd do it again', *Daily Mail*, 16th April 1988, page 12.

2. Bill Greig, 'The double life and double death of John Stonehouse', *Daily Express*, 15th April 1988, page 3.

3. Norman Leith, 'Flawed man of passion Stonehouse dies', *Evening Standard*, 14th April 1988, page 5.

4. Ian Waller, 'The rise and fall of John Stonehouse', *Daily Telegraph*, 15th April 1988, page 7.

5. 'Maverick MP dies of heart attack', *South China Morning Post*, 15th April 1988, page 14.

6. 'Stonehouse dies of heart attack', *Hong Kong Standard*, 15th April 1988, page 1.

Chapter 18

1. Museum of Communism, Prague, Information Board titled 'Basic Structure'.
2. Josef Frolik, *The Frolik Defection – Memoirs of an Intelligence Agent*, London: Leo Cooper, 1975, page 10.
3. Ibid, pages 80, 113–14.
4. Ibid, pages 78–9.
5. Josef Frolik interview by Peter Williams, 'The Czech Connection', 'This Week', Thames TV, 7th July 1977.
6. 43075_43075_000_0099, Security Services Archive, Prague: fond Foreign Intelligence Main Directorate – Operative Files (I. S – svazky): personal file reg. no. 43075 I. S, code names 'Kolón', 'Twister', including MTH 21968 I. S. Unless otherwise stated, all references within this chapter adhere to the above citation, and the file prefix: 43075_43075_. The seven digits in the references below shall indicate the individual file.
7. 21968_43075_020_0019, Security Services Archive, Prague: fond Foreign Intelligence Main Directorate – Operative Files (I. S – svazky): personal file reg. no. 43075 I. S, code names 'Kolón', 'Twister', including MTH 21968 I. S.
8. 020_0033.
9. Peter Benenson (Editor), *Gangrene*, London: John Calder, 1959, 'Kenya's Inhumanities,' page 94.
10. Peter Benenson (Editor), *Gangrene*, London: John Calder, 1959, 'From the Documents on Hola', page 96.
11. Ian Cobain, *The History Thieves – Secrets, Lies and the Shaping of a Modern Nation*, London: Portobello Books, 2016, page 110.
12. Ladislav Bittman, *The Deception Game*, New York: Ballantine Books, 1972, pages ix, 29.
13. 000_0285.
14. 000_0147.
15. 000_0295.
16. Josef Frolik, *The Frolik Defection – Memoirs of an Intelligence Agent*, London: Leo Cooper, 1975, page 50.
17. 000_0247.
18. Oleg Gordievsky, *Next Stop Execution, The autobiography of Oleg Gordievsky*, London: Macmillan, 1995, pages 221, 280. (Copyright © Oleg Gordievsky) Reprinted by permission of A.M. Heath & Co Ltd.
19. 000_0155.
20. 000_0155 and 000_0157.
21. Josef Frolik, *The Frolik Defection – Memoirs of an Intelligence Agent*, London: Leo Cooper, 1975, pages 98, 95.

22. 021_0033.
23. 000_0389.
24. 000_0389.
25. 21968_43075_020_0013, Security Services Archive, Prague: fond Foreign Intelligence Main Directorate – Operative Files (I. S – svazky): personal file reg. no. 43075 I. S, code names 'Kolón', 'Twister', including MTH 21968 I. S.
26. Josef Frolik, *The Frolik Defection – Memoirs of an Intelligence Agent*, London: Leo Cooper, 1975, pages 78, 85.
27. John Stonehouse, *Death of an Idealist*, London: WH Allen, 1975, pages 88–9.
28. 000_0061.
29. 021_0095.
30. 000_0579.
31. 021_0123.
32. 000_0151.
33. 000_0219.
34. 000_0385.
35. 000_0435.
36. 000_0439.
37. 000_0471.
38. 000_0479.
39. 000_0543.
40. 000_0037.
41. 021_0027.
42. 021_0029.
43. 021_0129.
44. 021_0269.
45. 021_0279.
46. 021_0281.
47. 000_0071.
48. 000_0067.
49. 000_0075.
50. 000_0077.

Chapter 19

1. Josef Frolik, *The Frolik Defection – Memoirs of an Intelligence Agent*, London: Leo Cooper, 1975, page 175.
2. David Leigh, *The Wilson Plot*, London: Heinemann – Mandarin, 1989, page 213.
3. Ibid, page 236.

4. Christopher Sweeney, 'Defector reveals MPs' part in spy ring', *The Times*, 25th January 1974, page 8.

5. Christopher Andrew, *The Defence of The Realm*, London: Allen Lane, 2009, page 668.

6. John Hunt to Ken Stowe, 3rd June 1975, The National Archives File PREM 16/1848, Document 2, pages 1–2.

7. Josef Frolik, *The Frolik Defection – Memoirs of an Intelligence Agent*, London: Leo Cooper, 1975, page 97.

8. Letter from Robert Armstrong to Sir Michael Hanley, 4th July 1974, The National Archives File PREM 16/1848, Document 1.

9. John Hunt to Ken Stowe, 3rd June 1975, The National Archives File PREM 16/1848, Document 2, pages 2–3.

10. Gordon Corera, BBC, 25th June 2012, https://www.bbc.co.uk/news/magazine-18556213, accessed 26th January 2021.

11. Richard Stott, 'MP Was Named as Spy Contact', *Daily Mirror*, 17th December 1974, page 1.

12. Josef Frolik quoted by Stephen Hastings MP in the House of Commons, 14th December 1977, Adjournment (Christmas), Hansard, volume 941 (508).

13. Sir John Hunt draft letter to Patrick Mayhew for signature of James Callaghan, 13th July 1978, The National Archives File PREM 16/1848, pages 1–2.

14. John Hunt to Mr Wood for the attention of Prime Minister James Callaghan, 15th December 1977, page 1, The National Archives File PREM 16/1848.

15. Stephen Hastings MP in the House of Commons, 14th December 1977, Adjournment (Christmas), Hansard, volume 941 (586).

16. Robert Armstrong to Ken Stowe, 24th January 1978, The National Archives File PREM 16/1848, Document 5.

17. Ken Stowe to James Callaghan, Compliment Slip, 27th January 1978, The National Archives File PREM 16/1848.

18. James Callaghan to Patrick Mayhew, 26th June 1978, The National Archives File PREM 16/1848.

19. Patrick Mayhew to James Callaghan, 11th July 1978, The National Archives File PREM 16/1848.

20. James Callaghan to Cranley Onslow, 28th June 1978, The National Archives File PREM 16/1848.

21. 'Note for the record' of meeting between Callaghan and Mayhew, prepared by Ken Stowe, 12th July 1978, The National Archives File PREM 16/1848, page 2.

22. Draft letter from James Callaghan to Patrick Mayhew, 18th July 1978 (attached to memo from John Hunt), The National Archives File PREM 16/1848, pages 1–3.

23. 'Note for the Record' prepared by Ken Stowe, 'The Frolik Affair Meeting' between James Callaghan and Margaret Thatcher, 18th July 1978, page 1, The National Archives File PREM 16/1848.

24. David Leigh, *The Wilson Plot*, London: Heinemann – Mandarin, 1989, page 240.

Chapter 20

1. John Hunt, interview Channel 4, *Secret History: Harold Wilson – The Final Days*, 15th August 1996.

2. Stephen Dorril, and Robin Ramsay, *Smear! Wilson and the Secret State*, London: Grafton, 1992, page 196.

3. Tony Benn, *Office Without Power, Diaries 1968–72*, London: Hutchinson, 1988, page 252.

4. Stephen Dorril, and Robin Ramsay, *Smear! Wilson and the Secret State*, London: Grafton, 1992, page 198.

5. Peter Wright, *Spycatcher*, Richmond: Heinemann Publishers Australia, 1987, page 364.

6. Ibid, pages 367–9.

7. Ibid, pages 369–70.

8. David Leigh, *The Wilson Plot*, London: Heinemann – Mandarin, 1989, page 236.

9. Ibid, page 239.

10. Ibid, page 193.

11. David Pallister, '*Private Eye* "may have been used by MI5"', *Guardian*, 14th May 2009, https://www.theguardian.com/books/2009/may/14/from-the-archive-private-eye, accessed 20th November 2021.

12. 'Diplomatic Bag', *Private Eye*, 20th September 1974, page 3.

Chapter 21

1. Linda Goldman and Michael Sherrard QC, *Wigs and Wherefores: A Biography of Michael Sherrard QC*, London: Wildy, Simmonds and Hill Publishing, 2008, pages 238–239. Reprinted with permission of Wildy & Sons Ltd.

2. Ibid, page 239.

3. Michael Sherrard, *London Capital Group (formerly British Bangladesh Trust Limited): investigation under section 165 (b) of the Companies Act*, London: H.M.S.O., pages 353–4.

4. Linda Goldman and Michael Sherrard QC, *Wigs and Wherefores: A Biography of Michael Sherrard QC*, London: Wildy, Simmonds and Hill Publishing, 2008, page 244.
5. Nigel Nelson, 'Stonehouse "Gave" Concorde Secrets to Russia', *The People*, 17th April 1988, page 2.
6. Chapman Pincher, 'Stonehouse was a Soviet Spy', *Daily Express*, Monday 2nd January 2006, pages 24–5.
7. Theo Barclay, 'Stonehouse, the MP who *was* a Czech spy', *The Times*, *Times2*, page 2, 22nd February 2018, and online at thetimes.co.uk as 'John Stonehouse, the MP who really was a Czech spy.'
8. Sarah Oliver and Katka Krosnar, 'Stonehouse was a Czech Spy', *The Mail on Sunday Review*, 15th January 2006, pages 55–8.
9. Chapman Pincher, 'Minister sold our Concorde secrets to KGB', *Daily Express*, 16th January 2006, page 10.
10. Ernest Prince, 'As immigration flood threatens to get out of hand … Midland MPs say where they stand', *Express & Star*, 17th February 1968, page 6.
11. John Stonehouse quoted in Ernest Prince, 'As immigration flood threatens to get out of hand … Midland MPs say where they stand', *Express & Star*, 17th February 1968, page 6.
12. Ferdinand Mount, 'Wedded to the Absolute', *London Review of Books*, 26th September 2019, page 3.

Acknowledgements

I consider myself very lucky to have Icon Books as my publisher as they have proved a joy to work with. In particular I'd like to thank Ellen Conlon who has, in addition to excellent editorial skills, an instinctive touch that identified otherwise invisible areas of weakness in my manuscript. I'd also like to thank the archivists who helped me in my research, and all archivists everywhere, because without them history would be lost and events more vulnerable to fabrication. Finally, I am grateful to my mother for supporting me through this process, sometimes having to recall her experiences despite the emotional cost.

Index

JS indicates John Stonehouse. A page number followed
by 'n' indicates a note on that page.